Printer's type in the twentieth century

Printer's type in the twentieth century
Manufacturing and design methods

Richard Southall

The British Library

Oak Knoll Press

First published in 2005 by

The British Library
96 Euston Road
London NW1 2DB

and

Oak Knoll Press
310 Delaware Street
New Castle
DE 19720

Text © 2005 Richard Southall

British Library Cataloguing-in-Publication Data
A catalogue record for this book is available from The British Library
ISBN 0 7123 4812 3

Library of Congress Cataloguing-in-Publication Data
Southall, Richard.
    Printer's type in the twentieth century / Richard Southall.
      p. cm.
    Includes bibliographical references and index.
    ISBN 1-58456-155-6
    1. Type and type-founding–History–20th century. 2. Type and type-founding–Digital techniques. 3. Computer fonts. 4. Typesetting–History–20th century. 5. Phototypesetting. 6. Computerized typesetting. 7. Typesetting machines–History–20th century. 8. Printing–History–20th century. I. Title.

Z250.A2S68 2005
686.2'24'0904–dc22

2004057520

Printed in Great Britain by St Edmundsbury Press
Jacket designed by Bob Elliott

Contents

	List of illustrations	vi
	Acknowledgments	xi
	Introduction	xiii
	Part 1: Metal type	
1	Cutting type by hand	3
2	Making designs for hand punchcutting	12
3	Cutting type by machine	19
4	Making designs for machine-cut type	26
5	Hot-metal typesetting	35
6	Fonts and typefaces in metal type	47
7	Perpetua and Lutetia	53
	Part 2: The photographic matrix	
8	Making type by photography	79
9	Drawing characters for the Lumitype	93
10	The design of Univers	102
11	The search for speed	121
12	Scanned-matrix photocomposition	129
13	Fonts and typefaces in photomatrix manufacture	136
	Part 3: Digital and numerical techniques	
14	Digital and numerical photocomposition	143
15	Digital and numerical fonts	150
16	Laser imagesetters and the PostScript revolution	161
17	The Stone typeface family	173
	Part 4: Making type with programs	
18	Computer science and typography	185
19	The Colorado typemaking project	204
	Conclusion	223
	References	225
	Index	231

List of illustrations

Chapter 1: Cutting type by hand
1 Bill of font for J W Haas's Garmont Schwabacher 4
2 Fournier's gauges for calibre and slope 6
3 Roman and italic on pearl body 7
4 Fournier's Bâtarde Coulée 8

Chapter 2: Making designs for hand punchcutting
5 Drawings by Jan van Krimpen and the types cut from them 17

Chapter 3: Cutting type by machine
6 Leavenworth's pantograph for wood type 20
7 Benton's punchcutting pantograph 20
8 Mechanical punchcutting: early stages 21
9 Mechanical punchcutting: final stages 22
10 'The celebrated Benton Matrix Engraving Machine' 23
11 Matrix-engraving pantograph 24
12 Punchcutting for display type manufacture 25
13 Matrix engraving for display type manufacture 25

Chapter 4: Making designs for machine-cut type
14 The pattern drawing from Figure 8 26
15 Sketches by Eric Gill on a proof of Monotype Perpetua italic 31
16 Corrections by Gill to a proof of Monotype Joanna 32

Chapter 5: Hot-metal typesetting
17 An early Monotype matrix-case 37
18 Unit width allocations for the matrix-case in Figure 17 37
19 Unit-counting mechanism for the Monotype C keyboard 38
20 Keybutton layout for the C keyboard 39
21 Matrix-case arrangements for early Monotype machines 40
22 Standard layout for an early D keyboard 40
23 Caslon's pica old face and 12 pt Monotype Caslon 128 43
24 Single-letter and two-letter Linotype matrices 44
25 Standard alignments for Intertype matrices 45
26 Logotypes for Linotype Caslon Old Face 45

Chapter 6: Fonts and typefaces in metal type
27 Size comparisons for Monotype Old Style Series 2 49
28 Caslon Old Face foundry type 50
29 Monotype Caslon Series 128 51

List of illustrations vii

Chapter 7: Perpetua and Lutetia

30	'Mr S Morison's Gill type'	56
31	Rubbed type in Figure 30	57
32	Different states of o in Figure 31	57
33	The synopsis from Figure 30	57
34	The first synopsis from *The Fleuron*	58
35	Alphabets from the Meynell drawings	59
36	14 pt type cut by Monotype from the Meynell drawings	59
37	The first characters cut by Monotype from Malin's work	60
38	Monotype's Trial No. 2	62
39	Monotype's Trial No. 4	63
40	Proof of 18-pt trial cutting	64
41	Comparison of 10, 13, 16 and 18-pt Perpetua characters	64
42	Monotype's Trial No. 6	65
43	Roman and italic in the text of Trial 6	66
44	Monotype's first cutting and Malin's type	67
45	Monotype's 14-pt cutting and the Meynell drawings	68
46	The type of Trial 2 compared with Monotype's first cutting	68
47	Minuscule alphabets from Trial 2 and Malin's cutting	69
48	Roman minuscule alphabets from Trials 2 and 6	69
49	The second synopsis from *The Fleuron*	70
50	Composition sizes of Monotype Perpetua 239 roman	70
51	Characters from Monotype's Trial 2 and Malin's cutting	71
52	Variations in m in Rädisch's cutting of Lutetia	72
53	The Monotype and Enschedé cuttings of Lutetia	73

Chapter 8: Making type by photography

54	Schematic layout of the Monophoto Filmsetter	79
55	Schematic layout of the Photon 200	81
56	The photographic unit of the Photon 200	82
57	Stepwedge exposure test for Monophoto composition	83
58	Mixing of styles and sizes on the Lumitype	83
59	Variations of set for a single nominal size	84
60	The disappearance of the type body in photocomposition	84
61	A matrix disc for the Lumitype 540	85
62	Closeup of the disc in Figure 61	86
63	Phototype of Univers medium m	87
64	Original designs, drawings and camera masters	88
65	Two-stage reduction in photographic matrix-making	88
66	The five-disc 'ferris wheel' of the Fototronic TxT	91
67	Part of the matrix assembly of a Photon Pacesetter	91
68	Interior view of the Monotype 600	91
69	Matrices for the Linofilm Europa	92

Chapter 9: Drawing characters for the Lumitype

70	The Lumitype numbering scheme for weights and widths	96
71	Standard alignments for Lumitype typefaces	97
72	Window outlines for the Lumitype	98
73	Checking designs at the Lumitype studio	99
74	Trial pasteup of Lumitype Clarendon 653-55	100
75	Scaled trial pasteups of Lumitype Modern 57	100
76	Repeated-character test of Autologic Times Roman	101

Chapter 10: The design of Univers

77	Relationships between upright variants of Univers	103
78	Deriving an oblique shape from the roman	104
79	Calibres for the Univers family	105
80	Early output from the Lumitype	106
81	Univers semibold capital M and W	106
82	Medium-weight normal-width variants of Univers	113
83	Light-weight normal-width variants of Univers	115
84	Semibold and bold normal-width variants of Univers	117

Chapter 11: The search for speed

85	The control unit of the Photon Zip 901	122
86	Interior view of the 901's photographic unit	123
87	One of the 901's three matrix plates	123
88	Another view of the 901's interior	124
89	The lens carriage of the 901	124
90	Another view of the lens carriage	125
91	The 901's flash-tube array	125
92	A matrix filmstrip for the Photon 713	126

Chapter 12: Scanned-matrix photocomposition

93	Schematic layout of the Linotron 505	130
94	Schematic layout of the Linotron 303's output end	131
95	A matrix for the Linotron 303	132
96	Positive intermediates for Magnaset matrix manufacture	133
97	A matrix for the Magnaset 226	133
98	Close-up view of the matrix strip in Figure 97	134

Chapter 13: Fonts and typefaces in photomatrix manufacture

99	The Visual Graphics Corporation's Photo Typositor	139

Chapter 14: Digital and numerical photocomposition

100	The Digiset 50T1	143
101	Drawing character images with a vertical raster scan	144
102	Enlarged printout from Digiset image data	145
103	Scaled character images from straight-line segments	147

List of illustrations ix

Chapter 15: Digital and numerical fonts

104	Printout from an uncorrected scan	152
105	Mechanical and manual digitizations of Galfra Regular	153
106	Half-bitting: a character from Autologic Athena	154
107	Corrections to image data for the Galfra design	155
108	A Camex LetterIP input terminal	158
109	Two stages in the construction of a Tiffany roman n	158
110	Variations on Letraset Aachen medium	159

Chapter 16: Laser imagesetters and the PostScript revolution

111	Variable-size character images from a single raster pattern	162
112	Different raster patterns for different image sizes	162
113	The Apple LaserWriter	167
114	Minuscule m from Helvetica Neue, with no hinting	168
115	Apple's vision for the LaserWriter	170

Chapter 17: The Stone typeface family

116	An early version of the informal minuscule n	174
117	Developing italic characters alongside the roman	175
118	'The very first drawings' for the Stone family	175
119	A finished drawing of the italic e	177
120	Laser-printed proof in 'raw' data format	178
121	The upper part of Figure 120 in close-up	178
122	Laser-printed proof in 'Bézier' data format	179
123	The upper part of Figure 122 in close-up	179
124	An early proof of six styles from the Stone family	180

Chapter 18: Computer science and typography

125	Handwritten designs for AMS Euler roman and greek	190
126	Outline drawings for AMS Euler medium	190
127	Handwritten designs for fraktur and script capitals	191
128	Metafont proof of Euler medium-weight A	192
129	Stages in the construction of the A of Figure 128	192
130	10 pt Modern Series 8A	193
131	10 pt Computer Modern Roman	193
132	The first word from Figure 131	193
133	Metafont proof of the M from Figures 131 and 132	194
134	10 pt Computer Modern Sanserif Bold	195
135	The first word from Figure 134	195
136	Metafont proof of the M from Figures 134 and 135	195
137	Knuth's Metafont rendering of the 23rd Psalm	196
138	A sheet of Zapf's production drawings for AMS Euler	198
139	10 pt M from old and new Computer Modern	200
140	10 pt a from Modern 8A and new Computer Modern	201

Chapter 19: The Colorado typemaking project

141	Ladislas Mandel's Univad and Edgware designs	204
142	The 'visual itinerary' in directory consultation	206
143	A practical realization of Figure 142	206
144	Mandel's first trial pasteups for the Colorado family	207
145	Early sketches for Colorado light condensed o and g	207
146	Part of the first-stage reduction for Figure 144	208
147	Trial pasteups superimposed on a printed directory page	208
148	Ladislas Mandel and the author	209
149	Three characters from Mandel's Clottes design	211
150	Continuous-curve character drawing for Colorado 55 a	214
151	Pre-digitized drawing for Colorado 55 a	214
152	Early corrections to Colorado 47 A	215
153	Mandel's design for e in Colorado 89	216
154	The seven variants of the Colorado family	217
155	Example entries from a residential listing	218
156	Example entries from a combined listing	218

Acknowledgments

I owe a great debt of gratitude to my students and colleagues at the University of Reading and Stanford University, who prompted and accompanied my early explorations of the ideas discussed in this book. The late Ernest Hoch, in particular, was an indispensable companion at the beginning of the journey.

Christine King dealt with all the intellectual-property issues encountered in the writing, and provided immeasurable support during the final stages of the work.

Ladislas Mandel has been a colleague and friend since 1965. His generosity in granting me access to his unique library and the material in his studio, together with many hours of discussion and argument, have left traces everywhere in the book.

It would have been impossible to fill in the details of the historical framework without two books by Lawrence Wallis: *Electronic typesetting* (1984) and *A concise chronology of typesetting developments 1886–1986* (1988).

I am grateful for generous help from the staff of the Cambridge University Library; the William Andrews Clark Memorial Library; the Houghton Library of the Harvard College Library; and above all the St Bride Printing Library. Wendy Richmond provided me with much useful information about the early days of Bitstream Inc, including the photographs used in Figure 109. Sumner Stone answered at long range many questions about his work at Adobe Systems; he also generously donated the fonts with which the text is composed. David Way, Lara Speicher and Tony Warshaw at the British Library saw the book through its longer-than-expected gestation with unfailing patience and cheerfulness. Paul Luna and John Trevitt read a first version of the completed text, and contributed many helpful comments.

Figures 113 and 115 are reproduced by permission of Apple Computer Inc, to whom I am indebted for the provision of scans from proprietary artwork.

Material from Monotype specimen-book pages in Figures 27, 29, 50, 53, 57 and 82–84 is reproduced by permission of Agfa Monotype.

Figure 39 is reproduced by permission of the Syndics of Cambridge University Library.

Some of the images in Figure 5 are from material in the Van Krimpen archive at the Museum Meermanno-Westreenianum, The Hague.

Figures 54, 55, 93 and 100, all from A H Phillips's *Computer Peripherals and typesetting*, are reproduced by kind permission of The Stationery Office.

The photograph in Figure 148 is by Lionel Roux, and is reproduced with his permission. Other photographs not otherwise acknowledged here or in the text are by the author. Permission from the Basler Papiermühle (the Swiss Museum of Paper, Writing and Printing) to include those in Figures 1 and 11 is gratefully acknowledged. The photographs in Figures 8, 9, 12, 13, 64 and 65 were taken in March 1978 at D Stempel AG in Frankfurt.

Introduction

The twentieth century saw a succession of profound technological changes that affected every aspect of the manufacture and composition of printer's type. The craft of hand punchcutting had survived into the early part of the century almost unchanged from its first recorded form. By the 1930s it had been entirely superseded by industrial techniques, and the hand composition of metal type by mechanical methods. In the second half of the century three-dimensional matrices and types were replaced first by photographic images, then by digital and finally by numerical data, thus dematerializing completely the objects with which a printed text is composed.

The technical aspects of this revolution are more or less well documented: its earlier phases much better than the later ones. Its effects on the ways in which type was designed, and the resulting changes in the relationships between the designers and manufacturers of type, have by contrast scarcely been considered in any systematic way. This book attempts to discuss some aspects of them.

The typographical century the book deals with is displaced by fifteen years from the chronological one. It begins in 1885, with Ottmar Mergenthaler's first working linecaster and Linn Boyd Benton's punchcutting pantograph. Without Benton's machine, and the ability it brought with it to produce large numbers of identical matrices, the Linotype and the other hot-metal composing machines that followed it would have remained interesting curiosities. The century ends with the year in which PostScript fonts and the Apple LaserWriter brought typesetting and publishing to the desktop for the first time.

There are two excursions outside this period. The first two chapters of the book discuss the technique of hand punchcutting, the problem of specifying the appearance of a new design and the punchcutter's interpretative role. The concept of a type manufacturing system, with its three principal personalities of client, designer and producer, develops from this discussion; Claude Garamont's production of the *grecs du Roy* in the years after 1540 provides an early illustration of it. The second excursion is in the final chapter. This describes another manufacturing system, situated in a different technological context: the Colorado typemaking project. The project's main phase, completed in 1997, brings the chronological century to a close; its story challenges some of the orthodoxies of late twentieth-century type manufacture.

Within the century it mainly deals with, the book does not attempt to be a comprehensive history of type manufacturing techniques. Instead, brief descriptions of important advances in the technology of text composition are interleaved with accounts of significant type-design projects that accompanied them. The similarities and contrasts between metal-type manufacture by hand and machine, and the tensions that they gave rise to in an industrial setting, are illustrated in the development of Eric Gill's Perpetua and Jan van Krimpen's Lutetia designs by the Lanston Monotype Corporation. Adrian Frutiger's design of Univers for the Lumitype photocomposing machine, and its adaptation for Monotype hot-metal composition, demonstrate some of the problems of moving from a more to a less capable composing system. The Stone typefaces, Donald Knuth's Computer Modern family and Ladislas Mandel's Colorado designs for telephone directory composition exemplify different approaches to the task of designing for composing technologies in which mechanical constraints on the designer's freedom of action seem to have all but disappeared.

The author joined Crosfield Electronics Ltd in north London in the summer of 1965, to work on the specification of matrices for Lumitype-Photon photocomposing machines. At the end of the 1960s he found himself in New England, building a large high-resolution camera for photomatrix manufacture at Photon Inc. In the early 1970s he was responsible for the typography of Crosfield's novel scanned-matrix photocomposing machine, the Magnaset 226. At the University of Reading later in the same decade he designed a series of directly generated subtitling fonts for broadcast television. In the 1980s he worked in California, at Stanford University, Adobe Systems Inc and the Xerox Palo Alto Research Center. Much of this work was at the disputed frontier across which computer science and traditional typography contemplated one another in an uneasy truce. In the 1990s he was closely involved with the Colorado typemaking project described in Chapter 19.

   These experiences have had their influence on a text that perhaps differs from other surveys in the emphasis it lays both on the technical aspects of type manufacture in its interaction with type design and on the importance of theory in understanding the issues involved. (They also mean that some topics, of which the author has no direct experience, are largely neglected: notably the design of multiple-master typefaces for PostScript, and the development of the TrueType language.) The fact is, though, that printer's type exists only in an industrial context: typefaces have to be designed before they are produced, and produced before they can be used. The manufacturing process always imposes its own requirements on the designer's work. These change as the nature of the process changes, and the process itself has to be understood in order to understand its demands.

   Text types are fundamentally conservative entities. The slow, difficult but uniquely flexible process of hand punchcutting by which they

Introduction

were first produced allowed their forms to evolve over four hundred years to achieve a close match with their circumstances of use while also adapting to developments in visual style. The mechanization of type manufacture and composition, described in the first part of this book, obliged the manufacturers to invent a completely new way of working to accommodate the strict mechanical constraints imposed by the new technology. Part of this development was the appearance of large, precise character drawings as necessary intermediates in the manufacturing process.

This transition from making to drawing – from files, gravers and steel to pencils, ink and paper – foreshadowed a radical change in the practice of type design. The change did not happen immediately. Neither Van Krimpen's 'immaculate and unambiguous' drawings for the Lutetia typeface, nor the Perpetua drawings that Gill made for Stanley Morison,[1] were 'things' in the sense of Gill's well-known phrase. They were indeed 'pictures of things' that had to be interpreted, whether by Van Krimpen's or Morison's punchcutters or the drawing-office staff at the Monotype works, to produce the things themselves: the forms of the manufactured letters. Van Krimpen's strictures on the drawing-office's performance stemmed from his reluctance to accept the constraints that production for the Monotype system inevitably imposed, and about which the drawing-office knew much more than he had been willing to learn.

In photocomposition, on the other hand, the designer's freedom of action was much less limited by the technology's demands. Frutiger could make his own production drawings for the Univers family, and modify them himself to compensate for the composing system's rendering characteristics. The same was true of design for cathode-ray-tube machines.[2] It was only with the advent of outline fonts and algorithmic rasterization in the late 1970s that the technology began to assert itself again. The balance swung back, though not all the way, towards the designer's side with the arrival of PostScript and its hinting mechanisms for controlling the rendering of character shapes.

To the onlooker, type design today appears to be a simple activity. The designer makes character shapes on a computer display, and character images come out of a laser printer. It goes without saying that these appearances are deceptive. The physical systems of the computer, and the virtual mechanisms of the programs that run on them, are vastly more complex than anything imagined by the engineers who built the punchcutting pantographs of the 1880s or the matrix cameras of the 1960s. This book is an exploration of what has changed since 1885 in the design and manufacture of printer's type, and what has remained the same.

---

[1] *cf.* Figure 5 and Chapter 7. Gill's drawings appear to be lost.
[2] *cf.* Figures 80, 81 and 105.

Part 1: Metal type

1 Cutting type by hand

The first recognizable description of making printer's type is in the *Dialogues francois pour les ieunes enfans*, a French reader and childrens' encyclopaedia published by Christopher Plantin in Antwerp in 1567.

> To the technical historian [Plantin's account] is reassuring: it shows that the tools, and therefore the methods, in use by the middle of the sixteenth century were those remembered by older men in the trade today [*i.e.* in the late 1960s].[1]

The classic accounts of the craft of hand punchcutting are Moxon's and Fournier's.[2] Paul Koch, writing in 1933, describes techniques learned from his father Rudolf, who cut punches for his own designs at the Klingspor typefoundry in Offenbach-am-Main in the 1920s. Stan Nelson's description of his work at the Smithsonian Institution, written in 1984, has excellent illustrations. Fred Smeijers in Arnhem and Christian Paput at the Imprimerie Nationale in Paris have written on the subject more recently.[3]

In the first stage of the process, an image of the character to be produced is cut on the narrow end of a steel bar to make a *punch*. For types intended for the composition of text the bar is 5 or 6 cm in length, and 5-10 mm square in cross-section. The metal of the bar has to be of uniform hardness, since otherwise the punch will break in use. Early punches were irregular in shape, because flaws were removed from the metal by hammering it while it was hot. Later, when high-quality steel became commercially available, punch blanks were cut in suitable lengths from rectangular bar stock.

One end of the blank is smoothed and polished to make the *face* on which the character image will be cut. The outer shape of the image is made by cutting away the face at its edges with files or engraving tools. The interior shapes of characters such as A B e or h are made by striking appropriately-shaped *counterpunches* into the face, or (for larger sizes, and in later versions of the technique) by cutting into it with drills and gravers.

---

[1] Harry Carter, *A view of early typography* (1969). A facsimile reproduction of the *Dialogues* is in *Calligraphy and printing in the sixteenth century*, edited by Ray Nash (1964).

[2] *Mechanick exercises on the whole art of printing* (1683); *Manuel typographique* (1764). Page references to Moxon given here are from the Dover Publications reproduction of the edition by Herbert Davis and Harry Carter (Oxford, 1962; second edition). Quotations from Fournier are in Harry Carter's translation: *Fournier on typefounding* (1930), reprinted as vol. 3 of *The Manuel Typographique of Pierre-Simon Fournier le jeune* (Darmstadt, 1995).

[3] *The Dolphin* no. 1 pp. 24-57 (1933); *Matrix* vol. 4 pp. 31-36 (1984); *Counterpunch* (1996); *La gravure du poinçon typographique* (1998).

The punchcutter tests the progress of the work by making *smoke-proofs*. The face of the punch is blackened in a sooty flame and pressed on to a piece of smooth card; this yields a very clearly defined reproduction of the image on the face. When the punchcutter is satisfied with the appearance of the character image on the smoke-proof the punch is hardened by heat treatment. Its configuration cannot be changed any further once this has been done.

The hardened punch is struck into a block of copper to make a *matrix*. The matrix is *justified* by filing its face and its edges, to ensure that it will produce type which has the correct width, alignment and height to paper, and is used with a *mould* to cast type.

1 Part of a bill of font for J W Haas's Garmont Schwabacher. Approximately 46% actual size.

The purpose of the punchcutter's work is to produce tooling (in the modern, mass-production, sense of the word) for use in a subsequent series of manufacturing processes whose product is the types the printer uses. If punchcutting and matrix justification by hand have always been craft processes, the typefounding to which they are a preliminary has always been an industrial one, in the sense that it produces large numbers of quasi-identical objects by repetitive operations. Figure 1, for example, shows part of a bill of font (a list of characters to be cast) for a Schwabacher cut by J W Haas in Basel in 1760. The complete bill calls for 4 200 e, 2 400 i, 1 550 a and so on; a total of 35 700 sorts of 74 characters, including some punctuation signs but with no numerals or diphthongs and with only three accented letters.

The sheer scale of the typefounding task means that the craft processes that come at the beginning of the type-manufacturing sequence cannot afford to leave any decisions to be taken later on in the industrial processes that follow them: not necessarily for lack of skill on the part of the casters, breakers-off, rubbers, kerners, setters-up or dressers whose trades make up the typefounder's work, but for lack of time. The matrices delivered to the founder must contain complete specifications for the configurations of the character images on the face of the types as well as the widths of the types themselves and the positions of the images on them. Width, sidebearings and alignment come from the dimensions of the justified matrix, while configuration comes from the punch.

To say that typefounding has always been an industrial process is not to denigrate the skills involved in casting type by hand. However, all but one of Moxon's 'Rules and Circumstances to be observed in *Casting*' are consequences of the use of a hand mould, rather than inbuilt requirements of the casting process itself, and become irrelevant once mechanical casters have taken over.[4] His remark makes clear the industrial nature of the caster's work: 'A Work-man will *Cast* about four thousand of these Letters ordinarily in one day'.

The skills and abilities needed to administer a system for producing printer's type are not by any means necessarily the same as those needed to design the types the system produces: less and less so as its processes become more industrialized. Thus in making a new type there will in general be two personalities, the *producer* and the *designer*, with different roles to play. The producer's task is to define precisely the configurations of a set of character images that are consistent in appearance with one another, and then to make types that reproduce the images' configurations. The designer's task complements the producer's: it is to specify the appearance that the whole set of images ought to have.

Designer and producer are not necessarily single individuals. In traditional type manufacture the producer's role embraces the distinct activities of punchcutter, justifier, caster, and their related trades. In discussing designer-producer relationships in this technology the producer is personified in the punchcutter, because the appearance of the new design is fixed when the punches have been cut and hardened. The processes that come after punchcutting in the production sequence, important as they are to the commercial success of the enterprise as a whole, serve only to reproduce the character image configurations that have already been defined on the punches.

Designers and producers cannot work in isolation from their surroundings. The amount of effort involved in bringing a new type to completion is always such that the work will not be carried through

---

[4] *Mechanick exercises*, pp. 172–173. The exception is the note on adding extra tin to the metal used for casting small sizes, to make it run more easily in the mould. Mechanical typecasting was fully developed by the mid-nineteenth century, well before the advent of mechanical punchcutting.

unless a specific requirement for it is felt to exist. A third personality therefore enters the picture: the *client*. The client's role is to know, whether vaguely or exactly, what kind of design is needed, and to support and encourage its manufacture.

Client, designer and producer together make up a *type manufacturing system*. This is a system that incorporates all the operations involved in developing new designs for type and producing the types that realize them. The client discovers and then formulates a requirement for the reproducible visual realization of a script that is not exactly matched by any available type. The designer develops a set of appearance specifications for the characters of a script that will match the requirements the client has expressed. The producer first develops tooling to produce objects that will give rise to character images whose appearance meets the designer's specifications, and then makes the objects themselves in whatever quantities are needed. The whole system is situated in a particular combination of technologies for type manufacture and printing.

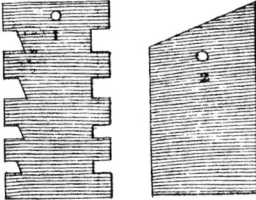

2 Fournier's gauges for calibre (left) and the slope of the italic (right). From Plate III of the Manuel typographique; *actual size*.

In the traditional technology of hand punchcutting, the first step in cutting a new character is to set out its principal dimensions on the polished face of the punch blank. To define the vertical dimensions of a new design, Moxon and Fournier both make notched gauges from thin sheets of metal (Figure 2). They agree on the proportions to be used for roman type: capitals and the ascending letters b d f h i k l should be five-sevenths of the body, and the short letters a c e m n o r s u v w x z three-sevenths. To set the height of the notches on his gauge, Fournier says simply that 'I divide the body of the letter which I am to cut into seven equal parts' without describing how he does so. Moxon's background as a mathematical author and instrument-maker reveals itself in his description of the same stage of the work.

> It may indeed be thought impossible to divide a Body into seven equal Parts, and much more difficult to divide each of those seven equal Parts into six equal Parts, which are Forty two, as aforesaid, especially if the Body be but small; but yet it is possible with curious Working...

He goes on to describe a sort of vernier system that begins with a thin space cast to such a thickness that seven of them exactly fill the body to

Cutting type by hand 7

be subdivided. Then he makes a full point . so that six of them fill the body exactly; then a colon : so that six fill the body and one thin space; then comma , so that six fill the body and two thin spaces; and so on with hyphen - and semicolon ; .

> If now you would make a *Gage* for any number of thin Spaces and sixth Parts of a thin Space [*i.e.* for 6/42 of the body (one thin space) or more], you must take one thin Space less than the number of thin Spaces proposed, and add . : , - ; according as the number of sixth Parts of a thin Space require; and to those complicated Thicknesses you may file a square Notch on the edge of the thin Plate aforesaid ... [5]

Moxon needs these small increments because the minuscules of his black-letter type are 22/42 of the body, as against three-sevenths (18/42) for roman and italic. Fournier makes an extra notch in the gauge, half the height of the body, that he uses for the small capitals of his normal styles or the short characters of a 'large face' [*gros œil*] design.

Both Moxon and Fournier state that the punchcutter continues by drawing an image in final size of the character to be cut. With his gauge ready Moxon prepares the face of the punch, files its bottom edge straight to make the foot-line of the letter, and marks off the letter's height from one of the notches on the gauge.

> Then on the face of the punch he [*i.e.* the punchcutter] draws or marks the exact shape of the Letter, with a Pen and Ink if the Letter be large, or with a smooth blunted Point of a Needle if it be small ... [6]

3 Roman and italic on pearl body. From a prayerbook printed at Oxford in 1708; actual size.

Defining the exact shape of a letter by scribing it freehand on a square of polished steel seems to me so difficult as to be almost impossible

---

[5] *Mechanick exercises*, pp. 92–93.
[6] *Ibid.*, p. 116.

in the sizes used for setting normal text (around 2.5 mm capital-letter height), and quite impossible for the smallest sizes in which type was cut by hand. The small roman and italic in Figure 3 are on pearl body (1.97 mm; 5.6 pt). The technique implied in Moxon's description, of making a drawing on the face of the punch which precisely defines the configuration of the character image and is followed exactly in its production, is clearly impracticable at this end of the size range.[7]

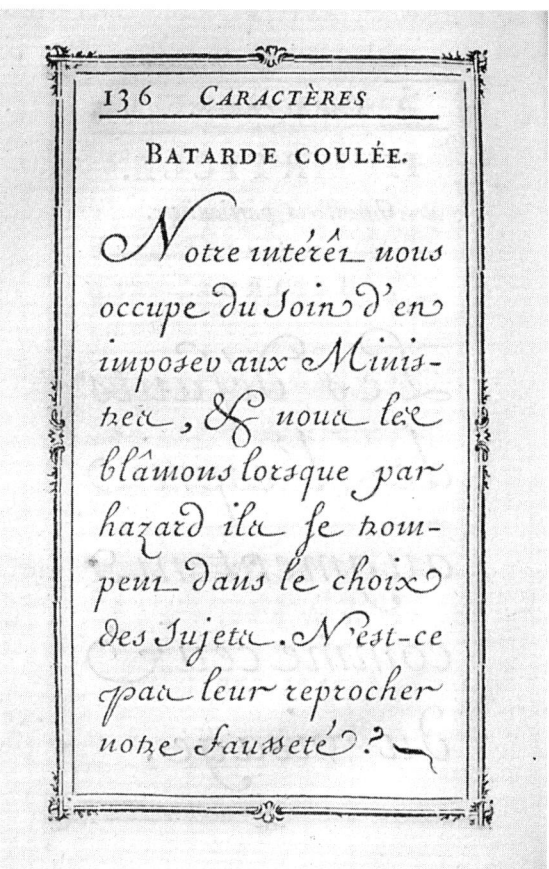

4 *Fournier's* Bâtarde Coulée. *From the* Manuel typographique; *actual size.*

Fournier checks the configuration of his counterpunches by drawing the outside shape of a character round the impression made by its counterpunch in soft metal.

The perfection of the letter's shape depends upon the accuracy with which

---

[7] The punchcutter and typefounder Dirck Voskens, who worked in Amsterdam, was a contemporary of Moxon's. The type specimen issued by his widow around 1695 shows black-letter (*Duyts*) faces, more complex in design than romans, on *Peerel*, *Robijn* and *Diamant* bodies: 2.0, 1.6 and 1.2 mm (5.69, 4.55 and 3.41 pt) respectively. The specimen is illustrated in *Type specimen facsimiles* (1963: edited by John Dreyfus).

the counterpunch is made. To make sure that it is right, the punchcutter strikes it lightly into a piece of lead or type-metal. After cutting away with a sharp penknife the burr due to the metal's being thrown up round the impression, he draws the letter outside it, with a steel point, then by testing it by the gauge in which the letter should fit he sees whether it is of the proper shape and size.

Smeijers is sharply critical of this technique. He points out that 'making a really good sketch [of the letter's intended shape] takes almost as much time as making the actual punch'. Also, because the sketch is made in soft metal rather than on the punch itself, making it does not help the punchcutter in the work of defining and then producing the eventual configuration of the character image. 'In practice you do not draw or scratch at all.'[8]

Fournier himself describes drawing on the punch itself only in one passage, where he discusses certain designs whose twisting strokes mean that counterpunches cannot be used:

> The punches are brought down to the exact width of the gauge, the end is faced, and the letter is drawn upon it the wrong way round with a steel point with all its correct and graceful lines.

The examples he gives are the capitals and some final letters of his *Caractère de Finance, dit Bâtarde Coulée* (Figure 4). These are around 5 mm (13 pt) high on a body of about 20 pt: larger than text types, with their capital-letter heights of 2.5 mm or thereabouts.

My own view is that, above all in small sizes, the only thing the punchcutter can realistically work on is the *appearance* of the character image that is being produced. Take for example the question of calibre: the actual distance from the top to the bottom of an image. For consistency in the line of text the short letters must all appear to have the same size and alignment; but to achieve this they must have a variety of different calibres. In ordinary roman type the feet of m n x stand on the baseline. To align visually with the top of x, the arches of m n go a little above the x-line. The tops of u v w z are on the x-line; to align visually with the feet of m n, the lower junctions of v w and the bowl of u go a little below the baseline. The round characters a c e o s go above the x-line at the top and below the baseline at the bottom.[9]

In the traditional technology, achieving visually consistent horizontal alignment between characters is part of the work of justifying the matrices. However, the justifier cannot get the alignments right unless the punchcutter has first got the differences in calibre right, and these differences are not large. In the early 1990s Jochen Schuchardt in Hamburg carried out a statistical study of 1 790 typefaces that had been converted

---

[8] *Counterpunch*, p. 107.

[9] The size of a character image is a visual attribute of the image rather than a metric one. It corresponds to, but is not identical with, the metric attribute of calibre.

to numerical outline descriptions. He found that for the overwhelming majority of these designs small o was between 3 and 5 percent larger in calibre than small x, with the difference being roughly equally distributed at the tops and bottoms of the characters. In a group of 644 upright roman typefaces the x-height averaged 69% of the capital-letter height, which was normalized for the whole set of designs at two-thirds of the nominal size. Ten Anglo-American points are 3.515 mm (0.138 in), so that for type of 10-pt nominal size the normalized capital-letter height for Schuchardt's samples is 2.343 mm (0.092 in). Hence in his upright romans the average calibre for x is 1.617 mm (0.064 in); the difference in calibre between this and o around 0.065 mm (0.0026 in); and the difference in alignment 0.033 mm (0.0013 in).[10]

Differences of this order are not so small as to be hard to detect once a punch has been cut. Equally, though, they are far too small to be set out consistently on the face of an uncut punch as offsets from dimensions defined by the sheet-metal gauges that Moxon and Fournier propose.[11] Gauges of the kind shown in Figure 2 can do no more than serve as a means of establishing the common dimensional framework on which the subtly varying configurations of successive character images are built. The actual dimensions of the images depart to a greater or lesser extent from this framework, and the amount by which they do so is governed by the appearance they need to have.

Present-day notions of accuracy have to do with the exact reproduction of previously specified dimensions or shapes. Accuracy in hand punchcutting is not the same. It is concerned with precise emulation of the appearance characteristics of existing images. The punchcutting process itself is capable of producing objects whose dimensions differ from one another by very small amounts; Smeijers measured the thickness of the flakes of steel cut from a punch by a graver at around 0.01 mm (0.0004 in).[12] But there is no equipment in traditional punchcutting that would allow internal features of character shapes to be made to dimensions specified *ab initio* with such a degree of accuracy. Instead, the punchcutter works in repeated cycles of cutting and smoke-proofing to approach a desired appearance more and more closely.

As Moxon says, describing work on the punch for capital A after the inside shapes have been produced by counterpunching:

> But if the Footing [the strokes below the crossbar] be too *Fat* or the Triangle of the Top too little in the Inside, he uses the Knife-backt Sculpter [one of his engraving tools], and with one of the edges or both ... he by degrees and with several proffers [*i.e.* smoke-proofs] Cuts away the Inside of the

---

[10] Peter Karow, *Typeface statistics* (1993). Fournier's x-height is three-fifths or 60% of the capital-letter height, smaller than Schuchardt's average figure.

[11] Smeijers says of Fournier's gauge that 'in practice it is quite hard to make, cumbersome, not very accurate and not necessary either' (*Counterpunch*, p. 101). He makes a punch-like gauge that he uses face-to-face with the punch being cut.

[12] *Counterpunch*, p. 86.

Footing, or opens the Triangle at the Top or both, till he hath made the Footing lean enough, and the Triangle big enough.[13]

'Enough' is judged by eye, not by measurement. Fournier says, of a punch being worked on after counterpunching, that

> The size is tested by means of the gauge, and the thickness of stroke by means of a punch finished to the punchcutter's satisfaction, which he uses as a pattern, constantly comparing it with the new one at which he is working.

He uses smoke-proofs to make sure the comparison is accurate:

> The letters m, M are the ones used as standards, the first for the lower-case and the second for capitals. It must be borne in mind that it is impossible to judge of the perfection of the punch without taking an impression of it, since the letters are all cut in reverse ... and are apt to look differently when seen the right way round; besides which the pleasing polish on the steel deceives the judgement, so that a punch which appears excellent that way round may prove not to be so at all when printed.

It is clear here that Fournier's criterion for the correctness of the new punch is that the appearance characteristics of the image it produces should accord with those of the image from a punch that has already been cut. His namesake Henri Fournier, writing in 1825, says that

> The engraver [i.e. the punchcutter] ought always to try to bring each punch into a single style of cutting, so that all the letters of a design, considered together, offer the most perfect harmony.[14]

It is true that by the time this was written the delicacy and elegance of pre-Revolutionary typography had been succeeded by the glacial formality of the Empire; but the point, that a type design has to be a single entity as well as a collection of individually identifiable character shapes, is valid nonetheless.

Consistency of appearance does sometimes follow on dimensional consistency: particularly with the weights of vertical strokes and the separations between them. Paput describes how the dimensions of stroke-weights and counters are checked with small sliding gauges, which are set to an existing dimension and verify another one against it.[15] But the punchcutter has to know which weights and widths should *be* the same, and which should vary in order to *look* the same.

A similar situation occurs in making an italic, where both Moxon and Fournier define the angle that ascending strokes make with the vertical by slanting the inner edge of the notches in their gauges.[16] In cutting the punches, once again, this angle has to be varied from character to character in order to achieve the appearance of a uniform slope.

---

[13] *Mechanick exercises*, p. 114.

[14] 'Les efforts du graveur doivent tendre constamment à ramener chaque poinçon à un système uniforme de gravure, de manière à ce que toutes les lettres d'un même caractère considerées collectivement offrent l'harmonie la plus parfaite': *Traité de la typographie* (1825).

[15] *La gravure du poinçon typographique*, pp. 58–59.

[16] Fournier also has a separate gauge for the slope of italic: *cf.* Figure 2.

2 Making designs for hand punchcutting

The central problem in a type manufacturing system is communication between the parties. The client has to make clear to the designer the requirements the new design is expected to fulfil. The designer has to convey to the producer the appearance the new types are to have. The producer, in consultation with the designer, has to ensure that the visual attributes of the character images the manufactured types give rise to will realize the appearance specifications the designer has in mind.

On 2 November 1540 the punchcutter Claude Garamont signed a contract before the notaries Jean and Claude Boreau in Paris. He was to 'make and cut punches for greek letters' (*faire et tailler poinssons de lectres grecques*) for Pierre Duchâtel, bishop of Tulle and librarian to the king of France. He took on an open-ended commitment to cut punches, and strike and justify matrices, to the number and in the sizes required by Duchâtel and Angelo Vergecio, 'the king's writer in greek' (*escripvain en lectre grecque pour le Roy*). But he was to be paid 22 *sols* 6 *deniers tournois* by the printer Robert Estienne on the delivery of each punch to Vergecio, and his obligation came to an end if he was not paid.[1]

Garamont worked on the types for ten years, though not continuously. He made three sizes: a *cicéro* (around 12 pt body), a *gros-romain* (16 pt) and a *gros-parangon* (20 pt). He must have invested a good deal of his own capital in the project, since Estienne did not get any funds for the work from the royal treasury until 1 May 1542, and even then there was only enough to pay for 200 punches at the contract rate. The performance incentives associated with commissions of this kind, though, are more than merely financial. The *gros-romain* was first used in 1543; the *cicéro* was completed in 1546 and the *gros-parangon* in 1550.

The *grecs du Roy* are interesting because they offer an early demonstration of a type manufacturing system in action. Duchâtel acts as client on the king's behalf. Vergecio plays the role of designer, and Garamont is the producer. We know something about the input to the production process, because examples of Vergecio's writing survive. Its appearance is extremely similar to that of text set in Garamont's types.[2] However,

---

[1] The contract is transcribed by Annie Parent in her article 'Les "Grecs du Roi"' in *L'Art du livre à l'Imprimerie Nationale* (1973). It reads, not surprisingly, as if the person who drew it up was unfamiliar with typemaking technique. Matrices are not mentioned specifically; the contract requires the punches themselves to be 'struck and justified and finished ready to cast' (*iceulx frapper et justiffier et mectre en poinct prestres à fondre*).

[2] *cf.* Figure 11 and Plate 5 of Elizabeth Armstrong's *Robert Estienne, royal printer* (1954). The 1986 edition, while not juxtaposing the illustrations as the earlier one does, adds a photograph of some of Garamont's punches at Plate 13.

Designs for hand punchcutting

the type does not copy the writing. In handwriting the configuration of a character's image varies from one occurrence to another in a text, whereas in type it is always the same. Garamont's punches give rise to images that have the same appearance as the characters in Vergecio's writing, while having configurations that differ from most of them in many respects.

Emulating Vergecio's handwriting required an enormous number of punches to be cut. According to Victor Scholderer,[3] Estienne estimated the *gros-romain* to have 347 punches, the *cicéro* 318 and the *gros-parangon* 430, of which 367 were ligatures and abbreviations. Defining character sets of such a size must have been a daunting task. Parent says that 'before beginning to cut the punches, the character set to be produced has to be precisely specified and drawn out'.[4] The character set does indeed have to be fixed at some stage in the production process, and one can imagine Vergecio making lists of the characters that were needed and writing them out individually by hand. However, I think that *dessiner* does not have the meaning in this context that it would have in a modern setting, where it implies a more or less exact definition of character shape. In 1540 there was no accurate way to reduce a drawn image to the size of a text type, or to transfer the result to the face of a punch before it was cut. In writing out the character sets, Vergecio is providing Garamont with models to work from. These specify the appearance of the new design: typeface and model should look alike. But Garamont is still free to decide on the actual configurations of the character images on the punches. Even if he were competent to do so, it is not part of Vergecio's role as designer to instruct Garamont on the details of calibre, weight and width that have to be taken into account in order to produce a set of images that will be technically satisfactory as type.

Although they play different roles in a type manufacturing system, client, designer and producer are not always separate individuals; nor is the separation between their roles always completely clear. Fournier cut his condensed *Caractères poétiques* '... for works to which it is desired to give an air of lightness by somewhat shortening the lines, especially for setting poetry, which, to gain elegance, needs a greater interval between the lines than usual'. Here Fournier is both client and producer. Whether he is designer as well depends on whether one believes him or Louis René Luce as to the origins of the design.[5] In any event, communication

---

[3] *Greek printing types* (1927).

[4] 'Avant de procéder à la taille des poinçons, il faut fixer avec précision et dessiner l'alphabet à reproduire ...' *Les métiers du livre à Paris au XVIe siècle* (1974), p. 70.

[5] The second volume of Fournier's *Manuel typographique*, in which he illustrated his *caractères poétiques*, appeared in 1766. In his *Essai d'une nouvelle typographie* of 1771, Luce implies that Fournier took the idea for the new design from specimens that Luce himself had published in 1732.

within the manufacturing system would not have been a problem while the type was being made.

In most circumstances, though, designer and producer are separate individuals or institutions, and communication between them has to be mediated by some means. At the beginning of the twenty-first century, conditioned by more than a hundred years of typemaking by machine, we tend to think of this means as being primarily graphic, with drawings going one way and proofs of type the other. But exchanges of graphic objects are not the only way to specify the appearance of character images. In 1819 Pierre Didot the elder published his *Spécimen des nouveaux caractères*: the culmination of French neo-classical type design, with a systematized range of body sizes and what D B Updike describes as 'marked and disagreeable peculiarities in some letters'.[6] In his introduction to the specimen Didot says that the types it shows were cut under his personal supervision by the punchcutter Vibert, with whom he spent time every day for a period of ten years.

> My most frequently repeated corrections, my most exacting demands, even my perfectionist whims, which often led me to begin the same character two or three times over, could not cool his enthusiasm, or allow me to discover the limits of his patience.[7]

We can imagine Vibert bringing yet another set of smoke-proofs to Didot, who says 'No, that's not quite right. I want . . . '. Producer-designer communication in this system, from Vibert to Didot, is indeed carried on graphically; but in the other direction Didot's description suggests that it was primarily verbal, perhaps with graphic-mode supplements in the form of sketches drawn by him on Vibert's proofs. The desired appearance of each successive version of the design is specified in terms of modifications to the appearance of the previous one.

When drawings do constitute the medium for designer-producer communication in a type design system, it is important for the success of the enterprise that their function is properly understood by all the parties involved. In the traditional technology of hand punchcutting, for the reasons discussed in Chapter 1 above, a designer's drawings can only serve as *models*: objects that convey information to the producer about the intended appearance of the new design. Difficulties will arise if attempts are made to use them as *patterns*, incorporating precise specifications of character image configuration.

In the summer of 1912 the calligrapher Edward Johnston was recruited by Harry Graf Kessler to help with the production of an italic type to

---

[6] *Printing types* (2nd edition, 1937), p. 179.

[7] 'Mes retouches les plus multipliées, mes indications les plus minutieuses, peut-être même mes caprices de perfectionnement, qui souvent m'ont porté à recommencer deux ou trois fois les mêmes types, n'ont pu refroidir son zèle, ni me laisser entrevoir le terme de sa patience.' Vibert must have been a very remarkable man.

match the roman that had been cut by the punchcutter E P Prince for Kessler's Cranach Press.[8] Prince had already cut some punches for the italic, using as his model a redrawing of the text type in G A Tagliente's writing-book of 1525, but Kessler considered these to be unsatisfactory.

Johnston approached the problem by making what he called 'character sketches'. He was emphatic that these were not to be taken as anything but guides to the appearance of the finished type. In his third set of sketches, for example, Johnston marks the dot of *i* with "Mr Prince may do what he likes with this", and the upper left terminal of *u* with "Mr P. may adapt this". Johnston understood the need for precise specifications of character image configuration in a type-manufacturing project, but considered that as a calligrapher he lacked the knowledge to produce them. His view, stated in a long letter to Kessler, was that

> ... [Prince] wants a *definite statement* to deal with, *from people who cannot give one*! I say we cannot give such a *definite statement*, because, in the first place, we do not know the true shapes of the type, and, in the second place, we cannot draw them exactly as we think they ought to be ... I know *that I cannot draw them with exactness* and, for example, Prince will say: – *'this letter has a different slope from that'* (which slope do you want?). *'The strokes of this letter are thicker than the strokes of the other in proportion'* (which thickness do you want?).

In this passage Johnston puts his finger exactly on the point where responsibility between designer and producer divides. The designer's task is to specify the appearance of the eventual types. The producer's task is to provide objects that will give rise to character images whose configurations give them the appearance the designer has specified. Johnston felt that he had already performed the designer's part satisfactorily with his character sketches:

> ... Prince should be given as free a hand with them as possible. This is what he managed to do with fair success in the case of the *a*. If you compare his smoke ... with my first 'character sketch' you will see that he only caught something of the character, the actual *punch letter* being strikingly different in almost every detail, from my *chalked letter*.

It is true that later on in the project Johnston made drawings in which the details of character shapes were more carefully specified; but in making them he had, in Dreyfus's words, 'been manœuvred into doing precisely what he had earlier refused to do'. Kessler persuaded Johnston to make detailed drawings of the complete alphabet because (in our terms) he felt that Prince was more at home with patterns than with models; with specifications of configuration, rather than guides to appearance.

> This reduction [of Johnston's new drawings] and your big sketches and remarks will *then only* be given to Prince to work on, so that he can have

---

[8] The story is told by John Dreyfus in his *Italic quartet* (1966). The book's text is reproduced, with one illustration omitted, in Dreyfus's *Into print* (1994). It is a *locus classicus* for any study of communication in type manufacture.

the letters before him the *exact size* and the *exact shape* (including slant, weight, colour etc.). This is what he has always been accustomed to …

However misconceived this may have been, Kessler needed to do something to move matters forward. The type had to be finished, and the project's earlier history had meant that Johnston had never been given the chance to deal with Prince on the terms he would have preferred.

Nineteenth-century developments in photographic technique made it possible to transfer reduced drawings of characters to the face of a punch in final size. In one version of the method a relief plate is made from the reduced drawing by photoengraving, and the character shape transferred to the punch as a smoke-proof.[9] Alternatively, the face can be coated with light-sensitive material and the character photographed on to it directly.

With these developments the function of drawings in hand punch-cutting undergoes a change. Whereas before they could only serve as models, they now have the potential to be patterns instead. Paul Koch describes both situations. Writing in 1933, he first describes how he works from letters that he has drawn himself. Like Fournier and Moxon, but with different tools, he begins by setting out the principal dimensions of the characters to be cut.

> With compasses I transfer the height of the letter from the glass gauge to a strip of paper … I paste a strip of paper next to the face of the punch in the screw-stock [*i.e.* the fixture in which his punch is held], lay on a small T-square from the left, and draw from the corresponding points of the paper fine lines upon the face of the punch, with an etching-needle. My written copy is then so placed that I see it in a small mirror, or it is held against the light [so that he sees the drawing laterally inverted, through the back of the paper]. With the etching needle I transfer the image, within the lines drawn previously, on the punch.[10]

Here his models, worked out with a broad pen beforehand, specify the appearance of the characters he wants to produce. However, he says,

> This method of transfer is only used when I am permitted some leeway in the fashioning of the final form of the characters. When working from carefully drawn copy I have a zinc etching made …

In this case the function of the drawing is to specify the intended configuration of the character image. Koch's subsequent account implies that he can follow the transferred shape very closely. He acknowledges, though, that he does not usually make punches for the type sizes used

---

[9] This technique is illustrated by Henk Drost in his 1983 demonstration at Stanford University: *Visible language* vol. 19 no. 1 (1985). Paput uses the same method of transfer from a relief impression to copy a character shape from an existing type to the face of a new punch for cutting: *La gravure du poinçon typographique*, pp. 38–40.

[10] 'The making of printing types', *The Dolphin* vol. 1 (1933). His 'glass gauge' is a small square of glass scribed with a grid of fine lines separated by multiples of printers' points.

Designs for hand punchcutting

for setting normal text. 'Generally I cut punches for type of 12- to 16-point size'.

a d e m o r s t — Drawings

a d e m o r s t — 24D

a d e m o r s t — 20D

a d e m o r s t — 16D

a d e m o r s t — 14D

a d e m o r s t — 12D

a d e m o r s t — 10D

5 *Comparison between drawings by Jan van Krimpen and types cut from them by P H Rädisch. The images in the first row are taken from the original drawings for Lutetia roman, which are in the Meermanno Museum in The Hague. The others are from the St Bride Printing Library's copy of the specimen published by Enschedé's in 1927. This is printed on a laid paper with a fairly heavy impression. Some of the increasing weight of the character images with decreasing size is attributable to the effects of impression and ink-squash. In the illustration the 16D type is twice actual size; the other examples are scaled to it so that the calibre of* o *is constant.*

P H Rädisch cut punches for Jan van Krimpen at Joh. Enschedé en Zonen in Haarlem between 1923 and his retirement in 1957. In his introduction to Van Krimpen's *Letter to Philip Hofer*[11] John Dreyfus describes the designer's working method:

> He made drawings for all his types on a hard, heavily-sized sheet of paper. This had rather a rough surface which, he said, gave him a good grip on the paper. Despite its surface, he was still able to make highly-finished designs upon it in one large size, approximately two inches high. Nearly all his designs were then cut by an extremely skilled punchcutter [*i.e.* Rädisch], who cut punches in every size for which types were required. Part of

---

[11] The *Letter* was a commissioned manuscript written between 1953 and 1955 for Philip Hofer, curator of the Department of Printing and Graphic Arts at the Houghton Library of Harvard University, and published with an introduction by John Dreyfus in 1972. Its full title is *A letter to Philip Hofer on certain problems connected with the mechanical cutting of punches*.

> the punchcutter's art is to make the small but important adjustments which *must* be made to a basic design if it is to serve for a whole range of sizes ... [12]

The range of sizes was wide: 6 to 48 Didot, for example, for the roman of Van Krimpen's Lutetia. In his review of Rädisch's autobiography *A tot Z*, G W Ovink adds some detail:

> [Rädisch] had photographic line-engravings made in copper – zinc was not sharp enough – of each sign in the desired size, from the original drawing, and with these he then made a smoke print on the blank steel bar. Then he scratched in the contours very lightly as guide-lines, with the possibility of deviating from them for adapting to the different sizes.[13]

Figure 5 compares some characters from Van Krimpen's drawings for the roman minuscule alphabet of Lutetia with the corresponding characters in part of the range of sizes cut by Rädisch. It is clear that as well as adjusting the configurations of the character images between one size and another in the way that Dreyfus describes, Rädisch has moved away from the drawings in settling some of their proportions: notably with a m and r. Although, as Walter Tracy says, Van Krimpen's drawings were 'immaculate and unambiguous', it is hardly true, at least in this first example of their collaboration, that Rädisch made 'a perfect copy on steel of the character on the drawing, without any deviation'.[14] Even with the help of photographic reduction, the drawings for Lutetia have served as models rather than patterns for the punchcutter.

One might speculate that Rädisch began work on the 16D size, the first to be cut, by making an m that owed something to his own experience as well as to the reduced image of Van Krimpen's drawing on the face of the punch blank. Van Krimpen, at the beginning of his type-designing career, was not yet ready to emulate Pierre Didot in his collaboration with Vibert: he accepted Rädisch's punch as it had been cut, and with it the effects of the narrowed character on the proportions of the alphabet as a whole. In the revised version of Lutetia, made in 1929 for the catalogue of the Frick collection, h m and n are wider than in the original, although s is much narrower.[15]

---

[12] *Letter*, p. 17; emphasis in the original.
[13] 'Grandeurs and miseries of the punchcutter's craft', *Quaerendo* vol. 10 no. 2 (1980).
[14] *Letters of credit* (1986), p. 118.
[15] *Ibid.*, p. 104.

3 Cutting type by machine

In the traditional technology of type manufacture by hand, the function of drawings is to specify the appearance of characters to the punchcutter. Drawings are not components of the manufacturing system, but serve as visual references against which the system's products are compared. In the latter part of the nineteenth century hand punchcutting began to be replaced by mechanical techniques of punchcutting and matrix engraving. With these developments the role of drawings in type manufacture evolves. Drawings of a new kind, produced in specialized premises by specialist workers, become embedded in the manufacturing system itself. These drawings are intermediates in the process of type manufacture, and their function is the specification of shape to other intermediates.

The transition from hand to mechanical methods of type manufacture which produced this evolution altered the whole conceptual basis of typography. By demanding the production of large drawings as the first stage in the manufacturing sequence the new methods marked the end of punchcutting as a craft, and brought about the separation between the activities of *designing* and *making* which is characteristic of industrial processes in general.[1]

The hot-metal composing machines that were being developed towards the end of the nineteenth century were primarily oriented towards the composition of text. The first to be commercially successful, Ottmar Mergenthaler's Linotype, demanded large numbers of identical matrices. 'The Mergenthaler Linotype machine has for its fundamental element about fifteen hundred brass matrices, which respond to the operator's touch upon the keyboard, and thus create the type-matter ready for use.'[2] Frequently occurring characters like e or a had 20 matrices each in the machine's magazine.

In this situation hand-cut punches had some serious disadvantages. A new alphabet took too long to cut in the first place, and an individual punch much too long to recut if it broke while a run of matrices was being struck. In addition, the newspaper publishers who were the principal potential customers for the new machines wanted the appearance of their existing pages to be reproduced exactly. The production of punches had to be mechanized in some way, and a method worked out

---

[1] The principal source for material on type manufacture by machine, as well as for the first phase of mechanical typesetting, is L A Legros & J C Grant's monumental *Typographical printing-surfaces: the technology and mechanism of their production* (1916).

[2] Information from the Mergenthaler Linotype Company, quoted in 1902 by T L De Vinne: *Plain printing types* (second edition).

of making exact reproductions of existing types, if the new composing machines were to succeed.[3]

The development that made this possible was the application of pantographic techniques to the manufacture of types intended for composing text. A pantograph is a device that reproduces the movements of a tracing point at a different scale by means of pivoted levers. In 1843 William Leavenworth of Allentown, New Jersey, had combined pantographic reduction with a high-speed rotating cutter to produce a machine for cutting wood type from relief patterns (Figure 6).

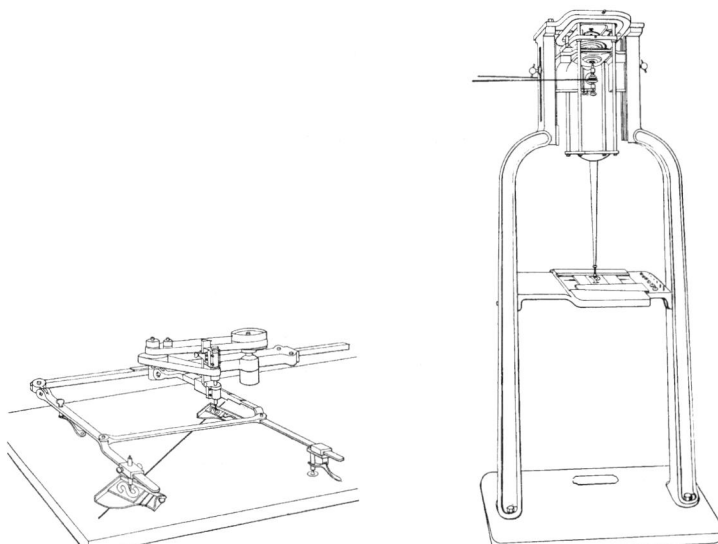

6, 7 Leavenworth's pantograph for wood type, and Benton's punchcutting pantograph. From Plain printing types *(second edition, 1902).*

In Leavenworth's machine the blank from which the letter was cut remained stationary, and the cutting head moved around it. This complicated the problem of driving the rotating cutter, and set an upper limit to the size and consequently the precision of the cutting head itself. Later machines achieved higher accuracies by keeping the cutting head fixed and allowing the pantograph's levers to move the workpiece that was being cut. In 1885 Linn Boyd Benton, of the typefounders Benton, Waldo & Co in Milwaukee, patented a pantographic type-

---

[3] Typefounders could already reproduce types exactly by electrotyping: depositing copper on the face of the type by electrolysis to build up a shell from which a matrix was made. The results were satisfactory for normal typecasting machines, but the process was too slow and its products not robust enough for the multiple circulating matrices of the new technology. Carl Schlesinger suggests in *The biography of Ottmar Mergenthaler* (1989) that Mergenthaler nevertheless made some electrotyped matrices when he was under pressure to reproduce the type of the New York *Tribune*.

cutting machine that could work in very small sizes (Figure 7). His machine was arranged vertically, rather than horizontally like Leavenworth's, with the workpiece held above the cutting head and the pivots for the pantograph levers at the top of the machine. Benton understood that the cutting tools themselves were crucial to the accuracy of the result, and made special devices for shaping and sharpening them.

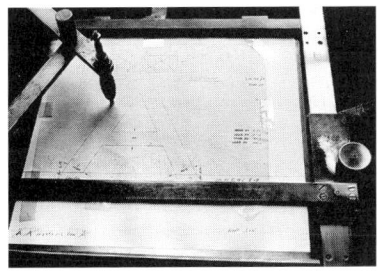

a

b

c

d

8 *Mechanical punchcutting: early stages.*
 a: *Pattern drawing.* b: *Pattern-cutting pantograph.*
 c: *The cut pattern.* d: *Retouching interior angles with a file.*

The original application of Benton's machine was to cut character masters in type-metal, which were used to produce copper matrices by electrotyping. The matrices were needed to cast the 'self-spacing' types, with systematized character widths, that Benton, Waldo & Co had introduced in 1883. However, the machine was soon improved and adapted to cut steel punches.[4]

---

[4] This is Legros & Grant's version of events: *Typographical printing-surfaces*, ch. 12. Richard Huss says in *The development of printers' mechanical composition methods* (1973) that Benton's 1885 patent was for a matrix-engraving machine, and the suggestion to modify it for punchcutting came from the Mergenthaler Printing Company, developers of the Linotype machine. In *The printer's composition matrix* (1985) he cites a Mergenthaler directors' report of 21 January 1888: '... by a contract recently completed with Benton, Waldo & Co., of Milwaukee, for the mechanical cutting of these dies [*i.e.* punches], it is believed that absolute accuracy in the reproduction of the best styles of type can now be secured.'

Linotype's version of the process is illustrated in Figures 8 and 9.[5] The starting-point is a large drawing around 25 cm high, on which a character shape is drawn as an outline. The first stage of the process is to make a reduction from the drawing on a horizontal pantograph fitted with a rotary cutter. This cuts into a plate made up of two layers of brass sweated together, and reproduces the shape on the drawing at a height of around 10 cm. The two layers of brass are then separated; the character shape, cut out of the upper layer, may be retouched by hand to sharpen up the rounded-out interior angles left by the cylindrical cutting tool. The finished pattern is riveted to a backing plate so that it stands in relief.

At the punchcutting machine the operator repeatedly traces round the pattern with circular 'followers' of progressively decreasing size, so that the path of the cutting tool approximates more and more closely, though on a reduced scale, to the outline of the pattern (Figure 9).

e   f

9 *Mechanical punchcutting: final stages.*
e: *The punchcutting pantograph.* f: *The tracing point, with followers of different sizes on the bed of the machine.*

The amount of reduction between pattern and punch can be varied by moving the cutting head and the workpiece up or down in the punchcutting machine, thus altering the ratio between the long and short levers of the pantograph. The vertical slides for the cutting head, and the chains at either side of the frame that support it, can be seen

---

[5] The photographs in these illustrations were taken in March 1978 at D Stempel AG in Frankfurt. The operator is Michael Wilhelm Schneider. The observer in the left-hand photograph of Figure 9 is the letter-cutter Ralph Beyer.

Cutting type by machine 23

in the left-hand photograph of Figure 9. A single set of patterns can thus be used to produce punches in a range of sizes.

In the Lanston Monotype Corporation's version of the technique the patternmaking pantograph cut into a layer of wax which was then electroplated with copper.[6] The copper shell was filled with type-metal to yield the pattern for the punchcutting machine.

Walter Wilkes describes another version still, in which the first stage is to cut the character shape from thin cardboard at the same size as the pattern drawing.

> Some typefounders do not use the working drawings for patternmaking directly, but transfer them at their original size on to cardboard of around 250 gsm substance and cut the character shape from that . . . The shape thus makes a useful pattern that is easy to trace round with the [patternmaking] pantograph . . .[7]

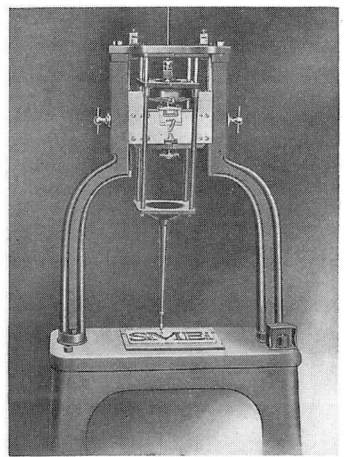

10 'The celebrated Benton Matrix Engraving Machine': from the 1923 ATF specimen book.

Matrices as well as punches were made by pantographic reduction from patterns that followed the shapes on large drawings. The 1923 specimen-book of the American Type Founders Company claims that

> During the last quarter century the entire process of making matrices has been revolutionized and greatly improved by the American Type Founders

---

[6] The process is illustrated in *Monotype Recorder* vol. 40 no. 3 (1956).

[7] 'Verschiedene Schriftgießereien benutzen die Werkzeichnungen nicht unmittelbar zur Schablonenherstellung, sondern übertragen sie in Originalgröße auf einen etwa 250 g/m² schweren Karton und schneiden die Figur anschließend aus . . . Die Figur bildet dann eine erhabene Schablone, die leicht mit dem Pantographen zu umfahren ist . . .': *Das Schriftgießen* (1990), p. 69. The board he describes is surprisingly light: only a little more than three times the substance of ordinary photocopier paper.

Company, by the development of the wonderful Benton Matrix Cutting Machine, of which it is the exclusive owner and sole manufacturer in America.

Like Benton's punchcutting pantograph the machine has a vertical layout, but with the blank matrix below the cutting head so that the depth of cut can be easily controlled (Figure 10).

F W Goudy used a matrix-engraving machine of a different design but with a similar layout in his own Village Type Foundery between 1925 and 1939.

> ...I contend that I can cut matrices for type from 8-point to 72-point from the same pattern and retain in each size the exact character of my original drawing, because each stem, hairline, serif or counter is enlarged or reduced proportionately.[8]

Matrices for types as small as 8 pt were not normally made by engraving. As Walter Tracy says, speaking of Goudy's designs, 'the action of the rotary cutting tool makes it impossible to obtain the precise angles and corners needed in hard-edge faces'.[9] Goudy was also unusual in cutting a 9:1 range of sizes from a single set of patterns.

11 *Matrix-engraving pantograph, with a close-up of the cutting head. The controls at the left of the head adjust the depth of cut.*

The matrix-engraving machines generally used in European foundries, unlike Benton's and Goudy's, were laid out horizontally. The patterns were outlines engraved in metal plates, rather than the relief letters that Benton's machines used. Different shapes of cutting tool were used for successive phases of the work, with the cutting head of the machine adjustable for depth of cut. Figure 11 shows a matrix-engraving pantograph made by Kämpf of Frankfurt.

The two pantographic processes, punchcutting and matrix engraving, are summarized in Figures 12 and 13.

---

[8] *Typologia* (1940), p. 114.

[9] *Letters of credit* (1986), p. 152. By 'hard-edge faces' Tracy means sanserif, slab-serif and modern-face designs.

Cutting type by machine 25

12 *Stages in display type manufacture by cutting punches. The patterns at the top of the photograph are for 20 pt Helvetica light expanded. The punches are below them. The leftmost objects in the bottom row are matrix blanks. Next to them are matrices that have been struck but not justified. The finished matrices, for use in a typecasting machine, are on the right.*

13 *Stages in display type manufacture by matrix engraving. The patterns are for 24 pt Univers bold. The one on the left is engraved but not finished; the one on the right is ready for use. At the left in the bottom row are matrix blanks. The right-hand one is finished ready for engraving. The matrix for* m *is as it comes from the engraving machine; that for* H *is ready for casting.*

4 Making designs for machine-cut type

The feature of mechanical punchcutting that made it a prerequisite for the development of mechanical composition was its reproducibility. Hot-metal composing machines use matrices which, for a given character of a given design, have to be strictly identical with one another; and this identity has to be preserved over the whole production run of each matrix, which may extend to thousands of copies over many years. Even if the punch that produces the matrices does not break in striking it will wear in the course of time, and when it does it has to be replaced with another punch which is identical to the first. The new punch has to be made from the same pattern as the old one, by procedures that will yield an identical configuration. Thus for each character the shape on the punch, and hence on the matrix and the type, is defined in mechanical terms by the shape on the pattern. However, the accuracy required on the pattern is such that it has to be produced from a drawing which is larger than the pattern itself.

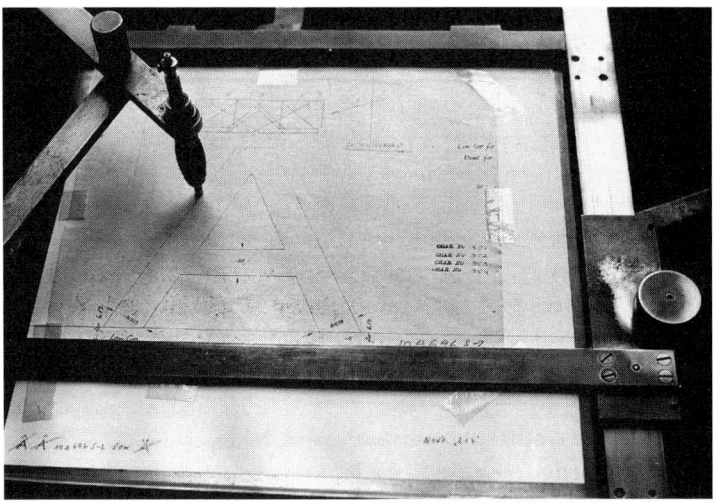

14 The pattern drawing from Figure 8.

Both the Lanston Monotype Corporation and the Mergenthaler Linotype Company used pattern drawings corresponding to a body size of about ten inches, and these needed to be made with an accuracy of around 0.2 mm (0.008 in).[1]

---

[1] The pattern drawings for Linotype designs were made to a nominal size of 768 pt (270 mm; 10.6 in). The capital **A** in Figure 14 is for a 6-pt type, and has the thicknesses in inches of its three strokes marked: .01275 and .01325 for the diagonals and .011 for the crossbar. This suggests that strokeweight measurements were on a scale whose minimum increment was 0.00025 in (0.00635 mm). Suppose

Making drawings to this degree of accuracy was a new requirement for type manufacturers. The first types made for mechanical composition were, in Stanley Morison's words, 'copied or stolen from the typefounders'.[2] This is not surprising, since from Gutenberg onwards new technologies for producing text have always begun by trying to match the appearance of the existing product. The typefounders themselves, when they had occasion to copy or steal one anothers' designs, had normally done so by electrotyping: a process that delivered exact copies of types without any drawing at all, but whose product was matrices rather than punches. The new composing machines needed punches; punches needed the pantograph; and the pantograph needed drawings.

Making large pattern drawings from existing types (or punches, when they were available) was reasonably straightforward. F H Pierpont was the first manager of the Lanston Monotype Corporation's works at Salfords near Redhill in Surrey. He came there in 1899 from Berlin, where he had come from America to set up a matrix-making facility for the Typograph linecasting machine.[3] During his time in Germany Pierpont had taken out a patent for a 'microscope with camera lucida for delineating typefaces'.[4]

We can imagine that this resembled the device that Beatrice Warde describes in 1935:

> ...each type [of a design to be copied] would have been placed in an epidiascope, which enlarges an image with an uncanny illusion of the third dimension, and each image would have been traced by someone who could tell whether, or how much, each type had been worn down by printing.[5]

Legros & Grant describe the same procedure in less sympathetic terms:

> Others working in this field [*i.e.* the reproduction of existing designs] use optical devices that give enlargements of the character which are of necessity neither exact nor sharp in outline. These require further correction by skilful manipulators to standardize the resulting drawing

---

we want to hold dimensional errors on the type itself to less than half of this amount, with a maximum of, say, 0.0001 in (0.00254 mm). The reduction from drawing to type is 128 times, so that an error of this size on the type corresponds to an error on the drawing of 0.0128 in (0.325 mm). However, each of the two stages of reduction (drawing to pattern; pattern to punch) introduces its own inaccuracies, making the maximum permissible error on the drawing less than this.

[2] *A tally of types* (1953), p. 19.

[3] Typograph AG were the manufacturers in Europe of the Rogers linecaster, of which the American rights had been bought up by Ottmar Mergenthaler in 1891 to secure some patents that were crucial to the development of his own invention.

[4] British patent 23397 of 1896: *Typographical printing-surfaces*, p. 598.

[5] 'Cutting type for the machines', *The Dolphin* no. 2 (1935).

for gauge, thickness of stroke, form of character and position to be ultimately occupied on the body of the type to be produced.[6]

They prefer to use a microscope with a bifilar eyepiece and calibrated cross-slides, with which they measure the principal dimensions of the character to be copied.[7]

Pierpont's projection microscope could be used to enlarge character images printed from type as well as the types themselves. Monotype Plantin Series 110, adapted from an example of Robert Granjon's Augustijn roman printed in 1905 at the Plantin-Moretus Museum, seems to be the first instance of its use at Salfords for this purpose. The design was considerably redrawn to make it suitable for printing on coated papers.[8]

Whether the traced images that were the input to the drawing office's work originated from type, punches, or printed images, they were redrawn with straight-edges and french curves. These were often specially made to fit the characteristic forms of a new design. Part of the objective in this work was to secure consistency between elements such as strokeweights and curve configurations in the different character shapes of the design. Drawings were also made at this stage for characters for which types, printed images or original designs were not available. When the large character drawings were traced on the pattern-cutting pantograph, the same curves that had been used to make the drawings themselves were used to guide the tracing point. This ensured that the shapes on the drawings were reproduced as accurately as possible on the pattern.[9]

An original design for mechanical composition normally arrived at the manufacturer's type-drawing office, in Beatrice Warde's words, 'in the form of inked-in drawings, preferably about two inches high'. These are not, and cannot be, accurate enough for punches and matrices to be made from them directly. Rather than being patterns, they are models: their purpose is to provide information about the intended appearance of the new design. The drawing office's task, in preparing large pattern drawings from the material provided by the designer, is once again to translate between appearance and shape. The translation is no longer implicit, as it was for the hand punchcutter working directly on the appearance of a character image at final size and almost

---

[6] *Typographical printing-surfaces*, p. 214.

[7] 'So far as the authors can ascertain, they are alone in using this method.' This is probably because it was impracticably slow. Tracing round the projected image of a type is much quicker than measuring the type itself with a microscope, and the results have to be reworked by the drawing office in any case.

[8] Christopher Burke, 'The early years: 1900–1922', *Monotype Recorder* new series no. 10 (1997), p. 9.

[9] David Saunders describes Monotype drawing office practice in 'The Type Drawing Office', *Monotype Recorder* new series no. 8 (1990).

Designs for machine-cut type

incidentally generating a shape on the face of the punch while doing so. The drawing-office staff have to make the translation explicit. The drawings they produce specify the appearance of character images indirectly, via the shapes of the patterns, punches, matrices and type that will be produced from them. The relationship that has to be worked out is that between a particular set of precisely defined shapes and the appearance of the character images they will give rise to.

An account of this process exists, given by an unusually articulate designer who worked in close collaboration with the producers of his designs: W A Dwiggins, who designed the Caledonia, Electra and Metro typefaces, among others, for the Mergenthaler Linotype Company between 1929 and 1946.[10]

In 1937 Linotype had commissioned Rudolf Ruzicka to design a typeface for bookwork composition. Ruzicka asked Dwiggins what his working methods were, and Dwiggins replied in a letter that he rewrote for publication in 1940 as *WAD to RR: a letter about designing type.*

> The way I work at present is to draw an alphabet 10 times 12 point size, the letters carefully finished... Ten times 12 point [*i.e.* 4.22 cm; 1.67 in] is a convenient size to work; and I have a diminishing glass that reduces the letters to something like 12 point size when I put the drawing on the floor and squint at it through the glass held belt high. This gives a rough idea of what the reduction does to curves and things. Having got a start on what I want by this means I turn the drawing over to G. [C H Griffith, in charge of typographic development at Linotype] and he puts a few of the characters through – possibly lowercase h and p. He makes his large pattern drawings (64 times 12 point), cuts, casts and proves the trial characters; and sends me his large drawings, my 10 times drawings, & proofs on smooth and rough paper... From the large pattern sheets I can see just how details behave when they get down to size, and can change the weights of serifs, thin lines, etc. etc. accordingly.

Once strokeweights and alignments had been decided between himself and Griffith, Dwiggins went on to make freehand outline drawings of the whole alphabet, based on accurately drawn horizontal alignments, at Linotype's pattern-drawing size of 768 pt. He worked from right-reading to wrong-reading and back again on either side of sheets of thin bond paper, erasing and redrawing until he arrived at 'a "positive" that is good enough to mark down on the other side of the paper as a "negative" in thin pencil line'. These wrong-reading outlines were given to the Linotype drawing-office staff 'as a guide for [their] French curves and straight edges'. At Linotype, as at Monotype's type-drawing office, nothing was left to the individual hand in making the production drawings.

In making the 120-pt filled-in character drawings with which the design process begins, Dwiggins is conducting a dialogue between shape and appearance. The characters in the drawings are large enough to have shapes; but the subject-matter of the drawings themselves is appearance.

---

[10] Walter Tracy, *Letters of credit* (1986), ch. 16.

Dwiggins's remark about the effects of reduction makes this clear. The finished 768-pt outlines that Dwiggins produces, on the other hand, are exclusively about shape, as are the pattern drawings derived from them at the drawing office.

The first step in the transition between the two is to make types whose actual shapes are reduced versions of the shapes in the 120-pt drawings. Doing this involves the whole manufacturing process: enlarging the 120-pt drawings, making pattern drawings from them, cutting brass patterns, reducing these on the pantograph to make punches, striking matrices and casting type. The pattern drawings returned with the type proofs show the designer in detail what the shapes are that give rise to the appearance of the character images in the proofs.

With this information the designer can make and revise his own large drawings, with a good chance of arriving at a shape that will give the characters their intended appearance. The results are submitted to the type producer, who reviews them in the light of established standards for calibres, alignments, strokeweights and sidebearing widths: obligatory requirements in the domain of shape, that have their effects in the domain of appearance. With these decided on, the designer goes ahead to make his working drawings at the large size. These are redrawn at the factory to the producer's own manufacturing standards, so that they are suitable for use as input to the next stage of the process. Dwiggins was comfortable with this reworking of his drawings:

> I haven't any complaint to make about the staff's French curves – they do a surprisingly faithful job. Just what happens in the next step – the reduction to the brass-pattern size . . . I don't know. I haven't compared working-drawing with brass yet; not easy to do. But so far as I can observe from the final proof they keep the original touch here too.

By the standards of the Lanston Monotype Corporation a working relationship of such closeness between designer and producer was most unusual, as was Dwiggins's detailed involvement with the technicalities of pattern drawing. In Salfords' practice the translation from appearance to shape – from the 'two-inch' drawings provided by the designer to the large outlines used at the pantograph – was exclusively the drawing office's affair. In *The letter forms and type designs of Eric Gill* (1976), Robert Harling illustrates Gill's drawing for the second version of the companion italic to his Perpetua typeface. Beatrice Warde, in her later description of matrix-making at Salfords, shows an operator tracing round the outlines of a projected image of the same drawing, enlarged to the 'ten-inch' size of Monotype's pattern drawings.[11]

The outlines that the Linotype drawing office sent to Dwiggins along with the types made from his 120-pt drawings in the first stage of his design's development must have been produced by similar means. At Salfords, though, outline drawings did not leave the drawing office,

---

[11] *Monotype Recorder* vol. 40 no. 3 (1956).

Designs for machine-cut type 31

and producer-designer communication in developing a design was conducted entirely by means of proofs of type. Figure 15 shows Eric Gill struggling to define modifications to his design for Perpetua italic, consequent on an experimental redesign of *f*, in a medium which is quite unsuitable for the task at hand.

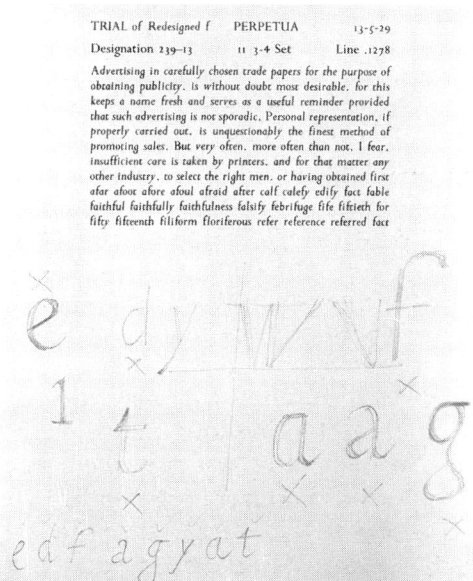

15 Sketches by Eric Gill on a trial proof of 13-pt Perpetua 239 italic (St Bride Printing Library).

Gill is confronted here by an extreme example of a problem faced by all designers of metal type: how to specify modifications to the appearance of a type that is under development. Because the images on a proof of text type are small, it is impossible for the designer to make quantitative modifications to them; in other words, to draw on to the proof a new shape for an image that will serve as a pattern for the producer. The designer has to be content with making qualitative comments on the image's appearance. These may be verbal, graphic or a mixture of the two, but in any event they cannot convey exact dimensional information to the producer.

    This presents no great difficulty to the hand punchcutter, who corrects the appearance of the images in the smoke-proofs directly by modifying the punches. With pantographic techniques the problem is not so simple. The producer has to carry out a reverse translation from appearance to shape, converting the designer's qualitative remarks about the appearance of the images into precise quantitative modifications to the shapes on the pattern drawings. Drawings and patterns are both much larger than the images that will eventually be produced from them. With matrix engraving there are no punches, so that the only way to make a reliable assessment of a character's appearance at final size is to cast type from its matrix and proof it. With mechanical punchcutting the whole production process, from modifying drawings to proofing type, has to be gone through at each stage of the development cycle. In either case, a multistage process needs to be invoked that has none of the responsiveness of cutting and smoke-proofing by hand.

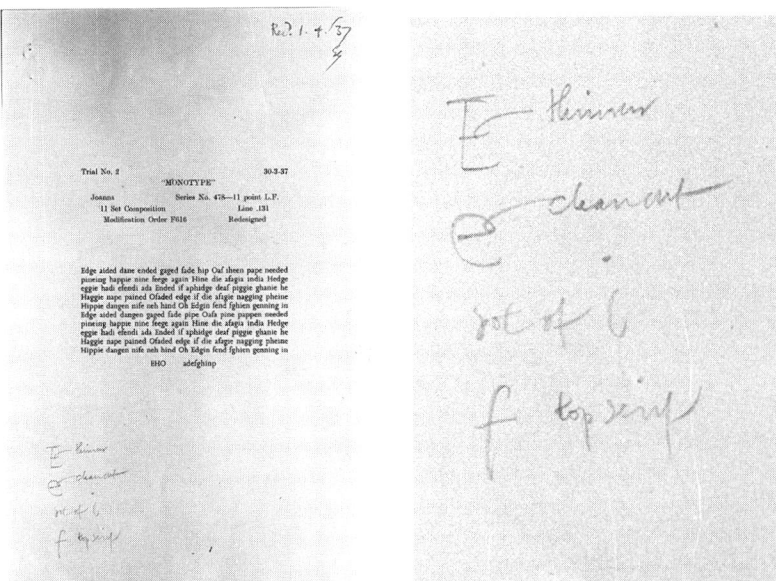

16 *Corrections by Eric Gill to a proof of Monotype Joanna (St Bride Printing Library).*

It is clear that designers took for granted the producers' ability to make this reverse translation satisfactorily. Eric Gill's correction to the centre stroke of E in an early trial of Monotype Joanna, shown in Figure 16, says simply *thinner*; not *how much* thinner the stroke ought to be. Hermann Zapf, correcting a foundry proof of 36-pt Optima, marks the inner bowl of ç with *Bogen schlecht*: 'curve bad'.[12] He relies on the Stempel drawing-office staff not only to make the curve less bad, but to see what details of its configuration made it bad in the first place.

The criticism levelled by designers in Stanley Morison's circle – Bruce Rogers, Eric Gill, and principally Jan van Krimpen – against the Lanston Monotype Corporation's type-drawing office was that its work traduced the quality of their designs by over-simplifying and over-regularizing them. In the words of Van Krimpen's memorandum of March 1956 to the Corporation, there were 'arbitrary encroachments from the side of the drawing office on the designer's work and intentions and

---

[12] *Hermann Zapf & his design philosophy* (1987), p. 195.

otherwise inevitable disappointments at the designer's end'.[13] With drawings as the input to the manufacturing process, it might have been expected that mechanical punchcutting would have led more designers to anticipate or follow Dwiggins's working methods and make large drawings themselves: 'definite statements', in Edward Johnston's phrase, of character shape, to be followed exactly in the production of the type.

One of the reasons why this did not happen has already been mentioned: printed character images are small. The appearance of a shape that has been drawn large changes when it is seen small, and it is very difficult to anticipate from the large drawing precisely what the changes will be. F W Goudy says of his first draft for the type that became University of California Old Style that 'it was one of those disappointments that occasionally (thank God, only "occasionally") come through the inability of any designer to visualize completely the effect of large drawings as type'.[14] Gill, in *An essay on typography* (1931), describes the same problem in his own style:

> It is difficult enough for the designer to draw a letter ten or twenty times as large as the actual type will be and at the same time in right proportion; it requires very great experience and understanding. It is quite impossible for a set of more or less tame employees, even if the local art school has done its poor best for them, to know what a letter enlarged a hundred times will look like when reduced to the size of the intended type.

Even Dwiggins, more at ease with himself and the technology than Gill, did not feel able to judge the effects of reduction accurately enough to make large drawings that would serve directly for making patterns. 'I am beginning to get the drift of it and to foresee from the large drawings what will happen in the type. I can *modify* in the large outline, but so far I can't *originate* in that medium.'[15]

In hand punchcutting this difficulty of anticipation is unimportant, because of the way the process works. Once the principal dimensions of a character image have been transferred to the face of a punch, developing the appearance of the image in its final size by modifying the punch and making smoke-proofs is fairly quick and very interactive. The punchcutter may follow a transferred shape to begin with, but the final shape on the face of the punch is unlikely to reproduce it exactly if the punch is part of a new design. With mechanical punchcutting, on the other hand, making corrections to a pattern drawing is the only way to modify a character shape, and the shape on the punch always follows the shape on the drawing. Corrections to the appearance of character images are no longer interactive: indeed, the interval between making corrections on a drawing and seeing their results in a proof

---

[13] Quoted by John Dreyfus in his introduction to Van Krimpen's *Letter to Philip Hofer* (1972).
[14] *Typologia*, p. 52.
[15] *WAD to RR*, p. [2] of text: emphasis in the original.

of the type becomes very long by comparison with the immediacy of hand punchcutting. The working drawing of the Caledonia italic *p* reproduced by Dwiggins in his *Letter* is dated by him 6 26 37 (26 June 1937). A note in his handwriting near the foot of the descender, dated 13 August 1937, remarks 'looks unfinished in proof', and another, three days later, says 'Change / add serif'. Nearly eight weeks, during which almost the whole italic minuscule alphabet was cut, went by between finishing the drawing and seeing the first proof of the type.

A further reason why designers did not draw patterns, for the Monotype system in particular, was the sheer amount of work involved. The matrix-case layout in Figure 17 contains 224 characters. Figure 27 suggests that three or four sets of drawings were made to cover even the restricted size-range of the early composing machines. Hence a minimum of 672 drawings, made to high technical standards and with the correct character widths for each size, would be needed for each new design. Designers like Gill or Van Krimpen were not equipped for this kind of work, even if they had been intellectually in sympathy with it.

5 Hot-metal typesetting

For the composing machine manufacturers' type-drawing offices, the work of making pattern drawings involved much more than the production of accurate and consistent renderings of existing character shapes. The mechanisms of hot-metal composing machines generated requirements of their own that had to be met by the matrices the machines used, and hence by the drawings from which the matrices were produced.

There are two principal systems to consider. The first, more complex and demanding in terms of the drawing task, is the system of single-type composition developed by Tolbert Lanston and J S Bancroft from 1890 and commercialized by the Lanston Monotype Machine Company in America and the Lanston Monotype Corporation in England.[1] The second is the linecasting system introduced by Ottmar Mergenthaler in 1885 and developed subsequently by the Mergenthaler Linotype Company.[2]

In the Monotype system text was composed at a keyboard that punched character codes into a paper ribbon. At the end of each keyboarded line, extra codes were added that specified the widths needed for the interword spaces in the line so that it would be correctly justified. The ribbon was then used in a separate operation to control the casting machine that produced composed type.

A system like this needs to share character width information between keyboard and caster, so that the former's calculations correspond to the dimensions of the types produced by the latter. This in turn means that character widths have to be quantified in some way. In normal Monotype practice the width of the widest character in a design was divided into eighteen parts, called 'units'. These were used to set the widths of the other characters in the design. Thus in Monotype Modern Series 1, for example, capital W Æ Œ, the widest characters, all have the same widths. The widths of M and H are 15/18ths of the width of W; small u and n are 10/18ths of W; and so on. The narrowest alphabetic characters such as i and l, and punctuation signs such as full point and comma, are 5/18ths of the width of W, or 5 units, wide.

In early Monotype designs the unit widths of characters do not vary

---

[1] The Lanston Monotype Corporation became the Monotype Corporation in 1931. Strictly speaking, the word "Monotype" is a trademark and should not be used descriptively. The Corporation's *Book of information* (1970) has a guide to its correct usage.

[2] Other machines working on the same principles, notably the Intertype, were produced after Mergenthaler's basic patents expired in 1912.

between one size and another.[3] The W of Modern 1 is always 18 units wide, the n 10 units, the i 5 units, and so on. The actual widths of the types that carry the characters vary with size, though, as they must. The width in points of the type carrying an 18-unit character of a given design at a particular size is called the *set value* of the design at that size. The widths of other types can be found by multiplying their characters' unit widths by a point dimension that is one-eighteenth of the set value.

A unit-based approach like this has many advantages. The width-counting mechanism in the keyboard can be kept simple, since it works with units that are independent of the size of the type being composed. The keyboard operator need be concerned with actual dimensions only when the measure for a new job is being set up. Conversion tables give the equivalents in ems and units of set (an em of set is 18 units) for the picas and points of the measure.

The overall proportions of a design can be varied between one size and another without changing the unit widths of its characters. The 6 pt size of Monotype Modern Series 1, for example, has a set value of $6\frac{3}{4}$; 7 and 8 pt have 7 and 8; 9 and 10 pt have $8\frac{1}{2}$ and $9\frac{1}{4}$ respectively. Thus the width of the type on which W is carried in 6 pt Modern 1 is $6\frac{3}{4}$ pt, more than the square of the body size; in 7 and 8 pt it is the width of the body; and in 9 and 10 pt it is narrower.

Old Style Series 2 is a wider design overall than Modern Series 1. Its set values for 6, 7, 8, 9 and 10 pt are $6\frac{1}{2}$ (narrower than Modern 1), $7\frac{3}{4}$, $8\frac{1}{2}$, $9\frac{1}{4}$ and $9\frac{3}{4}$ respectively. As with Modern 1, W is 18 units wide. Thus in every size except 6 pt the type that carries it is wider than the corresponding type in Modern 1, because the set value is larger.

At the Monotype caster, types are cast from matrices held in a rectangular matrix-case (Figure 17).[4] This moves in two dimensions, under the control of the punched codes in the paper ribbon, to position the required matrix over the aperture of the mould in the machine. The mould has a moveable side-wall or 'blade' so that it can cast types of different widths. The position of the mould blade, and hence the width of the cast type, is set by a sliding wedge that moves together with the matrix-case in one of its directions of travel. Thus each row of characters in the matrix-case (for example the row beginning *P R B F E T* in Figure 17) corresponds to a particular setting of the blade. All the types produced when the matrix-case is positioned at that row will have the same actual width; all the characters whose matrices are in the row, therefore, must have the same unit width. Figure 18 shows the allocation of widths to rows for the matrix-case in Figure 17.

---

[3] This restriction was subsequently relaxed for some designs, at a certain cost: see the discussions of Caslon Series 128 later in this chapter and Lutetia Series 255 in Chapter 7.

[4] Figures 17–22 are taken from *Typographical printing-surfaces*.

Hot-metal typesetting

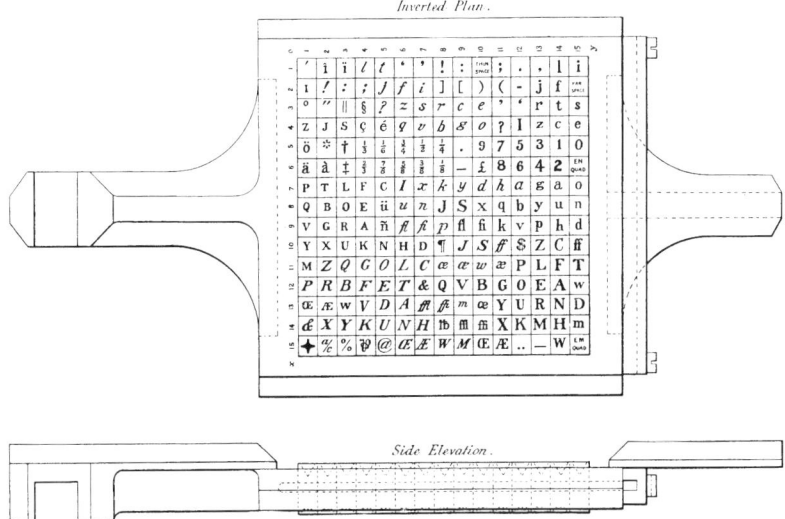

17 An early Monotype matrix-case. It has fifteen rows of matrices, with fifteen matrices in each row.

18 Unit width allocations for the matrix-case shown in Figure 17. The rows of characters in the diagram run vertically in the matrix-case.

Each character code in the paper ribbon produced at the keyboard is made up of two holes. At the caster, these control a pair of pins in the mechanism that positions the matrix-case over the mould. One pin selects a row of matrices in the case; the other a single matrix within the row. Thus each two-hole code in the ribbon corresponds to a particular position in the matrix-case, and the row-selecting part of the code carries information about the character's unit width.

Figure 19 illustrates the mechanism in the keyboard that uses a rack and pinion and 14 stopbars[5] to add up the unit width of each character as it is keyboarded and show the operator how much space remains in the line of text that is being set.

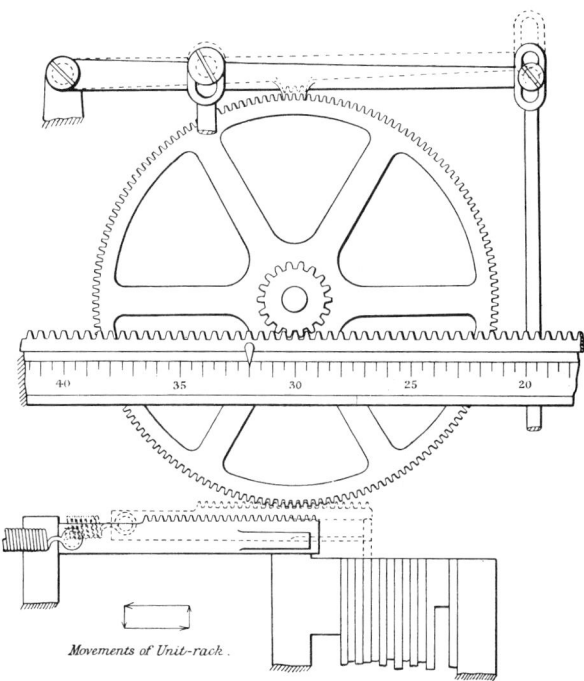

19 *Unit-counting mechanism for the Monotype C keyboard. The horizontal scale is calibrated in ems of set. The dotted lines show how a raised stopbar from the case at the lower right limits the travel of the rack that drives the unit wheel, on which each tooth represents one unit of set. Although the mechanism in the later D keyboard uses the same principles, its more compact design makes it difficult to illustrate.*

The actual widths of the types the caster produces are determined by the taper of the sliding wedge that fixes the position of the moveable side-wall in the mould. In Monotype terminology this is the 'normal wedge'. Each set value has a corresponding wedge with a different taper. In effect the normal wedge translates between unit widths and actual widths, leaving the keyboard free to make all its calculations in units independently of set value and size.

On the early A, B and C keyboards of the Monotype system (Figure 20) the layout of the buttons on the keyboard was the same as the arrangement of the matrices in the matrix-case, and the relationship between

---

[5] For 18-unit characters, in the last row of the matrix-case, the unit rack runs to the end of its travel.

Hot-metal typesetting 39

the two was fixed. Although this meant that the keyboard layout had no obvious logic, it was not too unsatisfactory a state of affairs as long as the arrangement of matrices in the matrix-case did not change. However, the need to cater for other kinds of typesetting than bookwork – 'railway timetables, trade circulars and even dictionaries', in Legros & Grant's words,[6] all of them well suited to single-type mechanical composition – meant that different selections of characters, and hence different matrix-case arrangements, had to be provided. This in turn meant that the characters and unit widths corresponding to several of the buttons on the keyboard changed with each new arrangement.

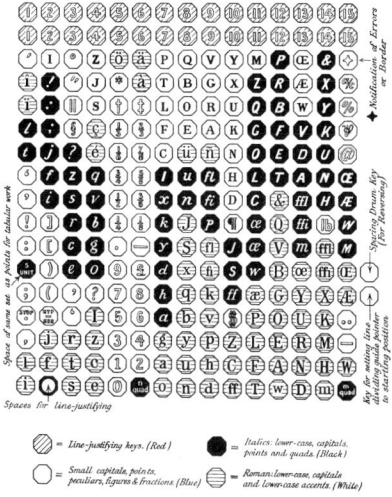

20 *Keybutton layout for the C keyboard. The arrangement of keys corresponds to the left-hand matrix-case arrangement in Figure 21.*

In Figure 21, for example, while roman capitals, small capitals, minuscules and numerals have the same positions in both standard and jobbing arrangements, italic and bold hardly match one another at all.[7] Operators had to remember the differences in character positions when changing from one matrix-case arrangement to another, and this made their work extremely difficult.

The problem was solved with the D keyboard, introduced in 1907. Its banks of keybuttons were arranged in the universal QWERTY typewriter layout (Figure 22). Interchangeable sets of keybars translated between keybutton positions and character codes at the paper-ribbon punch. Different matrix-case arrangements could be accommodated at a single keyboard by fitting it with appropriate keybars. The introduction of the D keyboard made the Monotype system a practical commercial proposition for the general printing trade.

---

[6] *Typographical printing-surfaces*, p. 396.

[7] Compare *P R B F E T* in the 13-unit row of the standard arrangement with **X U R D A w** in the same positions of the jobbing arrangement.

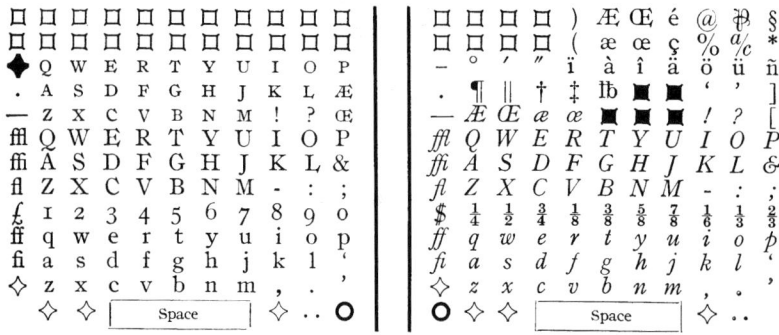

21 Matrix-case arrangements for early Monotype machines. Characters followed by a single dot are small capitals; numerals 1 and 0 are followed by two dots. The standard arrangement is the same as that of the matrix-case in Figure 17.

22 Standard (bookwork) layout for an early D keyboard. The layout corresponds to the standard matrix-case arrangement in Figure 21.

In Monotype terminology the allocation of unit widths to the characters of a design is called the *unit arrangement* of the design. Monotype designs intended for bookwork, like that shown in the standard layout in Figure 21, normally included roman and italic capitals, small capitals, roman and italic minuscules and roman numerals as well as punctuation and accented characters. Leaving aside characters such as fractions, foot and inch symbols and the degree sign, there are 196 face-related characters in the matrix-case. In the jobbing layout the italic is replaced by 82 bold characters.

The standard layout in Figure 21, and the arrangement of the bold in the jobbing layout, correspond to Monotype's unit arrangements 1 and 2 respectively. These two schemes for allocating unit widths to characters were used for the composition sizes of 77 series between 1901 and the 1940s.[8] The last designs to use them were Gravura 533 in 1939 and Old Style Bold 544 in 1943. Arrangement 3, another jobbing layout, was introduced in 1902 for the italic of Grotesque Bold Condensed 15 (the upright, like the bold in Figure 21, used arrangement 2) and arrangement 4, for bookwork, with Veronese 59 in 1911. Arrangement 4 was also used for Gloucester Old Style 99, Monotype's version of Cheltenham, and for the composition sizes of Imprint 101 (1912), Plantin 110 (1913) and Plantin Light 113 (1914). In fact the regular sizes of Imprint and Plantin from 6 to 12 pt share the same set values as well as having the same unit arrangement, so that the character widths in both designs are identical.[9]

The restrictions imposed on a design by fixed allocations of unit widths to characters are not necessarily burdensome. The fact that Imprint and Plantin share the same character widths has not generally been seen as detracting from the quality of their design. On the contrary: both are now taken as evidence of the kind of work that F M Steltzer, manager of the type-drawing office at the Monotype works, and his staff could produce when they were left to make their own decisions. James Mosley, for example, says of the two designs that 'they are deeply satisfying faces, beautifully fitted and ... "comfortable" to the eye'.[10] Working within the constraints of a width-allocation scheme they had come to know well, Steltzer and the drawing-office staff could concentrate on other aspects of the designs, such as evenness of colour and fitting, that were more important to their appearance. Drawing as they did with straightedges and french curves, they would also have been able to work quickly. Imprint was begun in November 1912, and was ready enough to set the first number of *The Imprint* in a single size in January 1913.

Walter Tracy points out the extent to which the character widths of Times New Roman 327 resemble those of Plantin 110.[11] He suggests that in making the finished drawings for Times the draughtsman Victor Lardent was instructed to work to the proportions of the earlier design. Once again the Corporation worked fast: the first trial cutting was put in hand on 8 April 1931 and proofed on 22 April.[12]

---

[8] The widths of alphanumeric characters for arrangements 1–425 are listed in *Unit arrangements of "Monotype" composition matrices* (1947).

[9] Plantin, unlike Imprint, has several long and short descender variants cast on different body sizes: 8 pt (long ascenders and descenders) on 10 pt, for example. These share the sets of their parent bodies. Sizes of 16 pt (sometimes 14 pt) and above, known as 'Large composition' in Monotype terminology, have fewer matrices in the matrix-case and consequently different unit arrangements.

[10] 'Eric Gill's Perpetua type', *Fine print* vol. 8 no. 3 (1982).

[11] *Letters of credit* (1986), ch. 17.

[12] John Dreyfus, 'The evolution of Times New Roman', *Penrose Annual* no. 66 (1973).

Existing schemes for character width allocation are an invaluable support when, as with Plantin, Imprint and Times, the type-drawing office is free to make detailed decisions about the proportions of a new design. The situation is different when its task is to reproduce an existing design as closely as possible.

The Edinburgh printers R & R Clark carried out a good deal of work for the publishers Macmillan & Co in the first decades of the twentieth century. They were early customers for Monotype equipment. One of Macmillan's authors was J W Fortescue, who had been at work since 1899 on his monumental *History of the British Army*. By 1914 seven volumes had been published, the fourth in two parts, and the first three volumes reissued in a second edition. The work was set by hand in pica old face type from H W Caslon & Co.

On 20 October 1914 Macmillan's wrote to Clark's:

Fortescue's History of the Army vol 4
An order should have been given you for resetting this in June last, but it was missed. We hope...you can put it in hand immediately as the present state of affairs is taking copies away...The whole book should be set up as quickly as possible and proofs sent to author who may have a few corrections.

We suppose it is not possible for you to set up by machine. It would not be advisable to have a type different from the rest of the volumes....[13]

On 8 April 1915 they wrote again:

Fortescue's Army vol 4: we are now out of this, and shall be glad if you hasten the completion of the new Edition.[14]

The second edition of Volume IV has 929 pages of text in its two parts. Sheets were delivered to Macmillan's at the beginning of May 1915.[15]

Further volumes of the first edition were in preparation at the same time. Two thousand copies of Volume VIII had been ordered from Clark's in July 1914,[16] and the manuscript for Volume IX was complete.

...Mr Clark has been asking for the Index [to Vol. VIII; set in a smaller size of type than the text] – but, as we have said before VIII and IX are to be published together and will probably have an Index for the two volumes.[17]

Volume VIII has 625 and Volume IX 516 pages of text. Thus by the end of April 1915 Clark's had almost a thousand pages set in Caslon's pica old face type – more, if earlier volumes of the second edition were still standing – and the imminent prospect of substantial further calls for it.

This is probably the situation that led Clark's to order matrices for a new type from the Lanston Monotype Corporation. Given that it 'would not be advisable to have a [machine-set] type different from the rest of the volumes', the new design needed to be as exact a visual match as

---

[13] *Macmillan archives* (1982), out letters vol. DLVII, no. 185.

[14] *Ibid.*, no. 530.

[15] *Ibid.*, no. 568.

[16] *Macmillan archives*, editions books vol. MCXXXVI, no. 61.

[17] *Macmillan archives*, out letters vol. DLVII, no. 798 (22 September 1915).

possible for the types that Clark's were already using for Fortescue's books. This ruled out Monotype's earlier versions of Caslon: Old Face Series 20 and 45, as well as their more recent Imprint. As Christopher Burke describes,[18]   Clark's requirements provided the Corporation with an incentive to move into new technical territory.

Every size of Monotype Caslon Old Face Series 128 has a different allocation of unit widths to characters: hence a different unit arrangement in the matrix-case, and a different set of keybars to translate between character codes and matrix-case positions. The widest characters are 20 units wide, cast on bodies of 11 or 12 units with high spaces next to them to support the overhanging part of the type. There are different allocations of unit widths to rows in the matrix-case for 8 pt, 11 pt and 14 pt small face; 9 pt; and 10 and 12 pt. Each group of sizes requires a separate stopbar case at the keyboard. Altogether a full installation of the composition sizes of Caslon 128 for one keyboard and one caster calls for six sets of keybars, three stopbar cases and six non-standard normal wedges as well as matrices and moulds. The capital cost would have been much higher than for installations of other designs.

> language wasted on both sides by scribblers of all descriptions; the actual combatants in the field treated each other with humanity and even with friendliness.
>
> principles but grave miscalculations of Windham, are one and all sad proof of the unteachable ignorance of our Governors. Their choice of fields of operations

23 *H W Caslon's pica old face (upper three rows) and 12-pt Monotype Caslon 128 (lower three rows). From Volume X of J W Fortescue's* History of the British Army *(1920), pp. 181 and 182. Actual size.*

Clark's went ahead nevertheless. The 12-pt size of the new type appears in Volume X of Fortescue's *History*, published in 1920. The changeover occurs between Chapters 20 and 21, on either side of a leaf in signature M (Figure 23).

The cost of the Caslon project does not seem to have acted as a deterrent to Clark's. Monotype Scotch Roman Series 137, produced for them in 1920, also has separate unit arrangements for each of its composition sizes. Their serial numbers (13–17) are continuous with those of Caslon 128.

The experience of Caslon 128 and Scotch Roman 137 gave the Corporation the technical flexibility and confidence it would need to deal with the programme of revivals and new designs urged on it by Stanley

---

[18] 'The early years: 1900–1922', *Monotype Recorder* new series no. 10 (1997), pp. 4–13.

Morison in the 1920s.[19] Until Jan van Krimpen's Lutetia Series 255 in 1928, though, none of them demanded a comparable number of special dispositions for a single series.

The essential innovation in the Monotype system was Lanston's idea of composing *and justifying* the line of text at the keyboard before it was sent to the caster. The corresponding intellectual leap in Mergenthaler's invention was the use of multiple circulating matrices to compose the text, with a means for sorting them back into the correct channels of the magazine so that they could be reused. Linecaster matrices were made of brass, with the character image punched into one edge (Figure 24). Mergenthaler's original machines, the 'blower' and 'square-base' Linotypes, used single-letter matrices. Two-letter matrices were introduced with the Linotype Model 1 in 1892.

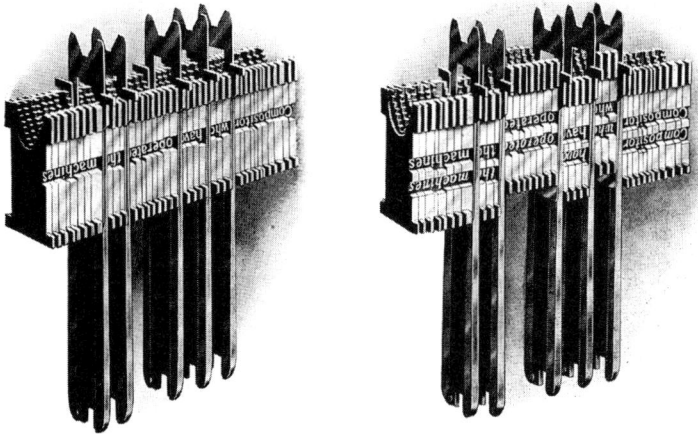

24 Single-letter and two-letter Linotype matrices, with spacebands. From Typographical printing-surfaces.

As a line of text was keyboarded, matrices and spacebands accumulated in the machine's assembler under the operator's eye. After a completed line was 'sent away' by the operator, the machine positioned it in front of the mould and justified it by expanding the opposed sliding wedges of the spacebands to make a metal-tight assembly. Metal was then pumped into the mould to cast the line as a single 'slug' of type. Thus in keyboarding a text the positions of line-endings had to be chosen so that after justification the lines would be neither too loose nor too tight. Because the widths of the justifying wedges were continuously variable between limits, though, there was no need for the widths of characters to be systematized as they were in the Monotype system, and the widths of interword spaces were not quantified at all.

Figure 25, which shows the standard alignments of matrices for Inter-

---

[19] Garamond Series 156, for example, has the same non-standard allocation of unit widths to matrix-case rows as 10-pt Caslon 128.

type machines, illustrates the constraints that the circulating-matrix principle inevitably imposed on any type design that was made for it.[20] The first and most significant is that the punched image of a character, whether upright or oblique, has to fit entirely on to the vertical edge of the matrix. This means that characters cannot kern either to the left or right of their width. In fact the sidewalls of the matrix have to be thick enough on both sides of the image to prevent them breaking down with wear: otherwise, type-metal would be forced into the resulting gap by the casting pump and print along with the characters. (Sidewall breakdown was a constant problem with early linecaster composition, made much of by contemporary critics of the new technology.) The second constraint applies to the pairs of designs on two-letter matrices. The two designs have to be 'duplexed': corresponding characters must have the same width.

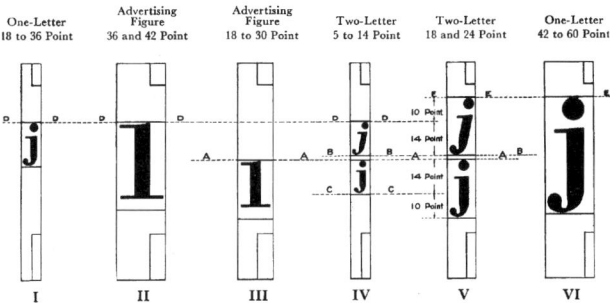

25 *Standard alignments for Intertype matrices. From the* Intertype *Book of instruction.*

F. P. Ta Te To Tr Tu Tw Ty T. Va Ve Vo V. Wa We Wi Wo Wr W. Ya Ye Yo Y.
F. P. Ta Te To Tr Tu Tw Ty T. Va Ve Vo V. Wa We Wi Wo Wr W. Ya Ye Yo Y.

fa fe fo fr fs ft fu fy ffa ffe ffo ffr ffs ffu ffy f, f. f- ff, ff. ff- f ff
fa fe fo fr fs ft fu fy ffa ffe ffo ffr ffs ffu ffy f, f. f- ff, ff. ff- f ff

26 *Logotypes for Linotype Caslon Old Face. From the Mergenthaler Linotype specimen book, c. 1937. Actual size.*

Non-kerning type had existed long before the Linotype. Earl Stanhope, who died in 1816, deplored the existence of kerns.[21] The Wicks typecasting machine, used for the daily production of new type at *The Times* newspaper between 1886 and 1908, could not produce them: the cast type was ejected through the mould, limiting its overall width to the

---

[20] The assembly, casting and distributing parts of the Intertype worked on identical principles to those of the Linotype.
[21] See Horace Hart's *Charles Earl Stanhope and the Oxford University Press* (1896; reprinted 1966).

width of the body.[22] When it was important for the manufacturers of linecasting machines to bring out designs that reproduced existing types, as with Mergenthaler Linotype's Caslon Old Face of 1921, special logotype matrices were made in which kerning characters were followed by another character or a space (Figure 26). But linecasters' inability to kern to the left of the matrix meant that such reproductions could never be truly faithful.

Duplexing presents different problems according to whether the pair of designs that have to work together are roman and bold or roman and italic. The relative proportions of bold characters are normally much the same as those of roman, and the problem in duplexing the two is to accommodate the extra stroke-weight of the bold without making its counters too narrow or forcing the roman to be too gappy or too wide. With italic the two variants can have substantially different proportions (compare 10-unit q and 8-unit *q* in Monotype Modern 1, by no means the most flamboyant of italics) and the problem is to reconcile their differing rhythms without doing too much violence to either. The sloped roman that was the first 'italic' of W A Dwiggins's Electra is one solution. Walter Tracy, however, suggests that it was poorly received by the trade, and it was indeed later supplemented with a more conventional cursive.[23]

In spite of its particular difficulties, though, the Linotype was far less demanding than the Monotype as regards the allocation of widths to characters.[24] The drawing-office staff at the Mergenthaler Linotype Company in Brooklyn were much less bound by metric considerations than were their counterparts at Salfords. They could vary the proportions of characters from one size to another in a way that would be impossible in a system in which the relationships between character widths had to remain constant over the whole range of composition sizes.

---

[22] *Typographical printing-surfaces*, p. 80.
[23] *Letters of credit*, p. 180.
[24] This became less true for newspaper typefaces after the arrival of 'unitized' fonts for the Teletypesetter system in the 1930s.

6 Fonts and typefaces in metal type

In hand composition, a *font* is a set of printing types that gives rise to character images of a particular size, with a particular set of appearance characteristics. By association the word identifies the moulds and matrices from which the types were cast, and hence the punches from which the matrices were struck.

For Moxon a font is 'the whole number of *Letters* that is cast of the same *Body* and *Face* at one time'.[1] He stipulates 'at one time' because, with the technology available to him, only types made in a single session of casting and dressing will have consistent body size and height to paper.

Fonts for hand composition have connotations of quantity. A *bill of font* (*cf.* Figure 1) is a list of the numbers of each type (or *sort*) in the font that are to be cast or supplied. The cost of a font depends on its weight in metal and the number of characters it contains. Typefounders charged separately for the two components: per thousand sorts for casting, and by unit of weight for the metal.

Moxon lists the type bodies that his master printer ought to provide: from great canon at the large end of the range to pearl at the small, although he acknowledges that this and nonpareil, the next larger size, are not found in every printing-house.

> These aforesaid *Bodies* are commonly *Cast* with a *Romain, Italica,* and sometimes an *English* [*i.e.* black-letter] *Face.*[2]

'Face' here denotes a very broad category of appearance. In the following sentence, indeed, Moxon uses the word where we would use 'script':

> He [the master printer] also provides some *Bodies* with the *Musick,* the *Greek,* the *Hebrew,* and the *Syriack Face...*

He does not imagine that there might be several roman or italic types, with different appearance characteristics, on a single body.

Fournier lists his designs by body size, qualified if necessary by a comment on their appearance: *Cicéro, gros œil,* with a larger x-height than normal; *Cicéro, gros œil, dans le goût Hollandois,* in the Dutch taste, narrower and with more marked contrast in strokeweights. He does not distinguish between romans and italics. Vincent Figgins, in his specimen book of 1815, names his faces first by body size and then by number in

---

[1] *Mechanick exercises,* p. 341. Moxon, like many later English authors, uses *fount.* The word denotes something that is cast in metal.

[2] *Mechanick exercises,* p. 20. He provides a table to convert between bodies and feet. In present-day terms his great canon, at $17\frac{1}{2}$ to the foot, is around 48 pt; pearl at 184 to the foot is 4.7 pt; nonpareil (he spells it phonetically as *nomparel*), at 150 to the foot, is 5.8 pt.

chronological order: Great Primer Nos. 3, 4 and 5, for example.³ Like Fournier, Figgins includes roman and italic variants under the same name.

De Vinne, writing in 1899, follows essentially the same scheme as Moxon's:

> Faces and styles have to be described by a ruder method [than the use of point dimensions to denote body sizes], with long names of two, three, or four words. The first word always describes the body. If no other word is added, this single word is always understood as the name of a body with roman face... The second word more plainly describes the face or style, as pica antique or pica gothic. The third word usually describes its form as to thickness or thinness... The fourth word is intended to describe its fashion of ornament, as pica antique condensed outline; but all ornamental types, and indeed many plain types, are named and classified in an unsatisfactory manner.⁴

Legros & Grant list three main groups of 'type faces': Old-style, Modern and Fancy. 'The faces used for the greater part of the printed matter of the day are either old-style, or modern, or follow the leading features of one or of the other very closely.'⁵

As more designs were developed for each appearance category (the 'face or style', in De Vinne's words) on a given body, the founders gave them serial numbers within each category; like Figgins's, but with the style name added to the body size. The epigraph to Legros & Grant's chapter on typefounding, for example, is set in Shanks & Sons' *Long primer* [body] *old-style antique* [style] *No. 2* [serial number].⁶

The first designs produced by the manufacturers of the new hot-metal composing machines were reproductions of types already popular in the trade. The Lanston Monotype Corporation's Modern Series 1 was adapted from Miller & Richard's Moderns 23 and 28, and Old Style Series 2 from Stephenson Blake's type of the same name.⁷ Like Fournier and Figgins, the Corporation included roman and italic variants under the same series number.⁸

Updike was almost certainly overstating typefounders' normal practice when he claimed that with the arrival of pantographic punchcutting techniques 'Sizes from 6-point to 120-point, or as large as desired, are

---

³ *Vincent Figgins type specimens, 1801 and 1815* (1967); edited by Berthold Wolpe.
⁴ *Plain printing types*, pp. 182–183.
⁵ *Typographical printing-surfaces*, p. 82.
⁶ *Ibid.*, p. 15.
⁷ C Burke, 'The early years: 1900–1922', *Monotype Recorder* new series no. 10 (1997). 'Adapted', because the machine's constraints on character widths did not permit direct copying.
⁸ The Mergenthaler Linotype Company, unlike the Lanston Monotype Corporation, did not use chronologically ordered series numbers as part of their design names. The 'triangle numbers' that identify Linotype matrices correlate in a complicated way with the names of designs.

Fonts and typefaces in metal type 49

often cut from the same model letter'.[9] De Vinne gives the possible range as being from 2 to 72 pt.[10] The fact is, though, that types in more than one size, carrying images of exactly the same shape in each size, could now be made from a single set of drawings. The composing-machine manufacturers offered designs in a range of sizes as a matter of course, and there was no longer any need to specify the body a type was cast on in order to characterize its appearance.

This development allowed the concept of *typeface* to acquire a precise meaning for the first time. In type manufacture for mechanical composition a typeface is a set of character shapes with common appearance characteristics, derived from a single original, that exist in a range of sizes and are identical for one or more subranges of size within the range. In the extracts from the specimen-book page for Monotype Old Style 2 shown in Figure 27, for example, the differences in configuration that exist between character images in the range from 10 to $13\frac{1}{2}$ pt, or between 8 and 9 pt, result only from the consequences of letterpress printing: that is, the increasing significance of ink-squash as the images themselves get smaller. The printed images in each range come from types carrying identical shapes that differ only in size. This identity of shape comes about because the punches from which the types are derived are produced from a single set of patterns. Figure 27 suggests that three or perhaps four different sets of patterns were made for Monotype Old Style 2 to cover the range from 6 to $13\frac{1}{2}$ pt.

margins	6 pt at 332%	margins	10 pt at 200%
margins	7 pt at 290%	angular	11 pt at 186%
margins	8 pt at 248%	margins	12 pt at 164%
margins	9 pt at 230%	margins	13.5 pt at 150%

27 *Monotype Old Style 2 roman: from a Monotype specimen-book page dated July 1960. The examples are scaled so that the calibre of* g *is constant. The word* margins *is not in the showing for 11 pt.*

In mechanical type manufacture the name of a typeface ultimately refers to the sets of outline drawings that are the first stage of the process from which the character images that realize the typeface eventually result. Thus there may not be, and indeed probably is not, any single set of graphic objects that realizes the typeface in its final form. The nearest

---

[9] *Printing types*, p. 12.
[10] *Plain printing types*, p. 352.

we can come to a definition of it is the type-specimen produced by the manufacturer, which provides the definitive realization of its appearance characteristics.

A *font* in mechanical composition is the set of matrices from which types of a particular typeface are cast in a particular size. Thus an early Monotype matrix-case, like the one at the right in Figure 21, could hold fonts for 10-pt Monotype Modern 1 (the roman) and Clarendon 12 (the bold). Each font has a single matrix for each character. In linecasting machines, with their circulating matrices, each character had several matrices and the font still retained its former association with quantity. 'The full-length 90-channel magazine... holds an average fount of 1,200-odd matrices, the remainder of the 1,500-matrix fount being held in a sidecase for insertion by hand...'.[11]

Composing-machine manufacturers quite soon began to make new designs as well as reproducing existing ones.[12] It was logical enough to give names to these new series that reflected their origin or purpose in some way. Thus Monotype Imprint 101, made for the periodical *The Imprint* founded in 1912 by F Ernest Jackson, J H Mason, Edward Johnston and Gerard Meynell; Monotype Plantin 110, adapted from types in a specimen issued by the Plantin-Moretus Museum in 1905. Names like these were a godsend to the composing-machine manufacturers' marketing departments.

ahemop	10 pt at 300%
ahemop	11 pt at 269%
ahemop	12 pt at 230%
ahemop	14 pt at 211%
ahemop	16 pt at 181%

28 *Caslon Old Face foundry type. The examples are scaled so that the calibre of* o *is constant.*

The fact that a design has similarities in appearance over a range of sizes does not of itself define it as a typeface. Figure 28, taken from the specimen printed for H W Caslon & Co by G W Jones in 1924, shows characters from several sizes of Caslon Old Face foundry type. The specimen claims, truthfully or not, that the types in it were 'cast

---

[11] Allen Hutt, *Newspaper design* (1967), p. 15.

[12] Monotype Grotesque Series 11, issued in 1908, was the first design that the Corporation acknowledged as its own (Burke, *op. cit.*).

Fonts and typefaces in metal type 51

entirely from matrices produced from the original punches engraved in the early part of the eighteenth century'. Their characters have many appearance characteristics in common; but they are only broadly similar in configuration. Even if Caslon himself had begun his work by making a single set of character drawings, the technology for transferring scaled images of them to the punches as a starting-point for cutting was not available to him. Hence, on the definition proposed above, the Caslon Old Face shown in Jones's specimen is not a typeface but a collection of fonts.

This can be true of some machine-cut designs as well. Monotype's adaptation of Caslon's Old Face to produce their Series 128 was discussed in Chapter 5 above. Figure 29 shows that there are indeed many differences in configuration between the same characters in the different sizes of Series 128. Each size will have been made from drawings; but if the drawings were faithfully enlarged (except for some minor liberties taken with character widths and projector lengths) from the corresponding sizes of foundry type, then the non-typeface-ness of the original is carried through into the reproduction.

margins   8 pt at 355%
margins   9 pt at 325%
margins   10 pt at 300%
margins   11 pt at 271%
originality 12 pt at 235%

29 *Monotype Caslon Series 128: from a specimen-book page dated June 1960. The examples are scaled so that the calibre of* n *is constant. The word* margins *is not in the showing for 12 pt.*

It is equally true that differences in character shape between sizes do not unequivocally characterize a design as a set of fonts rather than a typeface. P H Rädisch's work on Jan van Krimpen's Lutetia design was discussed above in Chapter 2. The type was cut in sizes from 6 to 48 Didot. The shapes of the characters vary to some extent for every size within this range; but all the sizes were derived directly, by simple photographic reduction in the first place, from a single set of drawings. The punchcutter, in making the necessary adjustments between sizes, is doing what a composing-machine manufacturer's type-drawing office would do if a separate set of pattern drawings was made from the same original for each size within the range. Thus the foundry version of

Lutetia is indeed a typeface rather than a set of fonts. There are no two sizes in which the shapes of all the characters are identical; but, unlike Caslon's designs, they are all descended from a single set of original designs.

7 Perpetua and Lutetia

The curious story of the production of Eric Gill's Perpetua type by the Lanston Monotype Corporation exists in several versions.[1] Another story, equally significant but less well documented, is that of the Corporation's production of Jan van Krimpen's Lutetia. In both cases a new design for machine composition was produced from existing punches and types: not as a copy made for commercial motives like the Corporation's early designs, but in a deliberate attempt to challenge and extend the capabilities of mechanical punchcutting.

The outline of the Perpetua story is as follows. In November 1925 Gill began work on a commission from Stanley Morison, typographic adviser to the Lanston Monotype Corporation, to draw alphabets for a new text type.[2] This was the first stage in a plan that Morison had hinted at in 1924, in his anonymous introduction to the first showing of the Corporation's Poliphilus type:

> It is hoped, in the course of time, to make available to the present day other distinguished faces of the past and in addition at least one original design...[3]

Gill invoiced Morison for three days' work at ten pounds a day for the drawings.[4] At this stage the project was a private affair between Morison and Gill. Morison's intention was to have punches cut from Gill's drawings and type cast from the punches, which he could then present to Monotype as a starting-point for the new design.

Morison sent the drawings to the Parisian punchcutter Charles Malin, who had been recommended to him by François Thibaudeau of the

---

[1] The official accounts are by Beatrice Warde: as Paul Beaujon in 'Eric Gill, sculptor of letters', *The Fleuron* 7 (1930), and anonymously in the special issue of the *Monotype Recorder* produced for the Corporation's exhibition of Gill's work: 'Eric Gill: master of lettering', *Monotype Recorder* vol. 41 no. 3 (1958). Nicolas Barker's *Stanley Morison* (1972) reproduces much correspondence between Morison and Gill. Robert Harling discusses Perpetua alongside Gill's other type designs in *The letter forms and type designs of Eric Gill* (1978). James Mosley's definitive 'Eric Gill's Perpetua type' is in *Fine print* vol. 8 no. 3 (1982). Sebastian Carter, in *Twentieth century type designers* (new edition, 1995), points out some inconsistencies in Morison's account in *A tally of types* (1953) of his motives in commissioning the design. In 'Eric Gill: the continuing tradition', *Monotype Recorder* new series no. 8 (1990), Carter summarizes the history of Gill's type designs for the Corporation. Articles by John Dreyfus and David Saunders in the same number of the *Recorder* provide more details of the relationship, as well as helpful illustrations of material from the Monotype archives.

[2] Barker, *Stanley Morison*, p. 197.

[3] *Monotype Recorder* vol. 24 no. 199 (1924).

[4] William Andrews Clark Memorial Library: Ms. Gill G475Z [1937?] Feb. 27.

Peignot typefoundry. Malin wrote to Morison on 13 May 1926, enclosing smoke-proofs of the first characters cut in the 12 Didot size.[5]

It is clear from Malin's letter that the project was already some way advanced:

> I have the honour to send you smokes of the new punches of Gill Roman on 12 pt [*i.e.* 12 Didot] body, as well as the smokes of the 14 pt that you have already seen, so that you can appreciate the difference between them.
>
> I have followed the directions you gave me and I hope the work will give you every satisfaction. I have given the whole design a slightly darker colour and widened the counters of h and m. In my view, this holds up much better than the first trial; that is to say, it looks more solid and more legible.[6]

On 4 September 1926 Malin sent Morison smoke-proofs of the whole roman minuscule alphabet in the 12 Didot size. In the same letter he mentioned a 'fairly long text' that he had composed (*i.e.* stamped by hand from the punches).[7] He wrote again on 13 September acknowledging a letter of 6 September from Morison, who had asked for modifications to e g q y and raised a question about the relative widths of h n m and b d o p q. Malin gave it as his opinion that h n m ought to be widened as an alternative to reducing the width of the round characters. 'The bowls of b d p q have an elegance which they would lose if they were made narrower.'[8]

Morison wrote to Gill on 14 September, enclosing the hand-stamped text that Malin had produced.

> I send you a smoke proof of a few lines made up by the punch cutter. With your permission, I will have the lower case h and the lower case n widened just a trifle, and the lower case g brought down to line with the p.

This is a trifle disingenuous, since it is clear from Malin's 13 September letter that Morison had already asked for the depth of g to be modified. His letter continues:

> As these lines are done with the punches you will appreciate that it is

---

[5] Malin's letters to Morison between 13 May and 23 December 1926 are in the Cambridge University Library: Morison III 13.

[6] 'J'ai l'honneur de vous envoyer le fumé des nouveaux poinçons que j'ai gravés en Romain Gill c.12, ainsi que le fumé du corps 14 que vous avez déja vu, pour que vous puissiez apprécier la différence.

J'ai suivi les indications que vous m'avez données et je pense que ce travail vous donnera toute satisfaction. J'ai donné à l'ensemble une couleur légèrement plus noire et élargi les contrepoinçons des h et m. A mon avis, cela se tient beaucoup mieux que le premier essai, c'est à dire présente un aspect plus solide et d'une lisibilité plus grande.'

[7] 'J'ai le plaisir de vous envoyer ci-inclus le fumé du bas de casse Gill Romain corps 12. J'ai composé un assez long texte pour que vous puissiez vous rendre compte de l'effet obtenu une fois ce caractère fondu et imprimé . . .'

[8] '. . . contrairement à votre opinion, je crois qu'il serait préférable d'*élargir* h m n plutôt que d'allonger légèrement les sortes rondes. Les panses de b d p q ont une élégance qu'elles perdraient étant resserrées.'

rather a fine achievement considering the difficulty of the job. The spacing between the letters is a trifle too liberal, otherwise the general aspect pleases me.

I forgot to say that the lower case e is being recut as at present the swell is a little too one-sided. Perhaps you will kindly return the proof to me when you have looked at it . . .[9]

Gill replied on 16 September:

I agree that the lower case H would be better wider as also the lower case N, though the latter does not seem so necessary. I do not feel that the lower case G wants bringing down, I rather like it tightly compacted though the shape of the lower bowl might be improved, neither do I see anything much wrong with the lower case E . . . It is difficult to judge the effect at present but it is, I think, a decent and legible type. I return the proof herewith and look forward to print from the actual type which will no doubt be better in effect. The smoke has so much the effect of photographic reduction, though it is extraordinarily well done.

On 1 October 1926 Malin sent Morison smoke-proofs of the completed roman. He enclosed 'a short text which I find satisfactory overall':

I have kept the first y that was cut, because it will perhaps be difficult to set gy (Egypt), depending on the sidebearing width [of the cast type]. Excuse the incorrect positioning of the accents; it is not at all easy to proof them exactly where they ought to be.

He asked Morison if there were any more changes to be made to the punches, or whether he could harden them as they were. He had cut 91 punches altogether: 31 capital letters, 36 lowercase, 10 numerals, 10 punctuation signs, and four lowercase (h m n g) cut twice, 'together with 8 accents'.[10]

John Dreyfus reproduces the smoke-proofed text in his *Monotype Recorder* article.[11]

---

[9] Correspondence between Morison and Gill on matters related to the Lanston Monotype Corporation is in the Cambridge University Library: Morison III 1 and 2.

[10] 'J'ai composé un petit texte dont l'ensemble me donne satisfaction . . . J'ai conservé le premier y gravé, car peut-être il sera difficile de composer gy (Egypte), cela dependra de la largeur d'approche. Excusez l'emplacement défectueux des accents, il n'est pas commode du tout de les fumer exactement à leur place.

Ce corps 12 est donc terminé. Ayez l'obligeance de me dire si vous y voyez encore quelques retouches à y faire, ou si je peux le tremper tel qu'il est.

Cela fait un total de 91 poinçons, se décomposant ainsi:
   31 Capitales
   36 bas de casse
   10 chiffres
   10 ponctuations
   4 bas de casse (h m n g) gravés deux fois
plus 8 accents.'

[11] 'Gill, Morison and Warde', *Monotype Recorder* new series no. 8 (1990); reprinted, though without this illustration and some others, in *Into print* (1994).

Matrices were struck from Malin's punches and type cast from them by the Ribaudeau Dumas foundry in Paris. Proofs in the Cambridge University Library show the type in two different states.[12] In one, marked '? 1st casting of 1st setting', the type is somewhat loosely fitted. The other, marked 'second casting of first cutting' in Gill's hand, is a setting of a passage from *The passion of St Perpetua and St Felicity*, the same work that was used for the first showing of Monotype's Perpetua in 1930. The type is more tightly fitted in this proof; there is a noticeable weight defect in the lower bowl of g.

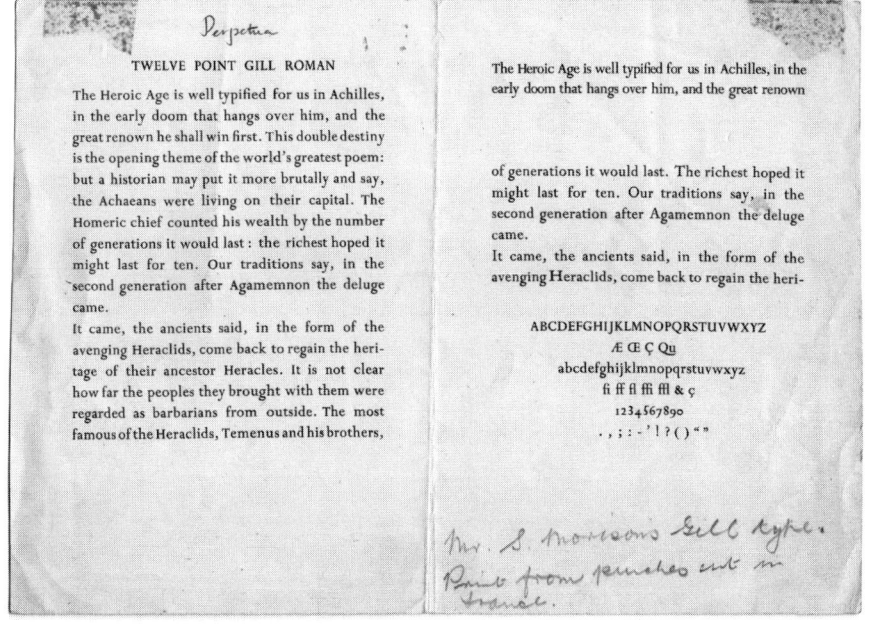

30 'Mr S Morison's Gill type' (St Bride Printing Library). Half actual size. The marks at the upper corners are residue left by adhesive tape.

In the special number of the *Monotype Recorder* published for the exhibition of Gill's work in October 1958, Figure 13 shows a text with the caption 'Facsimile of Malin's hand-stamped proof from the smoked punches mentioned in his letter'.[13] The letter in question is the one sent by Malin to Morison on 4 September 1926, which is quoted in the adjacent column.

Sebastian Carter reproduces the same text in *Twentieth century type designers*. He describes it more cautiously as 'Charles Malin's pilot cutting of Perpetua', and points out that the capitals in the second portion of the text are different in design from those in the first.[14]

The text that Warde and Carter reproduce is on the right-hand page

---

[12] The proofs are in Morison III 4.

[13] *Monotype Recorder* vol. 41 no. 3 (1958), p. 11.

[14] *Twentieth century type designers*, p. 74.

Perpetua and Lutetia 57

of the double-page spread shown in Figure 30.[15] The two pages are printed on one side of a leaf of cream laid paper. At the bottom of the right-hand page is a note in pencil: 'Mr S Morison's Gill type. Print from punches cut in France'. Both pages are printed from type, with an impression that is heavier at the bottom of each row of characters than at the top.

> The Heroic Age is well typified for us in Achilles, in the early doom that hangs over him, and the great renown

31 *The first two lines of the text on the right-hand page in Figure 30. Actual size.*

> Heroic for doom over renown

32 *Different states of* o *in the first two lines of the text in Figure 31. Twice actual size.*

The first two lines of the text on the right-hand page are set in type that has been rubbed to reduce its width (Figure 31). In the word Heroic the rubbing has cut into the left-hand curve of the o, and in for into both sides (Figure 32).

> ABCDEFGHIJKLMNOPQRSTUVWXYZ
> Æ Œ Ç Qu
> abcdefghijklmnopqrstuvwxyz
> fi ff fl ffi ffl & ç
> 1234567890
> . , ; : - ' ! ? ( ) " "

33 *The synopsis from the bottom of the right-hand page in Figure 30. Actual size.*

The text on the left-hand page of Figure 30 is set in the second state of the type cast by Ribaudeau Dumas. The first two items on the right-hand page are experiments, by Malin or someone else. The third item, the synopsis at the bottom of the page, shows the type as Morison submitted it, along with Malin's punches, to the Lanston Monotype Corporation in March 1927 for production as a new design (Figure 33).[16]

---

[15] The original of Figure 30 is in the Gill collection in the St Bride Printing Library.
[16] The date is given by James Mosley: *op. cit.* p. 94.

Figure 34 reproduces the first of two synopses shown by Beatrice Warde in the article she wrote as Paul Beaujon on Gill in *The Fleuron* 7. It is captioned 'First cutting of the *Perpetua* type (December 1927)'.[17] The type is the same as that of Figure 33 with the exception of the y, which has a straight tail.

> A B C D E F G H I J K L M N O P Q R S T U V W X Y Z
> Æ Œ Ç Qu
> a b c d e f g h i j k l m n o p q r s t u v w x y z
> fi ff fl ffi ffl &   1 2 3 4 5 6 7 8 9 0
> æ œ ç . : ; , ! ? - ' " " ( )

34 The first synopsis from Beatrice Warde's article in The Fleuron. *Actual size.*

In his *Monotype Recorder* article John Dreyfus illustrates a proof of the text on the left-hand page of Figure 30, with a note in Gill's hand 'N.B. Capitals to be raised g y e a to be revised'. He also reproduces a letter written by Morison on 11 April 1927 to W I Burch, managing director of the Corporation, enclosing a copy of a letter from Gill and clarifying the design of y r g for the new type. Morison asked for a straight tail to y instead of the round terminal that Malin had cut as his second version, a curved spur to r instead of Malin's flicked spur, and g with a narrower lower bowl. These changes reflect Gill's notes on the proof of Malin's type as well as comments he made in a letter to Morison, cited but not dated by James Mosley:

(i) The y must be altered—the blob removed...
(ii) The tail of the "g" is rather heavy. You see it all over the page...
(iii) I think the bow of the lower case "r" is too heavy.
(iv) I agree the space between the letters is too great.
(v) I agree that the capitals are too short...[18]

The drawings that Malin worked from seem not to have survived. They were sent to Monotype along with Malin's punches and type: James Mosley cites a note from the drawing-office records dated 13 May 1927, commenting on their condition. He goes on to suggest that they may have been destroyed when Morison's London apartment was burned in the air-raid of 10 May 1941.[19]

While Malin was working on the punches, however, Gill had made another set of alphabet drawings for Gerard Meynell of the Westminster Press (Figure 35).[20] Morison suggested to the Corporation in

---

[17] *The Fleuron* 7 (1930), p. 43.
[18] Mosley, p. 94.
[19] *Ibid.*; Barker, pp. 384–387.
[20] The drawings are in the St Bride Printing Library. They are on four sheets, signed 'Eric G' and dated 31.7.26 [31 July 1926].

Perpetua and Lutetia

August 1927 that these drawings were like enough to those from which Malin had worked to serve equally well as a basis for the production of the new design, and that 'Mr Meynell has no doubt that when the type is ready he will require considerable use of it'.[21]

ABCDEFGHI abcdefghijklmn
JKLMNOPQR opqrstuvwxyz &
STUVWXYZ
1234567890

*ABCDEFGHI abcdefghijklmn o
JKLMNOPQR opqrstuvwxyz
STUVW&XYZ*

35 Capitals, minuscules and numerals from the Meynell drawings (St Bride Printing Library).

239-14.   GILL FACE.   15-10-27.

BED HEN DON NOD HEED NEED DEED BONE
DONE HONE ONE BEEN NO BOB DOB HE
Beef Dip Nine Nip Hen Open Nippen Ninnen
hen jip fen pen hip pip nip ijifennie pippen in Oh
            BDEHNO   fehijnp

*BOG NOD NOB GOD DOG HOB NO GO GOOD BON
Ba Gab Ga Gap Ha Da a Hap Hab Na Bah Hah
pa ha ba ab bab pa bah hah pa appa ah ah abh
            BDGHNO   abhp*

36 14 pt roman and italic type cut by Monotype from the Meynell drawings (St Bride Printing Library). Actual size. The marks at the top and left of the proof are residue left by adhesive tape.

---

[21] Mosley, p. 94.

Roman and italic trial characters were cut from the Meynell drawings and proofed in 14 pt on 15 October 1927 (Figure 36). A few days later work on this size of the design was stopped.[22]

Malin's type had been with the Corporation since March 1927, but the first characters recut from it (D E H M e f g h m p) were not proofed until 14 January 1928 (Figure 37).[23]

239–13   Gill   14–1–27

DEEM MEED HEM MEDE HEED HE EM ME
Meg Hegge Def Emmeg phef mefg hemp feg
gemp heppeg pemp peg feg gep meg em gem

37 *The first characters cut by Monotype from Malin's work (St Bride Printing Library). Actual size.*

The proof is in 13 pt, corresponding to the 12 Didot size of the type cast in Paris. The p has a wide bowl and an asymmetrical lower terminal. The undated note in the drawing-office records quoted by Barker,[24] with its reference to the wide p and the design of g, makes sense with reference to this proof. On 19 March 1928 Pierpont instructed the drawing office to make the capitals of 13 pt Series 239 taller. The revision took 30 minutes.[25]

On 16 June 1928 Gill wrote to Morison thanking him for a letter of 14 June and for a proof of 'the new roman'. He considered it to be

> ... a great improvement on previous proofs, and the type wd. I think look better still when there's a bit of *impression*. The space between letters wants alteration, but, as you say, that can be done independently of me.[26]

Gill complained about the round terminal on small y:

> I won't say that the ball end is absolutely barred ... but the form you have at present is v. bad. But I certainly do think of the alphabet as a whole as being without balls tho. not without guts so to say. E.g. the l.c. a & the l.c. f and I'm thinking that in order to preserve the character we'd better make

---

[22] David Saunders, 'The Type Drawing Office', *Monotype Recorder* new series no. 8 (1990).

[23] The proof is dated 14-1-27 [14 January 1927]. It is an easy mistake to make at the beginning of the year.

[24] *Stanley Morison*, p. 226.

[25] Saunders, 'The Type Drawing Office'.

[26] Barker, p. 233; emphasis in the original.

Perpetua and Lutetia 61

the y do as the a & f do. I will try to make sketches to send herewith. Also I will draw sorts for fi and ffi.[27]

This is an odd comment to make at this stage of the work. At first sight it could be taken as referring to the type cast from Malin's punches, rather than to Monotype's recutting of it. Unfortunately Gill's letter no longer has the proof attached to it, so that we cannot tell which of Monotype's versions he was commenting on. It seems nevertheless that Gill's modification to the round-terminal y in the original type, passed on by Morison to Burch in his letter of 11 April 1927, had so far gone unremarked at Salfords.

Monotype's 'TRIAL No. 2 . . . Designation 239-13' is dated 14 August 1928 (Figure 38). It shows a type that has come a long way towards Malin's from the few characters cut by Monotype at the beginning of the year. The new type has two versions of y. One has a straight parallel-sided tail, and the other a rounded lower terminal cut off at the left with a straight line that makes the descender look rather like an ice-hockey stick. The note at the bottom of the synopsis lists B C H L S V U and two versions each of e and r as well as the two ys as 'New Characters'. This implies that the other characters in the synopsis are not new: in other words, that they would have been shown in a first trial of the design.[28]

A scenario that fits the evidence so far is that development of the type shown in Figure 37 was abandoned early in 1928 after it was realized that its characters were by no means a faithful interpretation of Malin's work. A second version was begun, closer to the original. Pierpont's instructions to the drawing office in March are about trial capitals for this version.[29] The 'new roman' that Morison sent to Gill on 14 June 1928 was its first trial. Changes had been made to g and perhaps r following Morison's letter of April 1927, but the round-terminal y of 'Mr S Morison's Gill type' had survived in the first trial of the new version along with round-terminal fi and ffi. Gill's remark about lack of impression would be justified if the Monotype trial had been proofed on supercalendered paper, as they very often were. Between June and August 1928 revised versions of e r y were cut and incorporated in Trial 2.

'Trial No. 4 . . . GILL MORISON' is dated 3 December 1928 (Figure 39). The copy in the Cambridge University Library, unlike the copies of Trial 2 there and in the St Bride Printing Library, is printed on wove paper.[30]

---

[27] Barker, p. 233.

[28] The chronology suggests that this first trial was the one on which Gill was commenting in his letter of 16 June 1928.

[29] Figures 37 and 40 show that only a few characters were cut to begin with for a new design.

[30] It is in Morison III 16, together with an incomplete copy of Trial 2 in which the synopsis and some of the text are missing.

> TRIAL No. 2　　　　　　　　14–8–28
>
> Designation 239–13　11¾ Set　Line .1278
>
> On the greatest and most useful of all inventions, the invention of alphabetical writing, Plato did not look with much complacency. He seems to have thought that the use of letters had operated on the human mind as the use of the go-cart in learning to walk, or of corks in learning to swim is said to operate on the human body. It was a support which soon became indispensable to those who used it, which made vigorous exertion first unnecessary and then impossible. The powers of the intellect would, he conceived, have been more fully developed without this delusive aid. Men would have been also compelled to exercise the understanding and the memory, and, by deep and assiduous meditation, to make truth thoroughly their own. Now, on
>
> ABCDEFGHIJKLMNOPQRSTUVWXYZÆŒ&
>
> abcdeefghijklmnopqrrstuvwxyyzæœfiffflffifﬄ
>
> 12345　.,:;!?-''-""()—Qu　67890
>
> New Characters:—
> 　　　B C H L S V U e e r r y y

38　*Trial No. 2, 14 August 1928 (St Bride Printing Library). Actual size.*

Trial 4 shows a revised a in which the flat serif-like lower terminal of Malin's cutting and Trial 2 is replaced by a hook. Both e and r are the second of the two new versions shown in Trial 2. The version of y shown in the text and the minuscule alphabet of the synopsis is a modified version of the hockey-stick y from Trial 2. The straight-tailed y shown as an alternative in the synopsis of Trial 4 now has a descender that swells towards its foot. In the earlier straight-tailed version shown in Trial 2 the descender is parallel-sided and somewhat thinner, following Malin's first version of the character.

Trial No. 4   11¾ Set   Line .1278   3-12-28

GILL MORISON

Designation 239—13 point

On the greatest and most useful of all inventions, the invention of alphabetical writing, Plato did not look with much complacency. He seems to have thought that the use of letters had operated on the human mind as the use of the go-cart in learning to walk, or of corks in learning to swim is said to operate on the human body. It was a support which soon became indispensable to those who used it, which made vigorous exertion first unnecessary and then impossible. The powers of the intellect would, he conceived, have been more fully developed without this delusive aid. Men would have been also compelled to exercise the understanding and the memory, and, by deep and assiduous meditation, to make truth thoroughly their own. Now, on the contrary, much knowledge is traced on paper, but little is engraved in the soul. A man is certain that he can find information at a moment's notice when he wants it. He therefore suffers it to fade from his mind. Such a man cannot in strictness be said to know anything. He has the show without the reality of wisdom. These opinions Plato has put into the mouth of an ancient king of Egypt. But it is evident from the context that they were his own; and so they were understood to be by Quinctilian.

ABCDEFGHIJKLMNOPQRSTUVWXYZ&

12345   abcdefghijklmnopqrstuvwxyzfifflflffiffl   67890

,.'"-:;)(!?— —   Çy   U   R   Qu   ""fiffi   ÆŒæœ

39 Trial No. 4, 3 December 1928 (Cambridge University Library). Actual size.

The capital alphabet in the synopsis of Trial 4 has U with a round bottom; the version with a serif at the foot of the right-hand stroke is shown as an alternative. All the capitals are now the same height as the B C H L S V shown as 'New Characters' in Trial 2, so that the ratios between the calibres of H p e are now 1.47 : 1.64 : 1. There is an alternative R with a wider bowl than the one in Trial 2. The f in fi and ffi has lost its ball terminal, and now has the same sheared terminal as the ff which in turn is the same as that in Trial 2. Alternatives for fi and ffi have a truncated terminal to f and a separate dot on the i. The alignments of 3 4 5 in Trial 4 are changed from those in Trial 2, so that the tops of 3 5 align a little way below the x-line while the foot of 4 stands on the baseline.

Display Matrices

Perpetua 239—18   20-4-29

Gefegh Ghefgh Gefgh Ggehefgh
Hehgf Hfegh Hefegh Hgef Hehf
ghef gfeh gefgh geh gef ghfefegh
hegfg hefegh hef hfeg hgef hegef
fegh feheg fgeh fehgf fehg fegeh

40 Proof of 18-pt trial cutting (St Bride Printing Library). Actual size.

GHefgh   10 pt at 384%

GHefgh   13 pt at 287% (from Trial 4)

GHefgh   16 pt at 227%

GHefgh   18 pt at 200%

41 Comparison of 10, 13, 16 and 18-pt characters. The 18-pt characters are twice actual size; the others are scaled to them so that the calibres of H h are constant.

With the design of the roman becoming stable, trial characters were cut in 10, 16 and 18 pt. The proofs of the two larger sizes are dated 20 April 1929, and the 10 pt 26 April. Figure 41 shows the three new sizes compared with characters from Trial 4. It seems that the four sizes were made from two sets of drawings. A new set was made for the 10 point, and the drawings for the Trial 4 type used for the two larger sizes.

TRIAL No. 6 1-5-29

PERPETUA

Designation 239—13   11 3-4 Set   Line .1278

On the greatest and most useful of all inventions, the invention of alphabetical writing, Plato did not look with much complacency. He seems to have thought that the use of letters had operated on the human mind as the use of the go-cart in learning to walk, or of corks in learning to swim is said to operate on the human body. It was a support which soon became indispensable to those who used it, which made vigorous exertion first unnecessary and then impossible. The powers of the intellect would, he conceived, have been more fully developed without this delusive aid. Men would have been also compelled to exercise the understanding and the memory, and, by deep and assiduous meditation, to make truth thoroughly their own. Now on the contrary, much knowledge is traced on paper, but little is engraved in the soul. A man is certain that he can find information AT A MOMENT'S NOTICE WHEN HE WANTS IT. HE THEREFORE SUFFERS IT TO FADE FROM HIS MIND. SUCH A MAN CANNOT IN STRICTNESS BE SAID TO KNOW ANYTHING. HE HAS THE SHOW WITHOUT THE REALITY OF WISDOM. these opinions plato has put into the mouth of an ancient king of Egypt. but it is evident from the context that they were his own and so they were understood to be by quinctilian indeed Each Every Eaten Evident Egypt Exercise Exertion Engraved Eat Heavy Here However Human Have His Here Heavy Heaven

abcdefghijklmnopqrstuvwxyyzæœ   fiffflffifflfiffi
ABCDEFGHIJKLMNOPQRRSTUUVWXYZÆŒ&ÇQu
12345   .,:;-''!?""–()—   67890
abcdefghijklmnopqrstuvwxyz   :;'!?   HE
ABCDEFGHIJKLMNOPQRSTUVWXYZÆŒ

Redesigned Characters: Hhmotu

42 *Monotype's Trial No. 6 (St Bride Printing Library). Actual size. A fold in the original runs through the upper part of the italic minuscule alphabet.*

Malin had asked Morison on 1 October 1926, and again on 23 December, whether he was to cut a companion italic to the 12 Didot roman.³¹ Because no more of Malin's letters survive it is not clear whether or not Morison ordered it from him. Pierpont had written to Burch in September 1927:

> The Meynall [sic] italics are good, but should be given a somewhat greater inclination, as it is a little difficult to distinguish them from the Roman. The Morison italics are worthless in my opinion.³²

This is unexpected, since several of the italic minuscules in the Meynell drawings, particularly *v w x y*, would need a good deal of modification to make them work satisfactorily alongside the roman. In January 1929 Burch reversed the Corporation's opinion and sent Gill's original drawings for the italic to the works for production.³³

'TRIAL No. 6 ... PERPETUA' (Figure 42) is dated 1 May 1929. It shows small capitals and an early state of the italic along with the roman from Trial 4. The text of the trial mixes roman and italic, sometimes within a word, no doubt to see whether the two are well enough differentiated (Figure 43).

became indispensable to

43 Roman and italic mixed in the text of Trial 6. 225% actual size.

The final form of the Trial 6 italic appeared as Felicity in *The Fleuron* in November 1930. In January 1931 Gill was asked to make drawings for a new italic.³⁴

A letter from Gill to Morison in March 1931 shows that he was still concerned with the design of roman minuscule y, in the context of the 18-point size that was being cut at the time:

> I do think it is a pity to have two sorts of l.c. y ... I see the need of the stronger tail – couldn't it be done by thickening ... ³⁵

He continues the discussion on a postcard written on 15 April, evidently in reply to an intervening letter from Morison:

---

[31] 'Pour l'organization de mon travail, j'aimerais aussi savoir si je dois m'occuper de l'Italique Gill c. 12 dans un avenir prochain' (1 October); 'Si vous jugez bon de vous occuper de l'Italique prochainment, vous voudrez bien me le faire savoir pour que je puisse prendre mes dispositions et m'en occuper' (23 December).

[32] Cited by Mosley: pp. 94–95.

[33] *Ibid.*

[34] Harling shows some of these: *The letter forms and type designs of Eric Gill*, p. 50. It is the design on the projector in the first illustration to Beatrice Warde's *Monotype Recorder* article about matrix production at Salfords: vol. 40 no. 3 (1956).

[35] William Andrews Clark Memorial Library, G475L M861 1931 Mar 21. The 'two sorts' of **y** that he sketches in the letter are similar to the straight-tailed and hockey-stick versions from Trial 4.

Perpetua and Lutetia 67

Many thanks for yours ... Re Perpetua y. I will come and talk about this with pleasure. I still intuish and think that the dotty y is out of keeping with the fount in spite of the round punctuation points (the end of the y's tail is not punctuation) ... [36]

Gill then sketches six variants of y with different tails, the last of which closely resembles the hockey-stick version of Trial 4, and writes 'What about no. 6?'.

The design of Perpetua Series 239, with roman and italic together in the same matrix-case, was finalized in March 1932.

Malin's type and punches were available to Monotype in March 1927, and Salfords had considerable experience in copying existing types. Given this, it is surprising that the few characters cut in January 1928 were such a heavy-handed interpretation of Malin's work. Figure 44 compares the two. It shows how many of their own conventions Monotype's drawing office had applied to this first machine-cut realization of the new design. The short letters were made larger relative to the ascenders and descenders, and the capitals taller.[37] The overall serif treatment was regularized, and Malin's sharp-pointed serifs rounded off. Almost the only details of Malin's type that survive, and those not without alteration, are the upper terminal of f and the lower terminal of p. The characters in the upper row of Figure 44 seem almost to be a declaration of independence from outside influences on the drawing office's part.

44 *Monotype's first cutting (upper row) compared with Malin's type. Four times actual size.*

The effect is less evident in Figure 45, which compares the 14-pt roman and italic trial characters cut in October 1927 with the drawings made by Gill for Gerard Meynell.

---

[36] William Andrews Clark Memorial Library, G475L M861 1931 Apr 15. The phrase 'intuish and think' has been changed with a proof-corrector's transposition mark from its original 'think and intuish'.

[37] In Malin's type the ratio between the calibres of **h**, **p** and **e** is 1.62 : 1.67 : 1; in the Monotype cutting it is 1.54 : 1.59 : 1. Malin's capitals are 0.82 of the calibre of **h**; Monotype's are 0.90.

BDEHNO fehijnp
BDEHNO fehijnp
BDGHNO abhp
BDGHNO abhp

45 *The 14-pt type of October 1927 (first and third rows) and the corresponding characters from Gill's drawings for Gerard Meynell. The type is twice actual size; the drawings have been scaled to it so that the calibres of* h h *are the same.*

The drawing office has missed the subtlety in the bowl of D as well as ignoring the curves at the inner foot of the verticals in D *D* and E, and the change in the proportions of B and H has made stolid characters out of sprightly ones. Overall, though, the type is much more like the drawings than the January 1928 type is like Malin's work.

Something must have changed Salfords' attitude between January and the summer of 1928. Figure 46 compares the type of Trial 2 with Monotype's first cutting. The serifs are much sharper, although the asymmetrical lower terminal to p has gone. The relative heights of short letters, ascenders and descenders have changed so that the short letters are actually smaller in relation to the others than they were in Malin's type.[38]

eefghmpDEHM

efghmpDEHM

46 *The type of Trial 2 (upper row) compared with Monotype's first cutting. Four times actual size. The oversized* H *was revised for Trial 2.*

Figure 47 shows how like each other are the minuscules of Trial 2 and Malin's type. Except for e r y, of which revised versions have been cut,

---

[38] In the new Monotype version the ratio between the calibres of **h, p** and **e** is 1.64:1.7:1. In the first Monotype cutting it is 1.54:1.59:1, and in Malin's type 1.62:1.67:1.

the characters of Trial 2 are those of the 'new roman' that Gill had commented on in June.

abcdeefghijklmnopqrrstuvwxyyz
abcdefghijklmnopqrstuvwxyz

47 Minuscule alphabets from Trial 2 (upper row) and Malin's cutting. Twice actual size.

Malin's wiry serifs, particularly those on d and u, have been regularized, but the overall sharpness of the design has been recovered. One new e follows Malin's, with a slight heaviness at the right-hand side of the bowl; the other is wider and more open. The g looks for the first time like a character Gill might have drawn. Monotype's h is wider than Malin's, though m and n are not. Both new versions of r have the curved spur that Morison had asked for more than a year before; one is narrower and heavier than the other.

The capitals in Trial 2 have been narrowed from Monotype's first cutting, and their serifs sharpened. B C H L S V have been revised, with the new versions taller than the other capitals: H is now 0.91 instead of 0.88 times the calibre of h, as against the 0.82 of Malin's type and the 0.90 of Monotype's first version.

abcdefghijklmnopqrstuvwxyyzæœ
abcdeefghijklmnopqrrstuvwxyyzæœ
fi ff fl ffi ffl fi ffi
fi ff fl ffi ffl

48 Roman minuscule alphabets from Trials 2 (second and fourth rows) and 6. Twice actual size.

The roman of Trial 4, carried through into Trial 6, firms up the revisions of Trial 2. Figure 48 compares the minuscules of the two. The serif at the foot of a in Malin's type and Trial 2 has been replaced by the hooked terminal that Gill had asked for on 1 September 1928 in a letter to Morison.[39] The wider e from Trial 2 has been adopted. The k has been revised to make it wider and lighter. The r is a compromise between Trial 2's two versions.

---

[39] Mosley, p. 94.

ABCDEFGHIJKLMNOPQRSTUVWXYZ
ÆŒÇQu
abcdefghijklmnopqrstuvwxyyz
fi fi ff fl ffi ffi ffl & ,— 1234567890
æœ.:;,!?-' ' " " ( )

49 *The second synopsis from* The Fleuron. *Actual size.*

Figure 49 shows the second synopsis from Beatrice Warde's *Fleuron* article. It is captioned 'Final Monotype cutting of the *Perpetua* type'.[40] The minuscules reproduce the type of Trial 6, including both versions of y and of fi ffi. The narrower of the two capital Rs is retained. The text of the *Fleuron* supplement that was the first showing of the Perpetua type uses straight-tailed y for initial and medial, and hockey-stick y for terminal, characters. Only the dotless fi is used.

In Perpetua 239, the type as it was finally issued, the hockey-stick y is the normal character, with the straight-tailed version offered as an alternative. The dotted fi ffi have disappeared. Figure 50 compares the principal composition sizes. It suggests that five sets of drawings were made to cover the range from 6 to 18 pt. 6, 8 and 9 pt each had their own set; there was one for 10 and 11 pt, and one for 13, 14 and 18 pt. The 16-pt size shown in Figure 41 did not find its way into production.

type	6 pt at 357%	type	11 pt at 222%
type	8 pt at 308%	type	12 pt at 200%
type	9 pt at 276%	type	13 pt at 194%
type	10 pt at 250%	type	14 pt at 172%
		type	18 pt at 137%

50 Composition sizes of Monotype Perpetua 239 roman: from a Monotype specimen-book page dated May 1960. The examples are scaled so that the calibre of p is constant.

Sebastian Carter says of Perpetua that it 'exhibits in an extreme form the tendency of the Monotype works to draw letters with ruler and compasses'. He reproduces the sketch of l with straight-sided and waisted stems – 'See how bloody the [straight-sided one] looks, and *is*' – that Gill made on the verso of a letter that he wrote to Morison on 31 December

---

[40] *The Fleuron* 7 (1930), p. 43.

1926.[41] The letter was about Malin's cutting of the titling capitals. E H O in the 30-pt size of Monotype's Perpetua Titling 258 exactly reproduce the smoke-proofs sent by Malin to Morison on 16 October 1926.

There may have been technical reasons for the regularizing tendency that Carter remarks on. Like all hand-cut punches, Malin's were intended to strike relatively few matrices. Machine-cut punches, on the other hand, had to make hundreds or (in Linotype's case) thousands of strikes. This meant that the physical structure of the punch itself had to be very strong.[42] Figure 51 shows some minuscules from Trial 2 and Malin's type. Even allowing for differences in inking and impression, the serifs of the Trial 2 type are shorter and more robust in shape than Malin's. His thin, wiry, curling serifs may simply have been mechanically unsuitable for repeated striking.

The drawing office's work also most often had to be used to make patterns for a range of sizes. Figure 50 suggests that the 13 and 14 pt composition sizes and the 18 pt display size of Perpetua 239 were derived from a single set of drawings. A detail like the downward-pointing lower serif in Malin's d, while it adds liveliness and sparkle to the type in the size for which it was intended, would be disagreeably obtrusive in a character half as large again.

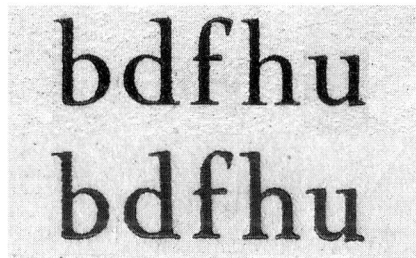

51 The type of Trial 2 (upper row) and Malin's type. Four times actual size.

These are two aspects of the problem that Morison wrestled with, Jan van Krimpen declared himself haunted by and Pierpont solved by ignoring it: how to make designs that were aesthetically as well as technically suitable for the means by which they were produced.

Van Krimpen had made his Lutetia design for Joh. Enschedé en Zonen in the early 1920s. The roman was cut in 1923–24 and the italic in 1924–25. The type was produced in a wide range of sizes, from 6 to 48 Didot for the roman and 8 to 16 Didot for the italic. Each font contained a large number of characters: the romans 142 (except for the 48 Didot size, which contained only capitals, numerals and punctua-

---

[41] *Twentieth century type designers*, p. 76; Barker, p. 211.

[42] David Saunders describes how the bevel or shoulder that a punch should have to make it robust was indicated on the pattern drawing along with the character outline: 'Two decades of change', *Monotype Recorder* new series no. 10 (1997).

tion) and the italics 149. Almost all the punches were cut by P H Rädisch from drawings made by the designer.⁴³ There was one set of drawings for the romans and another for the italics. Rädisch had them photographed to the correct size and used the resulting images as guides for cutting.⁴⁴

24D   20D   16D   14D   12D   10D

m m m m m m

52 *Variations in the configuration of* m *in different sizes of Rädisch's cutting of Lutetia; from a specimen booklet in the St Bride Printing Library, published by Enschedé's in 1927. The 16 Didot character is three times actual size; the others are scaled to it so that the height of the first vertical is constant.*

Figure 52 shows the differences between m in the size range from 10 to 24 Didot.

Morison and Van Krimpen first made contact in January 1926, following on a review of *The Fleuron* 4 that Van Krimpen had written in the Dutch journal *Het Boek*.⁴⁵ They discovered an immediate sympathy of views. Morison's mention of the Lutetia type in no. 5 of *The Fleuron* was followed up with an enthusiastic review of the italic in no. 6.⁴⁶ This contains the much-quoted phrase that the design of the roman 'was in no recognizable way purloined from ancient times but instead rose freshly from the reasoned canons of type design'. The same could equally, and with more justice, have been said of any of the contemporary German sanserifs: Futura or Kabel, for example. If it means anything, it is that Lutetia fitted in with Morison's views on the design of roman type at a time when he was involved with the production of Perpetua, and about to become so with Bembo and Bruce Rogers's Centaur, for Monotype.

On 28 February 1928 Morison wote to D B Updike, telling him among other things that

> ... I was visited recently by some very decent people from the Enschedé foundry, who desired my advice about one or two things, and as a result of several conversations a concordat between our Monotype Company [i.e. the English, not the American company] and Enschedé has been arrived at. This means that the Lutetia, roman and italics, will be reproduced for use on the English machines... ⁴⁷

Morison's use of the word 'reproduced' is interesting. Van Krimpen's view of the same agreement, written some time after the event, differed in a few respects:

> Messrs Joh. Enschedé en Zonen and I were asked, early in 1928, by the late

---

⁴³ Walter Tracy says that some of the punches were cut in Germany: *Letters of credit*, pp. 102–103.

⁴⁴ See Chapter 2 above.

⁴⁵ Barker, pp. 195–196.

⁴⁶ *The Fleuron* 5 (1926), pp. 191–192; *ibid.* 6 (1928), pp. 215–216.

⁴⁷ Barker, p. 228.

W. I. Burch, then Managing Director of the (English) Monotype Corporation, and by Mr Stanley Morison . . . to allow the Corporation to produce the type for use on their machine. My first impulse was to decline: I told my friends that I was afraid that they would not be able to make a rendering that would satisfy me. This reply was, in particular by Burch, taken as a challenge and he answered it with a counter-challenge: if I would only take into account the limitations of the Monotype unit-system, and allow for certain minor differences which are thought and said to be technically unavoidable, he authorised me to disapprove and reject unlimitedly.[48]

Monotype Lutetia 255 was finished in 1930. Its smallest size is larger than Rädisch's: 8 Didot as against 6 Didot. There is no 24 Didot size. The 48 Didot, like Rädisch's, has no minuscules.

Monotype		Enschedé
ahemop	10D	ahemop
ahemop	12D	ahemop
ahemog	14D	ahemog
ahemop	16D	ahemop
ademop	20D	ademop

53 *The Monotype and Enschedé cuttings of Lutetia compared. The Monotype examples are taken from a specimen-book page dated July 1960; the Enschedé ones from the same foundry specimen as the characters in Figures 5 and 52. The differences in weight between the two are largely due to differences in the papers on which they are printed. The 12 Didot Monotype characters are three times actual size; the others are scaled to them so that the calibre of* o *is constant.*

John Dreyfus describes how the punches cut by Rädisch were used in the Monotype Corporation's production of Van Krimpen's design.[49] Figure 53 shows how closely the Monotype cutting of Lutetia 255 followed Rädisch's work. The character widths tell the same story. Van Krimpen was obliged to take account of the Monotype unit system to the extent that the widths of the characters in each size were multiples of one

---

[48] *On designing and devising type* (1957), pp. 26-27.
[49] *The work of Jan van Krimpen* (1952), pp. 21-22.

eighteenth of the set-width for that size; but that was as far as he would go. Not only does the allocation of widths to characters, and hence the unit arrangement, differ for every one of the composition sizes: the allocation of widths to matrix-case rows is different for each size as well.

In Van Krimpen's own words, 'this makes the type unfit for practical use'.[50] Every size requires a different set of keybars and a different stopbar case for the keyboard, so that, as with Caslon 128, the capital cost of setting up for composition over the whole range of sizes is much higher than usual. In addition, and unlike Caslon, the selection of characters that overhang their body widths and have to be cast with a supporting space is different for each size, so that keyboarding becomes very difficult. 'If I had then understood and known the Monotype system better I should never have assented to this strange experiment and Monotype Lutetia would have become a different face altogether.'[51]

Morison, first in the Perpetua and then in the Lutetia project, was trying to do something new. He was searching for a way to incorporate into machine-cut type the quality that for him had so far existed only in types cast in matrices made from punches cut by hand: the particular sets of appearance characteristics that gave them a 'second nature which is so strong as to be unchangeable', as he described it in a letter to Van Krimpen thirty years later.[52]

The approach he chose for Perpetua was to have a hand-cut type made, and give it to the Monotype works at Salfords as an example for them to follow along with the designer's drawings. With hindsight, we can see that this could not have had the result that Morison intended. Leaving aside for the moment the personal tensions that existed between Morison and the works,[53] the ambiguous role of Malin's work in the production of the new design was bound to cause problems.

Morison's intentions in having Malin cut the type were 'to preserve absolutely the chiselled quality of Gill's capitals and lower case'.[54] His view of the drawing office at Salfords, then and later, was that if left to itself it would always over-simplify and over-regularize the shapes of characters. Morison may have intended Malin's type to be a model, serving as a guide to the interpretation of the drawings that accompanied it. This is Dreyfus's view;[55] but if that were so, then the task that Morison was inviting the drawing office to perform was

---

[50] *On designing and devising type*, p. 27.

[51] *Ibid.*, pp. 27–28.

[52] Reproduced by John Dreyfus in Appendix 2 of *A letter to Philip Hofer* (1972).

[53] *cf.* L W Wallis, 'Frank Hinman Pierpont (1860–1937): an unsung pioneer of mechanical typesetting', *Printing Historical Society Bulletin* (1994), no. 36 pp. 8–14.

[54] *A tally of types* (1953), p. 85. The chapter about Perpetua in the *Tally* contains a few errors of fact, understandable at such a distance of time. There seems no reason, though, to doubt Morison's account of his intentions for the project.

[55] *Monotype Recorder* new series no. 8 (1990), p. 15.

Perpetua and Lutetia

exactly the one he considered them to be incapable of. There were no technical reasons, apart perhaps from the question of serif robustness discussed above, why the configuration of the verticals, upright curves and terminals of Malin's punches should not have been reproduced exactly in a machine-cut version at the same, or indeed at any other, size.[56] Figure 51 shows how much of the individuality of the design resides in these features. Some of the character shapes would need to be widened or narrowed to accommodate the design to the Monotype unit system; but this could have been done without traducing the quality of Malin's work. (Compare the arches and foot-serifs of Malin's and Monotype's h in the same illustration.) All of this, though, would have involved the drawing office in interpreting the design of Malin's type rather than simply reproducing the configurations of its characters; and this was what Morison was trying to avoid.[57]

In the event, though, it is what happened. The works made good use of Malin's type once the defiant gesture of the January 1928 cutting was out of the way. Almost all the appearance characteristics of Malin's characters are preserved in the Perpetua type as it was issued.

On the other hand, Morison may have intended Malin's type to be a pattern: a set of character shapes to be reproduced exactly in a single size as the first stage of the drawing office's work. This would explain why the first types derived from it were made in the unusual body size of 13 pt, 'most unwelcome to the English trade', as opposed to the more conventional 14 pt of the trial characters cut from the Meynell drawings. If this was so, the single size that Malin cut was not, and could not be, enough to achieve Morison's objectives. The logic of his position *vis-à-vis* Salfords' capabilities required that if the qualities that he found only in hand-cut type were to be preserved in a machine-cut reproduction, a separate hand-cut original should be provided for each size of a new design for the drawing office to work from.

This is what he did with Lutetia. The type could have been a technical success, and with Monotype's publicity behind it an economic success

---

[56] As Beatrice Warde says, the cutting radius of the rotating tool in the punchcutting pantograph on its last cut 'is so infinitesmal that it can make a Bodoni serif appear, even under a strong glass, to be meeting the upright stroke at a perfect right angle': *The Dolphin* no. 2 (1935), p. 68. Whether or not this is the right thing for a Bodoni serif to do is a separate question.

[57] Gill's view of the personnel at Salfords, written in 1930 while he was still engaged with Perpetua as well as Gill Sans, is revealing. 'Enlargement operators, pantograph operators, pattern makers, electrotypers and machine operators are all necessarily completely tame and dependent on their overseers. Such interest as they have in the business... necessarily tends to be that of conscientious machine-minders, interested more in the good working of their machine than in the intellectual quality of the product': *An essay on typography* (1931), ch. 4. It has to be said that Gill was less uncomplimentary about the Corporation in Chapter 7 of his *Autobiography* (1940).

as well. We do not know the details of Van Krimpen's interactions with the works; but if he was intransigent, as the evidence suggests he was, then the project was doomed from the beginning. The drawing office indeed copied Rädisch's punches as exactly as they could; but they were not allowed to modify the characters' widths to the extent that all the sizes could be fitted into rational matrix-case layouts. There was no reason other than Van Krimpen's obstinacy why they should not have done so. A competent drawing office, and Salfords was nothing if not competent, would not have found it hard to alter the widths of character shapes while retaining all their other features: particularly since all the sizes were derived from a single set of drawings.

G W Ovink, in his review of Van Krimpen's *Letter to Philip Hofer*, locates the problem precisely.

> [Van Krimpen's] difficulties stemmed, in the last resort, from the fact that he shirked his responsibilities. On the one hand he exaggerated in his romantic notions the virtues of the craftsman wrestling with the hard metal, thereby producing sprightliness, and of the 'secret' skills that only the experienced craftsman, reared in a tradition, can acquire in judging the specific needs of the various sizes... On the other hand he refused to exercise his own judgment in the matter, which he could have done by patiently and laboriously drawing and redrawing for mechanical cutting until the result had all the sprightliness and specific suitability for size that he wished. Rädisch's judgment [in cutting a range of sizes from a single set of drawings] was no better than that which Van Krimpen could have undoubtedly acquired, had he taken the trouble to sit down and do at least the fundamental part of the dirty work himself.[58]

Morison might be said to have shirked his responsibilities in the same way. He could write, in his letter to Van Krimpen, that 'the engineers [*sc*. Pierpont] knew nothing about letter design fifty years ago – and know nothing to this day.' This was untrue: Monotype Imprint 101 and Plantin 110, both produced at Salfords before Morison's time and under Pierpont's supervision, demonstrate its falsity clearly enough. But if Morison felt it to be true, it was because he had not taken the trouble to build up good relationships with the authorities at Salfords, nor to explain to them adequately what his intentions were.

---

[58] *Quaerendo* vol. 3 no. 3 (1973), pp. 239–242.

Part 2: The photographic matrix

8 Making type by photography

In the early 1960s a new technology for composing type, that had been maturing since the 1940s, began to become a significant force. This was *direct-photography photocomposition*. Characters are imaged from a photographically produced matrix on to photosensitive output material which is then used to make a printing surface.[1]

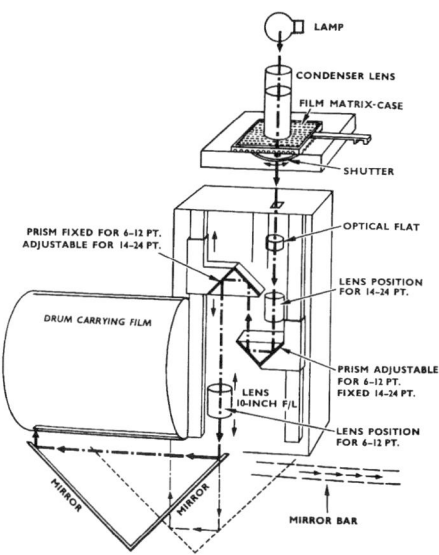

54 *Schematic layout of a first-generation machine: the Monophoto Filmsetter. From* Computer peripherals and typesetting.

In principle, direct-photography photocomposing machines are very simple. Character images are projected from a matrix on to photosensitive output material by means of an *optical system* of some kind. The images on the matrix are invariably negatives: transparent images on an opaque ground. There is a *light source* that illuminates the image to be composed, and a *selection mechanism* that makes sure the illuminated

---

[1] J W Seybold's *Fundamentals of modern photocomposition* (1979) is a good introduction to the area. A H Phillips's *Computer peripherals and typesetting* (1968) gives details of a wide range of composing machines, both hot-metal and photographic, from the point of view of someone setting up a computer-based typesetting system in the pioneer days. For the history of Higonnet's and Moyroud's inventions two works by Alan Marshall, *Ruptures et continuités dans un changement de système technique* (1992) and *Du plomb à la lumière* (2003), are the principal sources. Marshall also edited *La Lumitype-Photon* (1995), the proceedings of a colloquium held at Lyon to mark the fiftieth anniversary of the filing of the inventors' first patents.

image is the right one and that it is correctly positioned relative to the machine's optical axis. The optical system may, and usually does, alter the size of the image that is projected on the output material. The projected image is positioned by an *escapement system*, which in many cases is itself part of the optical system. There is also a means of positioning the output material to receive successive rows of character images. For convenience we can call this the *film transport mechanism*, though the output material is very often photosensitive paper rather than film.

In real machines this simple recipe is interpreted in a number of ways. The first photocomposing machines to achieve commercial success were closely modelled, both mechanically and conceptually, on their hot-metal equivalents. A Monotype caster, for example, has to have its mould and wedges replaced in order to change the body size of the type it casts. Its photographic analogue, the Monophoto Filmsetter, had to have its optical system reconfigured by hand, and elements of its gearbox replaced, to change the size and set of the character images it produced. Although the Monophoto's matrix started off as a single piece of glass carrying 272 character images, it was soon replaced by a metal carrier holding the same number of individual negatives, much more closely analogous to the Monotype matrix-case: a move which, according to Lawrence Wallis, 'signalled the commercial acceptance of the machine' in 1957.[2]

There were understandable reasons for this conservatism, which was matched in a different technical context by the Fotosetter, the photographic analogue of the Intertype linecaster. The mechanical composition of metal type had revolutionized the work of the compositor at the case, but had had much less effect elsewhere in the composing-room or in the letterpress machine-room. Photocomposition, on the other hand, along with the offset lithographic printing that was its natural associate, overturned all the practices that five hundred years of printing with metal type had established. Machines that looked like their predecessors, used many of the same mechanical principles, and were driven by the same keyboards – even if they smelled and sounded different – provided something familiar to hold on to in the face of the terrifying changes that were going on all round them. But these machines of the so-called 'first generation' could never be anything but a backwater. They were all vulnerable to the criticism attributed by Wallis to Ted Emery of Linotype: 'The use of a ton and a half of casting machinery to manipulate beams of light was not the correct approach'.

The second generation of direct-photography photocomposing machines broke away from the mechanical constraints of their predecessors – or rather, they never took them into account. René A Higonnet and Louis Moyroud, the inventors of the Photon-Lumitype range of machines

---

[2] *A concise chronology of typesetting developments 1886–1986* (1988), p. 29.

Making type by photography

among others, had no background in the printing industry, and hence no preconceptions about what type-composing machinery ought to be like. The machine they developed between 1944 and 1956, simultaneously with but conceptually far away from the development of the first-generation machines, was novel in every respect. Its matrix was a continuously rotating disc carrying concentric rows of character images. These were illuminated by a xenon flash tube, and projected on to the photographic material via one of a selection of sizing lenses and an electromechanical escapement that positioned the output character images successively along the line.

With this layout the machine could do something that had not previously been possible with mechanical composition: mix character images of different nominal sizes in a line of text, with correct lateral relationships and on a common baseline. To do this, the machine had to incorporate something completely new to composing technology: a calculator that would work out the space occupied by each character image in the output line by multiplying together its width and size. This in turn meant that the machine had to have some way of storing character widths... It is not surprising that Higonnet and Moyroud, along with the Graphic Arts Research Foundation in Massachusetts where the Photon machine was developed, held so many of the key patents in direct-photography photocomposition.

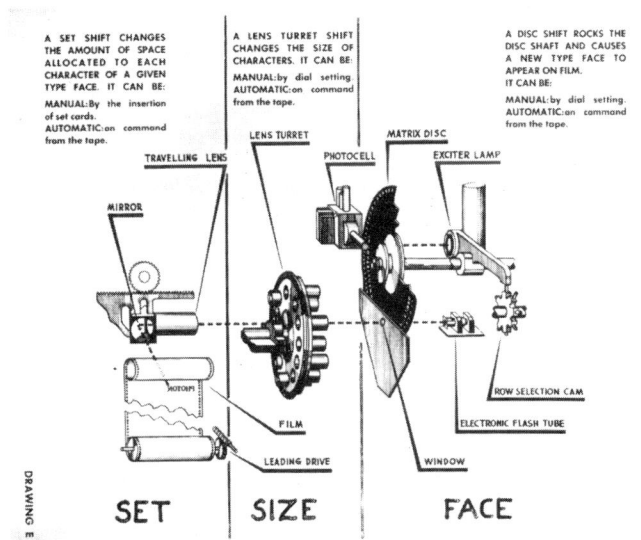

55 *Schematic layout of a second-generation machine: the Lumitype-Photon 200. From* Computer peripherals and typesetting.

If the Lumitype-Photon series of machines are used to illustrate the discussion that follows it is largely because Higonnet and Moyroud were the pioneers of modern photocomposition. They encountered its problems first, and developed the solutions that the designers of later systems made use of. It is also because their machines provided the technical background for the development of Adrian Frutiger's Univers family of typefaces, discussed in Chapter 10 below.

56 *The practical realization of Figure 55: the photographic unit of the Lumitype-Photon 200 machine. The solenoids, gears and friction clutches that make up the escapement are at the upper left. Below them and to the right is the mounting plate for the film magazine, which has been removed. The travelling lens and mirror are visible through the slot in the plate. The lens turret is to the right of the slot. Above it and further to the right is the matrix disc, seen almost edge-on in this view. The large assembly to the right of the disc contains the exciter lamp for the flash timing photocell; the decoder for resolving the rotational position of the disc; the row selection mechanism; the lens turret drive; and the drive for the film transport mechanism (inappropriately marked 'leading drive' in Figure 55). From a photograph in the Musée de l'Imprimerie de Lyon.*

In metal-type composition the solid body of the type itself defines the parameters of the printing surface. The image on the face of the type directly specifies the image that appears on the paper, and is effectively identical in every respect with the image in the matrix from which it is derived. The width of the type body locates the images to either side of it, and its height determines the minimum vertical distance between the baselines of successive rows of images.

In photocomposition with photographic matrices, all these parameters are defined by separate parts of the composing system. The character images that arrive at the output material are derived from the image on the matrix at one remove, modified in size and perhaps in slant and width as well by the optical system of the composing machine. Because the process that produces them is photographic, the eventual configuration of the output images depends on settings in the machine's optical system as well as on the chemical processes that follow composition (Figure 57).

To enable the Operative to exercise accurate control over the quality of the exposed film, a "test step wedge" is provided with each machine. It is a glass negative

To enable the Operative to exercise accurate control over the quality of the exposed film, a "test step wedge" is provided with each machine. It is a glass negative

57 *Underexposed and correctly exposed images: adapted from 'The quality of filmset text',* Monotype Recorder *vol. 42 no. 2 (1961). Actual size; laterally reversed.*

The vertical alignment of successive images in the line of output text depends on the precision with which the matrix is located in the machine: precision that often has to coexist with rapid movement of the matrix. Their horizontal positioning depends primarily on the escapement, which in second-generation machines is mechanically independent of the matrix, and secondarily, in machines with continuously moving matrices, on the accuracy with which the illuminating flash is timed. The vertical separation between rows depends on the film transport mechanism.

Le centrage est
indépend**ant**
du corps
et
indépend*ant*
du style

On peut aussi
mélanger
S t*y*les et **C** *o*rp s
dans la même ligne

58 *'Centering is independent of size and style. Styles and sizes can also be mixed in the same line.'*

This separation of functions makes for much greater capability in the composing system itself: for example, in allowing different sizes to be mixed and justified in the line, or the set-width of characters to be varied independently of their size (Figures 58 and 59). It also renders obsolete any model of the composition process that depends on the inviolability of the space occupied by the type body, by calling into question the notion of the body itself (Figure 60).[3]

---

[3] The concept of the type body has proved to be surprisingly robust. It survived the disappearance of its physical correlate, and persists to this day as a convenient,

Ceci est une ligne de corps onze sur set dix et demi
Ceci est une ligne de corps onze sur set dix trois quarts
Ceci est une ligne de corps onze sur set onze
Ceci est une ligne de corps onze sur set onze un quart
Ceci est une ligne de corps onze sur set onze et demi
Ceci est une ligne de corps onze sur set onze trois quarts

59 'This is a line of 11 pt on . . .' The set values vary from 10.25 to 11.75.

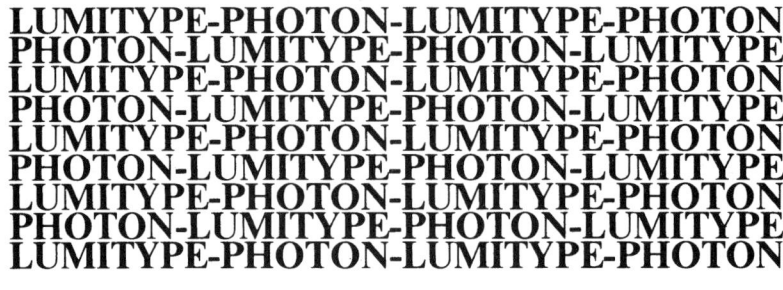

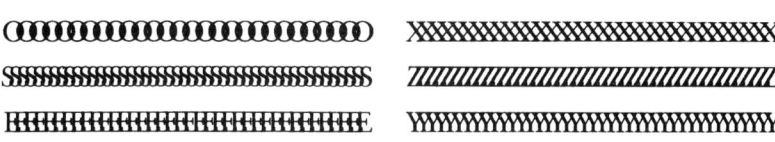

60 Above: 14 pt Lumitype Times 451-65 (semibold) on 10.25 Didot film feed. Below: characters of 12 pt Lumitype Baskerville 401-55 (medium) on half their normal set-widths.

Figures 58–60, taken from the Lumitype type-specimen book published by Deberny & Peignot in 1961, demonstrate the amount of flexibility permitted by the new technology: genuine advances in typographic capability, even if, like most advances, they were open to misuse.

However, the fact that the various parameters of the composed text were determined by different parts of the composing machine's mechanism meant that these had to have some way of communicating with one another. With first-generation machines the communication could be mechanical and direct, as with the gears of the Monophoto Filmsetter. With machines of the second generation, the calculations involved in mixing variants and sizes in the line meant that mechanics were no longer adequate. The machine had to have some computing capability that could function independently of the operator. The 200 and 500-series Lumitype-Photon machines used binary calculators implemented with electromechanical relays and stepping switches. These were replaced in later series of machines, first by special-purpose circuits built up from standard solid-state electronic modules and then by small stored-program computers when these became available.

though illogical and inaccurate, method of denoting character image size.

Making type by photography 85

61 A matrix disc for the Lumitype 540 photocomposing machine.

The matrices used in the 200/500 machines were glass discs around 25 cm (10 in) in diameter.[4] They carried eight concentric rows of 180 images (Figure 61). These were grouped into 16 'alphabets' of 90 characters each, with two alphabets per row, giving the machine a repertory of 1440 characters. In normal disc layouts each alphabet was a different typeface variant, so that a single disc carried 16 variants altogether.

The disc rotated continuously in the machine at eight revolutions per second. Characters within a row were selected for composition by keeping track of the rotational position of the matrix disc, and triggering the illuminating flash when the required character was aligned with the machine's optical axis. The triggering was done by detecting a pulse of light from one of the timing slits arranged round the periphery of the disc.[5]

As long as the characters being composed came from the pair of variants in a single row (roman and italic, for example) changing between variants had no effect on composition speed. To change from one row of characters to another the shaft on which the disc rotated was raised or lowered by a cam in the machine, and composition had to pause for a second or two while this 'level change' took place. The machine's character repertory could be changed by replacing the matrix disc itself. This involved shutting the machine down and, for the 200-series machines in which keyboard and photographic unit were integrated, replacing

---

[4] The discs were cut from photographic plates. For a short time in the late 1960s discs made from plastics were used. These were easier to machine, and more resistant to damage, than glass discs, but the photographic emulsion with which they were coated had unacceptably high levels of surface defects.

[5] This is the function of the components marked 'Exciter lamp' and 'Photocell' in Figure 55. The patent for this method of triggering an electronic flash to illuminate a single character on a continuously-moving matrix (the *brevet des fentes*) was one of the two most significant held by Higonnet and Moyroud. The other was the *brevet des cartes*, which protected the method of storing character widths by patterns of connections on printed-circuit cards.

the carrier holding the printed-circuit cards on which character widths were stored.

The output character images were sized by rotating a turret of twelve lenses to locate the correct one on the optical axis. The image was positioned on the output material by a travelling lens and prism whose movement along the line was controlled by a train of gears and solenoid-operated friction clutches. This allowed character images to be positioned laterally in increments of 1/128 cm (0.078 mm; 0.003 in). There were no restrictions on the allocation of widths to characters; a notable difference from the contemporary Monophoto, whose gear-driven escapement exactly reproduced the constraints of its hot-metal analogue.

In contrast with the multistaged and laborious processes of matrix-making for metal type, matrix-making for direct-photography photo-composing machines is conceptually very simple. Large character images – *character masters* – are photographed to produce small character images on the matrix.

In practical terms, the complexity of a matrix-making process depends largely on the amount of reduction from the character master to the image on the matrix. In second-generation photocomposing machines there is always an incentive to keep the matrix images small, so as to fit a large number on a matrix which is small and light enough to be moved around easily both within and outside the machine.

62 Close-up of the disc in Figure 61, showing arcs of character images with the same identity.

The disc matrices for the Lumitype-Photon machines were photographed with a single stage of reduction from positive character masters, known as *phototypes*, with a nominal size of 512 pt. The images on the disc had a nominal size of 6 pt. This was small enough to fit a large number of character images on a matrix of reasonable size, but not so small as to place excessive demands on the photographic performance of the matrix-making camera. Characters were photographed eight at a time,

Making type by photography

in an arc across the disc corresponding to the path along which it moved in the composing machine to select one or another row of characters (Figure 62). The length of this arc meant that a lens of around 5 cm focal length was needed in the camera to preserve image quality for the characters at its ends. This in turn meant that the camera itself was physically large. With a reduction ratio of 84:1 and a 5 cm lens, the distance from the panel carrying the character masters to the lens was around 14 ft (4.2 m).

Making the discs was a labour-intensive process. The Lumitype camera, with its single stage of reduction and separate character masters, offered the possibility of making matrices individually to order. Indeed, with the 1440-character repertory of the Lumitype's disc matrix (contrasted, for example, with the 88 characters of a single matrix for the early Linofilm machines) it would have been difficult to offer European customers, with their wide variety of needs, a standard product.[6] In these circumstances it was important to be sure that the images on a matrix were the ones the customer had specified.

63 *Phototype of Univers 751-55 (medium)* m. *One-fifth actual size.*

The camera masters from which the discs were made were photographically produced images on card, known in the Lumitype studio as *phototypes*. They were about 30 cm square, with a metal bar along the top which was punched with register pin holes for mounting in the camera (Figure 63). Assembling the 1440 phototypes required for each new disc and checking them against the specification was a considerable task in itself. The disc itself was made with 180 exposures of eight characters each, and took around three hours of continuous work to photograph.[7]

---

[6] For an extended discussion of this point, see 'Towards the present-day font' in *La Lumitype-Photon* (1995), pp. 143–154.

[7] *cf. Du plomb à la lumière*, pp. 242–245.

64 Original designs, character drawings and negative camera masters for matrix-making: photographed in the type-drawing office at D Stempel AG in 1978. The two masters are from Adrian Frutiger's Serifa 45.

65 Two-stage reduction in photographic matrix-making for the Linotype VIP photocomposing machine: photographed in 1978 at D Stempel AG. At the top of the picture is part of an intermediate plaque carrying 32 character images. Below, to the left and right respectively, are 'A' and 'B' matrices for the machine, with differently-sized character images. The characters from the plaque are visible in the eight columns at the left of the 'B' matrix. The Stempel system used reversal photographic processing throughout.

It is difficult to make a high-performance matrix camera with a single-stage reduction ratio of more than around 90:1, particularly if several characters are to be photographed at the same time. The matrix-making operation at D Stempel AG, set up in 1968[8] to produce matrices for Linotype's photocomposing machines from character masters at their standard size of 768 pt, used a process with two stages of reduction. The first stage used negative masters: transparencies cut from two-layer laminated film, yielding clear images on a photo-opaque red ground (Figure 64). These were photographed on to glass 'plaques' around

---

[8] The date is given by Frutiger: 'Letterforms in photo-typography', *Journal of typographic research* vol. 4 no. 4 (1970).

Making type by photography 89

20 cm (8 in) square, carrying 16, 32 or 40 negative images depending on the type of matrix they were intended for. Several of these plaques were then photographed together to produce the final matrix (Figure 65).

The VIP's filmstrip matrices, like the Lumitype's discs, are *unitary matrices*. The whole of the matrix's repertory of characters is carried on a single piece of photographic material, and its contents cannot be changed. While the earliest versions of the Monophoto Filmsetter also used unitary matrices with 272 character images, *discrete matrices* were used on production machines. The matrix-case was an assembly of individual elements, any of which could be removed or exchanged without affecting the others. This allowed the machine's character repertory to be modified to a greater or lesser extent to meet the requirements of particular jobs.

The design decision about which type of matrix to use is a complex one. It is easy to sympathize, for example, with the motives that led to the use of a unitary matrix in the prototype Monophoto. The machine's character-selection mechanism was closely modelled on that of its hot-metal predecessor, while the engineering difficulties involved in making a large array of precisely located photographic images with the same small size (0.2 in or 5 mm square) as the brass matrices of the earlier technology were formidable. With hindsight, though, it is clear that an unalterable assortment of 272 characters from one or a pair of typeface families is much too small for a machine that was directly aimed at the complex typography of Monotype's traditional markets: particularly as keyboard and caster operators in the hot-metal era had taken it for granted that they could build up the contents of the matrix-case according to the requirements of particular jobs. It was only when the machine was fitted with a discrete-matrix assembly with the same number of characters (increased to 340 in later models) that it became acceptable in the market.

The direct-photography Linofilm KE18 of the early 1960s was also equipped with unitary matrices: rectangular glass 'grids' carrying 88 character images each. Once again the influence of existing practice is clear. Unlike the Monophoto Filmsetter or the Intertype Fotosetter, though, the KE18 marked an advance on its hot-metal predecessors by using no fewer than 18 matrix grids, giving it a maximum repertory of 1584 characters: more than the Lumitype's 1440. Its successor, the Linofilm COL-28, had 28 grids and 2464 characters.[9]

---

[9] This was not necessarily quite the advantage it seemed. All the characters on the Lumitype's matrix were available in each of the machine's twelve output image sizes. The limited magnification range of the Linofilm's zoom-lens optical system meant that a total of five grids with different character image sizes were needed to cover the whole of the machine's size range, from 6 to 54 pt, for a single typeface (*Computer peripherals and typesetting*, p. 497).

Considerations of intellectual property sometimes played a part in deciding matrix configurations. Higonnet and Moyroud's *brevet des fentes* – their patent for timing an illuminating flash by means of slits on the periphery of a continuously moving matrix – led Linotype to adopt a stationary matrix and an intimidatingly complex prism-and-shutter character selection mechanism for the Linofilm. The mechanism became more complex still in 1964 with the 184-character matrix of the Linofilm Quick.[10] (Like Photon's 200 and 500-series machines, the Linofilm used connections on printed-circuit cards to store character widths. Photon saw this as a violation of Higonnet and Moyroud's *brevet des cartes*, and brought an action that after long negotiations was finally settled in Photon's favour in 1970.[11]) The Linotype VIP, whose drum-mounted filmstrip matrices were superficially very much like those of Photon's 713-series machines, circumvented the *brevet des fentes* by driving the matrix drum with a bidirectional stepping motor, using the slits on the edge of the filmstrip to monitor its position and bringing it to a halt at the instant of exposure.

In the final years of direct-photography photocomposition the trend of development was more towards the Linofilm's approach than the Lumitype's. Cynics might say that a still-conservative printing trade found it easier to come to terms with a machine that emulated a battery of high-speed linecasters than with one that offered 'a composing-room in a box'.[12] In some ways the 1440-character capacity of the Lumitype's discs made the problem of specifying their contents more difficult than it would have been for a matrix with a smaller repertory. There was a good deal to be said for the simplicity of choosing from a range of matrices with fixed small character sets – as long as these were properly chosen for the range of languages being composed, which was not always the case for the European market.

To achieve reasonable composition speed on anything but the simplest material, though, machines using the multiple-matrix approach needed some way of switching quickly between matrices. Harris-Intertype adopted a novel approach to this problem in 1968 when they extended the single-disc Fototronic 480 to the five-disc 1200: an approach reused in 1970 for the Fototronic TxT (Figure 66). A more elegant solution to the same problem was the segmented-disc matrix assembly of Photon's Pacesetter series, introduced in 1973 (Figure 67). The Monotype Corporation persisted in its attachment to discrete matrices, mounting them in 100-character arrays on lightweight metal discs in the Monophoto 600 machine of 1969 (Figure 68).

---

[10] The Quick's optical system is illustrated in Diagram 24.6 of *Computer peripherals and typesetting* and opposite p. 9 of Lawrence Wallis's *Electronic typesetting* (1984).

[11] *Du plomb à la lumière*, p. 185.

[12] The phrase was used to characterize the Lumitype 550 machine: *Du plomb à la lumière*, p. 234.

Making type by photography 91

66 The five-disc 'ferris wheel' of the Fototronic TxT. The turret of sizing lenses is at the lower left.

67 Part of the matrix assembly of a Photon Pacesetter.

68 Interior view of the Monotype 600. The pairs of 100-character carrier discs are swung out at either side, with the carousel of pi characters centrally below them.

The four discs gave the machine its substantial repertory of 400 characters, with 200 additional pi characters in the carousel. Images from all the discs and the carousel could be mixed in a line of composed text, although because the machine's five optical paths incorporated different numbers of reflections it was difficult to achieve uniform photographic density on the output material. The 400/31 and 400/8 machines, of 1973 and 1974 respectively, returned to the Corporation's traditions of a rectangular assembly of discrete matrices and a single optical path, while retaining the 400-character repertory of the Monophoto 600.

In Germany, Mergenthaler Linotype GmbH also clung to tradition and the discrete-matrix approach. The Linofilm Europa, released in 1970, had 480 glass matrices (Figure 69), each carrying a pair of characters, mounted magnetically on a large drum rotating on a vertical axis.

69 *Three matrices for the Linofilm Europa. Actual size. Each has its own magnet to hold it on the rotating matrix drum. The matrix characters are imaged photographically on a chromium film, which offers very high resolution and is also extremely robust. The uppermost of the three rows of slits below each pair of images is for flash timing; the others carry information for character identity and width.*

The turn of the decade was a hectic time for composing-machine development. As well as the Europa, 1970 saw the introduction by the Linotype group both of the Model 794, the last and fastest of their hot-metal linecasters, and of the VIP, the first photocomposing machine to be controlled by a programmable minicomputer.

But changes more radical than these were in the wind. Cathode-ray tube output, the successor technology to direct-photography photocomposition, was becoming established, with the scanned-matrix Linotron 505 already available and digital-font machines from several manufacturers occupying the top end of the market. Although new direct-photography machines were still being introduced in the late 1970s they had moved down the market by that time, almost to the extent of competing with direct-impression machines like the IBM Selectric Composer. The last direct-photography machine listed by Lawrence Wallis is the standalone Compugraphic 8200 of 1981.[13]

---

[13] *Electronic typesetting*, p. 34.

9 Drawing characters for the Lumitype

Photography has been used as an aid to typeface development at least since the beginning of the twentieth century. P H Rädisch's use of photographically reduced character drawings in cutting the punches for Enschedé's Lutetia type was mentioned above in Chapter 2. But the photographs used by Rädisch and his contemporaries were images made as adjuncts to the development of a design in a different medium, in which the final products – punches, matrices and types – were all three-dimensional objects. In photocomposition, on the other hand, the whole process of type design, design development, matrix-making and type composition is carried on in two dimensions. It is natural to use photography to develop designs that will be composed by photographic means, particularly since all the actions of the composing machine can be more or less faithfully reproduced 'off-line' in the darkroom.

In 1946 Higonnet and Moyroud had demonstrated the first prototype of their new photocomposing machine to Lucien Sauvage, director of the École Estienne in Paris. Sauvage saw that the inventors, coming from outside the printing industry, had no conception of the impact that a machine that set type photographically might have on the existing structures of metal-type manufacture and supply. He gave them an explicit warning to avoid contact with Deberny & Peignot, the principal French typefoundry, in case the latter attempted to buy up their invention and suppress it.[1]

In fact the opposite happened. Charles Peignot had become artistic director of Deberny & Peignot in 1931, and was anxious to keep the foundry technically up to date in the period of reconstruction after the second world war. 'I remembered that my father had let mechanical composition get away from him [in the years before 1914] and I decided not to let myself be overtaken by photocomposition.'[2] He took the initiative in making contact with Higonnet and Moyroud in the early 1950s, following the successful demonstration of their first industrial prototype in New York. In 1953 Peignot became chairman and managing director of the foundry, and in March 1954 an agreement was concluded that allowed Deberny & Peignot to manufacture and market Photon machines in France, the Benelux countries and Switzerland under the name Lumitype. An example of the first series to be commercialized,

---

[1] 'Surtout n'en parlez pas à Deberny & Peignot. Ils vous étoufferaient.' (*Ruptures et continuités*, p. 158; *Du plomb à la lumière*, p. 195.)

[2] 'Je me suis souvenu que mon père avait laissé échapper la composition mécanique et j'ai décidé de ne pas me laisser dépasser par la photocomposition.' *Caractère* December 1975, p. 51.

the Photon 200, was shown at the TPG exhibition[3] in Paris in May of the same year. A new company, Lumitype SA, was set up in the spring of 1955 in Deberny & Peignot's premises at 18 rue Ferrus in the 14th *arrondissement*.[4]

Adrian Frutiger was born at Unterseen in Switzerland in 1928. He began his apprenticeship as a compositor in 1944, and in 1948 went to the Kunstgewerbeschule in Zürich. He finished his course in 1951, and came to work in the drawing office at Deberny & Peignot in 1953.

Frutiger's first designs for the foundry were for metal type: Ondine, Phoebus and Président. But Peignot soon involved him in his plans for the Lumitype.

> My brief was precisely defined: photocomposed type printed by offset lithography should appear to the reader as being similar to conventional [*i.e.* letterpress] printing.[5]

In the spring of 1954 Frutiger began his work on the Lumitype project by defining a dimensional system for the new drawings he would have to make.

He took as his point of departure the pattern drawings for a group of designs from Deberny & Peignot's existing repertory, covering the whole range of widths from very wide (Normande) via Baskerville, Garamont and three variants of Europe to very narrow (Antique Simple Étroite).[6] With capital-letter heights scaled to a uniform 11 cm, he found that the widths of W ranged from 25.3 to 7.7 cm, and of i from 2.7 to 8.9 cm. For the text designs the widths of W and i were 18.05 and 5.32 cm respectively for Garamont, and 14.75 and 3.95 cm for Europe Light. The Photon machines built in America used a width allocation system similar to the Monotype's, with 18 units to the em square, and Frutiger had already decided to make his character drawings at a scale of 1 unit to 1 cm. He had also convinced René Gréa, the engineer responsible for the development of the Lumitype at Deberny & Peignot, to halve the smallest step of the machine's escapement, thus allowing 36 increments of character width to the em square.[7] The 11-cm capital-letter height would give him character widths for

---

[3] *Techniques papetières et graphiques*: the principal French printing trade exhibition.

[4] *Du plomb à la lumière*, pp. 203, 208–213.

[5] 'Ma responsabilité était précise: la composition photographique imprimée par le procédé offset devait apparaître aux yeux du lecteur semblable à l'impression conventionelle.' Frutiger's own account of this period is in 'Du plomb à la photocomposition: une mutation profonde', *La Lumitype-Photon*, pp. 137–142.

[6] Europe was Deberny & Peignot's recutting of Futura. The memorandum, dated 14 June 1954, in which Frutiger develops his conclusions is in the Lumitype collection in the Musée de l'Imprimerie de Lyon.

[7] In spite of the fact that all the Lumitype machines had 36 width increments to the em, character widths in the studio at 18 rue Ferrus were always described in terms of an 18-unit system with units and half-units.

text typefaces that fitted comfortably into this scheme; the wider and narrower designs could be accommodated by the variable-set facility the machine provided.

Frutiger recognized that his approach represented 'a definite commitment to designs with a single cap height for a given size, whether the designs themselves are narrow, normal or wide'.[8] This move towards the standardization of character dimensions was unique for its period.

Frutiger's memorandum also shows him coming to grips with the independence of baseline separation, setwise escapement and the dimensions of the character image itself that photocomposition makes inevitable.

> Until now the terms "body" or "size" have been used without distinction in discussions about the Lumitype to denote what is in fact the enlargement [*i.e.* from the character image on the matrix disc to the image on the output material]. Typographically, the significant thing is the amount of vertical space occupied by a line of text composed on the Lumitype, that is to say the distance from the bottom of the descenders to the top of the accented capitals; in practical terms this is the same as the body size in metal-type composition . . .[9]

Frutiger proposes the word *envergure* ('span' or 'scope') for this quantity, which in Photon's usage of the time was called 'leading' and is now known as minimum baseline separation. He points out that it is not the same thing as size, which in his terminology denotes the enlargement from the image on the matrix disc.

The optical system of the Photon machine could not accommodate characters wider than 7/6 of the em square (21 units), and the maximum distance the travelling lens could advance in a single step was just over 28 pt. Frutiger's initial proposal for handling designs such as Normande with very wide characters was to draw them with a reduced capital-letter height, so that the physical dimensions of the widest characters did not exceed these limits. (He seems to have been envisaging a maximum value of 18 units for stored character widths.) In the event, wide designs were drawn at the standard capital-letter height with the widths of the widest characters reduced to the 21-unit limit; extra space was set at the keyboard to the right of wide characters in large sizes.

An advantage of starting a typeface-drawing program from scratch was that a rational series-numbering scheme for the new designs could be

---

[8] 'Ceci équivaut à prendre définitivement partie pour des caractères ayant, dans un corps donné, une même hauteur pour les capitales, que ces caractères soient étroits, normaux ou larges.'

[9] 'Jusqu'ici, les termes de "corps" ou "size" ont été utilisés dans la Lumitype indifféremment pour signifier en fait l'agrandissement. Typographiquement, ce qui importera sera de connaître l'encombrement vertical de la ligne des textes composés en Lumitype, c'est-à-dire, la distance qui sépare la base des longues du bas du sommet des capitales accentuées; c'est ce qui correspond "pratiquement" à la force de corps en typographie . . .'

adopted from the beginning. This was made easier because in the 1950s the Lumitype was ahead of its time, and Peignot's initial estimates of sales were over-optimistic.[10] Three years went by between the agreement with Photon and the installation of the first machine for a European customer, Berger-Levrault in Nancy; so that the studio was not bedevilled early on by urgent demands for copies of existing typefaces in the way that the pioneers of hot-metal composition had been. Frutiger developed a scheme that located designs in a historical classification as well as describing their weight and width. Every variant had a serial number consisting of a three-digit series number and a two-digit 'descriptive number' (*numéro d'adjectif*): 751-55, for example. The first digit of the series number followed Maximilien Vox's scheme for typeface classification, which also appeared in 1954. 300-series designs were Garaldes; 400s were Réales (transitionals); 500s Didones; 600s Mécanes (slab-serifs); 700s Linéales (sanserifs). The second digit was 0 for adaptations of historical designs or 5 for new designs; the third gave the production sequence of the design within the category defined by the first two. Thus the Garamont family's variants shared the series number 301; Janson's were 302; and Méridien's 351. The first digit of the two-digit group gave the variant's weight, on a scale running from extra-light (3) to extrabold (8). The second indicated width and italicness or slantedness together: from 3 for wide upright, through 5 and 6 for normal-width upright and italic, 7 and 8 condensed upright and italic, to 9 extracondensed.

The typefaces of Lumitype origin are grouped by families and identified by a family number, for example Baskerville = 401, and a series number (2 figures) which has the following meaning:
— odd numbers = Roman (45, 47, 55, etc.);
— even numbers = Italic (46, 48, 56, etc.).

Weight	Tens	Units	Width	
Light	4	3	Roman . . .	Wide
		4	Italic	
Medium	5	5	Roman . . .	Medium
		6	Italic	
Bold	6	7	Roman . . .	Condensed
Extrabold	7	8	Italic	
Ultrabold	8	9	Roman . . .	Extracondensed

70 *The final version of the numbering scheme for weights and widths that was used for all the Lumitype designs. From the Lumitype-Photon specimen book of 1961; half actual size.*

This part of the scheme, summarized in Figure 70, clearly foreshadows the structure of the new family of sanserif typefaces that Frutiger already had in mind.[11]

---

[10] *Ruptures et continuités*, p. 239.

[11] An earlier version of the scheme, preserved in the Lumitype collection, adds 8 and 9 as the first digit of the series number for Vox's categories of Incises and Scriptes, and 9 as the first digit of the descriptive number for inline or shaded variants like Frutiger's own Phoebus. No designs in any of these categories were

Drawing for the Lumitype

Another advantage of starting with a blank slate was that a coherent approach could be developed to all the 'outside' characters that are needed in a real composing system. Starting from the 11 cm capital-letter height, a set of alignments was worked out that defined the vertical positions of dashes, accents, fraction bars and superior and inferior characters (Figure 71).

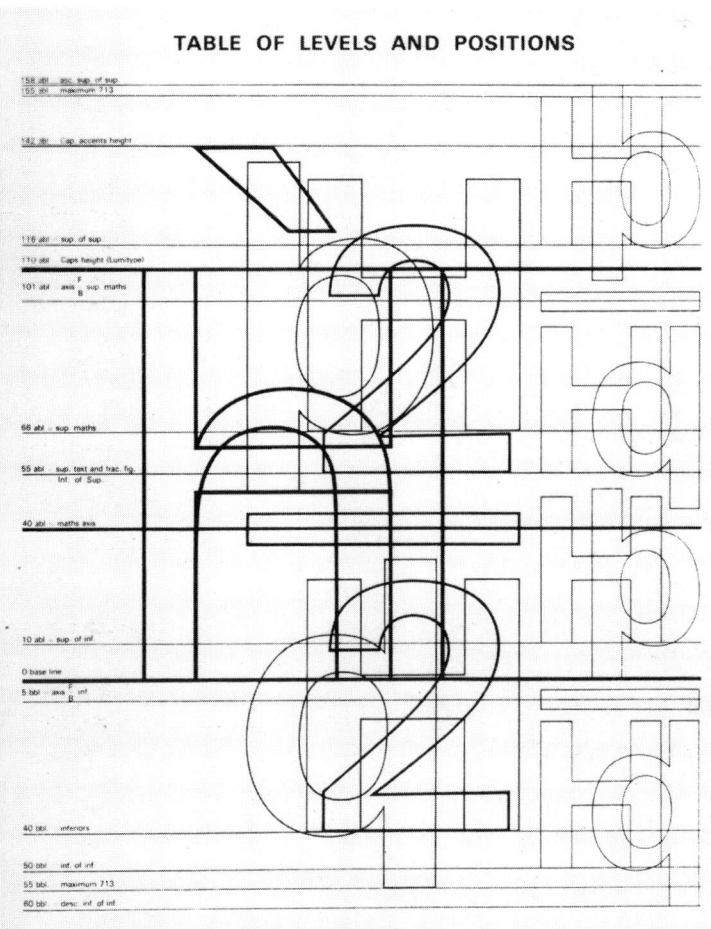

71 Standard alignments for Lumitype typefaces. From the Lumitype-Photon specimen book: half actual size.

Standardizing alignments in this way had the desirable side-effect of greatly reducing the number of special signs that were needed. A single set of hollow and solid squares and circles, for example, would work with all the Lumitype designs. This contrasted sharply with Photon's approach in the United States. They offered to reproduce customers'

---

produced for the Lumitype. The sequence of the second digits in the descriptive number is reversed in this version, with 1 for extracondensed (*serré*) and 9 for extra wide (*double large*).

character repertories exactly, so that output from the new machine would reproduce their existing metal-type composition as closely as possible.[12] The consequence was that the Photon typeface library filled up with many similar, but not identical, versions of the same signs.

The only externally-imposed restrictions that had to be observed in drawing characters for the Lumitype were those dictated by the dimensions of the 'windows' in the composing machine's optical system. These delimited the area of the illuminated matrix that was imaged on the output material. They were narrower for the rows of character images towards the centre of the matrix disc, because the images themselves were closer together. This meant that some wide designs, or those that kerned extensively to the left of their widths, could only be placed on the outer rows of a disc. Figure 72 shows the relationship of the window outlines for the eight rows on the disc to the standard position of character images in the machine's optical path.

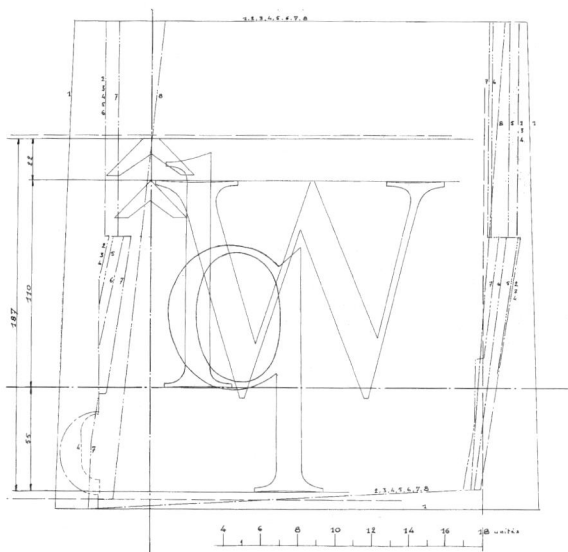

72 *Window outlines and character dimensions: a drawing made by the Compagnie Générale des Constructions Téléphoniques, who built the Lumitype machines in France. From the Lumitype collection in the Musée de l'Imprimerie de Lyon; one-quarter actual size.*

Frutiger was joined at Lumitype SA in 1954 by Ladislas Mandel, who after studying fine art at Rouen and Paris before 1939 had been working as a painter and stonecutter since the Liberation. While Frutiger, working on his own, had made his character drawings 'with extraordinary

---

[12] 'Photon will provide any other special character, within machine mechanical limitations, at a modest fixed charge per character regardless of the art work that needs to be done': from a specimen book published by Photon Inc in the late 1960s.

Drawing for the Lumitype 99

skill... with a brush, like a painter',[13] Mandel understood that the volume of work the Lumitype studio would necessarily have to produce demanded a different and more industrialized approach. He developed a technique of drawing on white scraper-board in indian ink, finishing the contours of the character shapes with french curves and a sharp blade to achieve a smooth high-contrast edge. The drawings were scaled to an em square of 18 cm, with reference lines ruled at the baseline and at the left and right limits of the character's width.[14]

These drawings, like those for other direct-photography composing systems but unlike those for pantographic punchcutting, were real pictures of letters: solid shapes on a contrasting ground. The first stage in testing a new alphabet was to put the drawings up on a vertical surface and look at them from a distance (Figure 73).

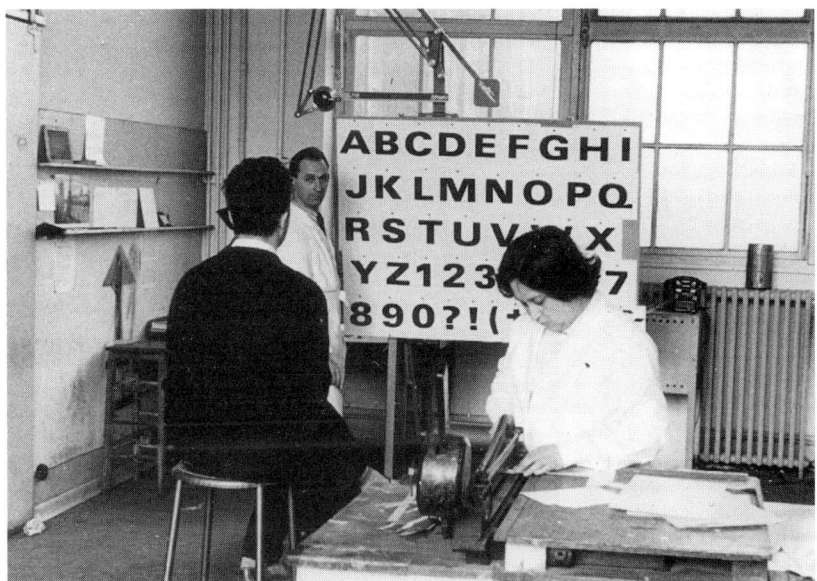

73 Checking designs for Univers 75: a photograph from Ladislas Mandel's collection taken at 18 rue Ferrus, probably in 1956. Frutiger is sitting with his back to the camera; Mandel is standing by the drawing board. In the foreground, Lucette Girard is trimming phototypes with a card-cutter.

Primitive as this method might seem, it is effective in showing up the differences in character weight or the shapes of curves. These are hard to avoid in a workgroup whose members were permitted a good deal of

---

[13] 'Frutiger dessinait avec une virtuosité extraordinaire, avant l'organisation en studio, il peignait des lettres au pinceau comme un artiste peintre': *Étapes graphiques* no. 55 (October 1999), p. 48.

[14] In *Une vie consacrée à l'écriture typographique* (2004) Frutiger gives a short description of his work at 18 rue Ferrus: though, curiously, without mentioning any of his collaborators in the Lumitype studio.

individual freedom, as those in the Lumitype studio were: much more so than the staff of type-drawing offices in the earlier technology.

The next stage in developing a design was to photograph the drawings on to 35-mm film in a fixed camera at ten times reduction. Contact prints from the film were pasted up to make short passages of text (Figure 74).

> portez ce vieux whisky
> au juge blond qui fume
> septembre 1963
>
> PORTEZ CE VIEUX WHISKY
> AU JUGE BLOND QUI FUME.
>
> ÆŒ&   780£   245$
> æœßflfiff«ffl»(ffi)-§,;:?!*

74 Trial pasteup of Clarendon 653-55, made with photographic prints reduced ten times from the character drawings. From the Lumitype collection in the Musée de l'Imprimerie de Lyon; 40% actual size.

75 Scaled trial pasteups of Modern 57, developed in the Lumitype studio in 1969–70 for dictionary composition under Ladislas Mandel's supervision. Half actual size.

Drawing for the Lumitype　　101

The pasteups were then rephotographed at the same reduction to produce images at a nominal size of 5.12 pt. These could be enlarged to show the appearance of the design at a range of sizes (Figure 75).

With its photographic parameters carefully standardized, this process could carry the development of a new design a long way before it became necessary to make a test matrix. However, it was incapable by its nature of producing long passages of text. Checking the fitting of a typeface involves setting every character next to every other, as well as between standard characters such as n or H. Tests like this, carried out in several sizes, generate so much output that they need a machine to produce it. The same tests, with their repeating patterns of character images, also allow the effects of the machine's optical system on character weights to be taken into account.

```
aaabacadaeafagahaiajakalamanaoapaqarasatauavawaxayaza
babbbcbdbebfbgbhbibjbkblbmbnbobpbqbrbsbtbubvbwbxbybzb
cacbcccdcecfcgchcicjckclcmcncocpcqcrcsctcucvcwcxcyczc
dadbdcdddedfdgdhdidjdkdldmdndodpdqdrdsdtdudvdwdxdydzd
eaebecedeeefegeheiejekelemeneoepeqereseteuevewexeyeze
fafbfcfdfefffgfhfifjfkflfmfnfofpfqfrfsftfufvfwfxfyfzf
gagbgcgdgegfgggghgigjgkglgmgngogpgqgrgsgtgugvgwgxgygzg
hahbhchdhehfhghhhihjhkhlhmhnhohphqhrhshthuhvhwhxhyhzh
iaibicidieifigihiiijikiliminioipiqirisitiuiviwixiyizi
jajbjcjdjejfjgjhjijjjkjljmjnjojpjqjrjsjtjujvjwjxjyjzj
kakbkckdkekfkgkhkikjkkklkmknkokpkqkrksktkukvkwkxkykzk
lalblcldlelflglhliljlklllmlnlolplqlrlsltlulvlwlxlylzl
mambmcmdmemfmgmhmimjmkmlmmmnmompmqmrmsmtmumvmwmxmymzm
nanbncndnenfngnhninjnknlnmnnnonpnqnrnsntnunvnwnxnynzn
oaobocodoeofogohoiojokolomonooopoqorosotouovowoxoyozo
papbpcpdpepfpgphpipjpkplpmpnpopppqprpsptpupvpwpxpypzp
qaqbqcqdqeqfqgqhqiqjqkqlqmqnqoqpqqqrqsqtquqvqwqxqyqzq
rarbrcrdrerfrgrhrirjrkrlrmrnrorprqrrrsrtrurvrwrxryrzr
sasbscsdsesfsgshsisjsksismsnsospsqsrssstsusvswsxsyszs
tatbtctdtetftgthtitjtktltmtntotptqtrtsttlutvtwtxtytzt
uaubucuduefuguhuiujukulumunuoupuqurusutuuuvuwuxuyuzu
vavbvcvdvevfvgvhvivjvkvlvmvnvovpvqvrvsvtvuvvvwvxvyvzv
wawbwcwdwewfwgwhwiwjwkwlwmwnwowpwqwrwswtwuwvwwwxwywzw
xaxbxcxdxexfxgxhxixjxkxlxmxnxoxpxqxrxsxtxuxvxwxxxyxzx
yaybycydyeyfygyhyiyjykylymynyoypyqyrysytyuyvywyxyyyzy
zazbzczdzezfzgzhzizjzkzlzmznzozpzqzrzsztzuzvzwzxzyzzz
```

76 *Part of a test of Autologic Inc's version of Times Roman, revised for the American Mathematical Society in 1987. Two-thirds actual size. The reduced size of the illustration has accentuated the weight defects already present in* g *and* k.

Machine-produced tests of new designs have not survived in the Lumitype archives. Figure 76 shows part of a similar test produced much later for a different project, on an Autologic APS-5 photocomposing machine at the American Mathematical Society in 1987.

10 The design of Univers

Frutiger's first designs for the Lumitype were adaptations of classical text faces: Garamont 301, Baskerville 401 and Bodoni 501. There was also a version of Times that had been made at Photon Inc by copying from metal type.[1] A sanserif would be needed for the machine as well, and from Deberny & Peignot's point of view an obvious candidate was already in place. Charles Peignot had negotiated a licence for Paul Renner's Futura with the Bauer typefoundry in 1928, and marketed it in France under the name of Europe. Frutiger, however, succeeded in persuading him that in the mid-1950s the days of constructivist typefaces were over.

In contrast with some traditional perspectives, Frutiger's view of the emerging 'Swiss style' of the early post-war period had been that it stemmed from a reaction against constructivism in typographic design, rather than being a development of it. During his apprenticeship

> ...a climate of opposition to the very aggressive and mechanistic style created by the Bauhaus began to make itself felt [in Switzerland]. Under the influence of teachers such as Emil Ruder, Armin Hoffmann and others we searched the cellars of our printing works for the old 'grotesques' from the beginning of the century. We found Haas's, and above all Berthold's... [These designs] had nothing of the constructed in their shapes. They were based on classical forms, modulated, with thick and thin strokes.[2]

At the Kunstgewerbeschule in Zürich Frutiger had been greatly influenced by Alfred Willimann and Walter Käch. From Willimann he learned that 'writing was also architecture in which the quality of space was as important as that of substance'.[3] From Käch, who taught signwriting, he learned to draw with 'an extreme purity of line' and also that type characters were based on grid structures.[4] As well as the wood-

---

[1] This version, Times 451, had a capital-letter height larger than the standard 11 cm. The typeface was later redrawn to Lumitype standards under Ladislas Mandel's supervision as Times 452D, with bold roman and italic variants added to the semibold of Times 451.

[2] '... une atmosphère de résistance au style très agressif et mécanisé créé par le Bauhaus commença à se faire sentir. Sous l'influence des maîtres comme Emil Ruder, Armin Hoffmann et autres, nous avons cherché, au fond des caves de notre imprimerie, les vieux 'Grotesk' du début du siècle. Nous avons trouvé le 'Grotesk' de Haas, et surtout celui de Berthold. Ces fonderies, déja à la fin du dix-neuvième siècle, avaient créé des écritures sans empattements, mais celles-ci n'avaient rien de construit dans leur forme. C'était des caractères appuyés sur les classiques modelés avec pleins et déliés': *La Lumitype-Photon* (1955), p. 141.

[3] 'J'ai appris chez lui que l'écriture était aussi architecture dans laquelle la qualité de l'espace comptait autant que la matière' (*ibid.*).

[4] '... j'ai appris le tracé travaillé jusqu'à l'extrême pureté de la ligne. Avec lui j'ai également compris qu'un alphabet se concevait sur une grille' (*ibid.*).

The design of Univers

cut history of the Western alphabet that won him an award from the Swiss ministry of the interior, his work at Zürich had included designs for a set of sanserif characters. Armed with this experience, Frutiger began to make studies for a new family of sanserifs for the Lumitype.

It was not a modest undertaking. 'I extended the normal set of roman, italic, semibold and bold to make a large family going from wide to very narrow and from light to bold.'[5]

77 *Relationships between the upright variants of the Univers family: from* Type sign symbol *(1980). The medium weight is at the upper right.*

Figure 77 shows the relationships between the different weights and widths of the new family. In the upright variants the increments in width between condensed, normal and wide are the same for the light, medium and semibold weights. The bold weight has no condensed variant; the increment between normal and wide is the same as for the other weights.

---

[5] 'J'ai entendu l'habituel minimum des séries romain, italique, demi-gras et gras à un vaste ensemble de toute une famille allant d'une version large à une version très étroite et d'une version maigre à une version grasse': *La Lumitype-Photon*, p. 141.

The oblique variants were based on the shapes of their upright analogues, sheared around an axis halfway up the x-height (Figure 78).

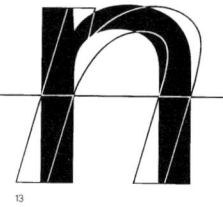

78 Deriving the oblique shape from the roman. From Type sign symbol.

This ensured that spacing between upright and oblique within a line of text was correct. It also meant that the two variants shared the same set of character widths. In linecaster terms, they were duplexed; but, because of the lack of mechanical constraints in the Lumitype imaging system, without any of the restrictions on character shape that the term suggested in the earlier technology.

Although Frutiger's approach to the design was systematic, it was not over-constrained. Capitals with horizontal strokes at the cap line (E F Z) are not quite as tall as those with vertical strokes (H I J), so that they look the same height. Converging strokes, in E F K M N W X Y Z for example, are slightly tapered so that they do not appear to thicken as they approach the junction. The actual strokeweights of 'busy' characters such as B are lighter than those of 'quiet' ones such as H, so that their apparent weights are the same.

Figure 79, which reproduces a page from the table of calibres used in the Lumitype studio, shows the extent to which the actual dimensions of characters in the Univers family departed from their nominal values in the cause of visual consistency. The annotations in the two right-hand columns show characters that are taller than I or lower than j: f in Univers 63, 66 and 76, and g in many variants.[6]

It appears from Frutiger's account of his early experiments with the Lumitype that the optical quality of the equipment he was working with left something to be desired. The deformations of character shape which he attributes to the effect of a short, bright flash (Figure 80) seem to me more likely to have resulted from a combination of light-scattering at the many glass-air interfaces in the composing machine's optical system and irradiation in the photographic emulsions, both of the output material and the matrix itself. In his original drawings for the Lumitype Frutiger opened out interior angles and exaggerated external corners to overcome these effects. The consequence is that the internal strokes of diagonal characters have no straight edges (Figure 81).[7]

---

[6] The height of H is standardized at 110 mm, following normal Lumitype practice.

[7] Optical design moved forward rapidly in the 1960s. When the Lumitype matrix-making camera was rebuilt at Photon Inc in 1968–69 (*Du plomb à la lumière,*

The design of Univers

CARACTÈRES	O	Î	o	Ilj	Îj
751-45 UNIVERS rom.maigre	113 mm	142	80 mm	141	g 24	113
46 UNIVERS ital.maigre	112,5	142	80	141,5	g 21,5	113,5
47 UNIVERS étroit maig.	112	142	75	140	g 24	111
48 UNIVERS ét.ital.maig.	111	142	77,5	139,5	↓ 21,5	110,5
49 UNIVERS serré maigre	112	142	75,5	139,5	↓ 21,5	110,5
53 UNIVERS large	117,5	142	81	141,5	g 20,5	112,5
55 UNIVERS romain	116	142	80	143	g 22	114
56 UNIVERS italique	115	142	80,5	142	g 21	113
57 UNIVERS étroit	114	142	75,5	139	g 24	111
58 UNIVERS étroit ital.	113	142	79,5	139	↓ 24	111
59 UNIVERS serré	114,5	142	75	139,5	↓ 21,5	111,5
63 UNIVERS large 1/2 gr.	117	142	82	140,5	g 24,5	111,5
64 UNIVERS rom.1/2 gras	115,5	142	81	141,5	g 24,5	113,5
66 UNIVERS ital.1/2 gr.	114	142	81,5	ſ 111 142	g 24	113
67 UNIVERS étr. 1/2 gras	113	142	79	140,5	g 24,5	111,5
68 UNIVERS étr.ital.1/2	. 114	142	78,5	139,5	↓ 24,5	111,5
73 UNIVERS large gras	117,5	142	82,5	139	↓ 24	111
75 UNIVERS romain gras	116	142	82,5	141,5	g 24,5	113,5
7. UNIVERS ital. gras	115,5	142	82,5	ſ 114,5 143	g 21,5	111,5
83 UNIVERS large double gr	117	142	83	142	g 22	114

79 Calibres for members of the Univers family. A working document from the Lumitype studio; half actual size. The handwriting is that of Ladislas Mandel.

Frutiger later questioned the appropriateness of this approach, in a letter quoted by Dreyfus:

> ... it has to be said that right at the beginning of photocomposition we had to do an enormous amount of trickery with all the characters with closed angles like v, w, M, W etc ... Later, the reproduction quality of [Photon's] machines improved, but the original drawings were not changed; for that reason v y etc ... became very light.[8]

---

p. 368) its lens was replaced with one of higher quality. I vividly recall Higonnet's remark at the time about the original camera, 'Nous l'avons bricolé dans un weekend': 'We built it ourselves [almost 'threw it together'] over a weekend.'

[8] '... il faut dire qu'au tout début de la photocomposition, nous avons dû faire d'énormes tricheries pour tous les caractères avec des angles fermés comme v, w, M, W etc ... Depuis, leurs machines [*i.e.* Photon's] ont progressé en qualité de reproduction, mais les dessins d'origine n'ont pas été changés ; pour cette raison

quents, n'ayant que les montagnes pour asiles contre les inondations, chassés souvent de ces mêmes asiles par le feu des volcans, tremblants

80 Early output from the Lumitype: from La Lumitype-Photon.

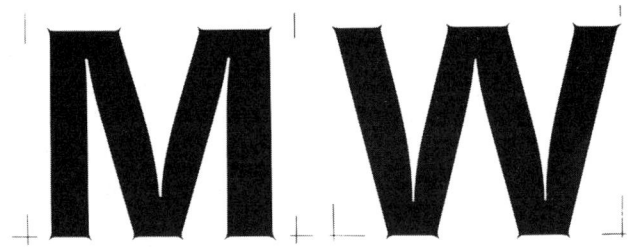

81 Univers 751-65 capital M and W. Reproduced from prints made at Crosfield Electronics Ltd in London for the Magnaset 226 composing-machine project, from microfilm originating at Lumitype SA. One-quarter actual size.

The issue that Frutiger's comment raises – the extent to which it is advisable to modify the details of a design to take into account the characteristics of a particular composing system – is one that was to become important with the development of digital and numerical systems later on (see Chapter 14).

Frutiger's subtle and delicate design was perfectly adapted to the Lumitype system, with its flexibility of character width allocation and the simplicity and directness of its matrix-making process. But sales of the machine for which it was intended did not come quickly enough to support the cost of its development.[9] The decision was taken in 1956 to produce the Univers family as foundry type.[10]

Designers of the 1950s, both in Europe and the United States, had learned about the new typography and were looking around for families

v y etc . . . sont devenus très maigres': *La Lumitype-Photon*, p. 164. Unfortunately Dreyfus does not give a date for this letter.

[9] The first French-built Lumitype was presented at the TPG exhibition of June 1956 (*Du plomb à la lumière*, p. 208).

[10] 'Designer's profile: Adrian Frutiger', *Print in Britain* vol. 9 no. 9 (January 1962), pp. 258–261.

of related sanserifs to use in machine composition. Among the requests that John Dreyfus had to consider when he became the Monotype Corporation's second typographic adviser in 1955 was the adaptation and extension of two existing Monotype series, Grotesque No. 1–215 and Grotesque Bold 216.[11]

These had been derived from designs produced by the Berthold foundry at the end of the previous century, and were much in demand as alternatives, with a less markedly English flavour, to Gill Sans.[12] Their age was beginning to tell against them, though; Grotesque 215 had been released in 1926, the year before Futura and Kabel. Also, with only a medium and a bold weight, they did not constitute a family in the way that the related variants of the German sanserifs – or, indeed, those of Gill Sans – did. Frutiger's new design met all of Dreyfus's requirements for an up-to-date sanserif.

Dreyfus and Charles Peignot had first met in 1948. In 1957 the two were involved with the launch of the Association Typographique Internationale (ATypI), which Peignot had been instrumental in setting up to unite the established type manufacturers against the threat of unauthorised copying of their designs. In the autumn of the same year Peignot and Jack Matson, General Manager of the Monotype Corporation's works at Salfords, met in London to discuss a possible grant by Deberny & Peignot to the Corporation of a licence to manufacture the Univers family for Monotype composing machines. A report by Frutiger, written after the meeting and dated 27 November 1957, begins by noting that it had been agreed within the foundry to offer the Corporation reproduction rights for text sizes of the Univers family, up to and including 14 pt.[13]

The reason for the restriction placed on the size range at this stage of the negotiations is clear from Peignot's reminiscences, published on the occasion of Deberny & Peignot's closure in 1975.

> At that moment [i.e. the announcement of Univers] I played a very dangerous game, that often kept me awake at night. I entered into negotiations with the Monotype, who needed a sanserif, telling myself that if they did not take Univers they would take another one. But it was very risky, because trade typesetters cast fonts on Monotype machines and sold them

---

[11] John Dreyfus, 'Histoire d'une collaboration: Deberny Peignot, Monotype et la commercialisation du caractère Univers', *La Lumitype-Photon*, pp. 155–165.

[12] Although the Corporation had cut several similarly-named series of comparable ancestry (Grotesque Bold Condensed 15; Grotesque Condensed No. 2–33; Grotesque 51; Grotesque Bold Extended 150; Grotesque Light Condensed 274; Grotesque Condensed No. 3–318; Grotesque Condensed 383), only 'Grot 215 and 216' could be set together from the same matrix-case.

[13] 'Il a été convenu de donner à la Monotype le droit de reproduction pour l'ensemble de l'Univers petits corps jusqu'au 14 inclus.' The report, with other correspondence related to the Univers negotiations, is in the Musée de l'Imprimerie de Lyon. In the correspondence the word 'Univers' is often set in all capitals; I have transcribed it here uniformly in capitals and minuscules.

> to letterpress printers. On the face of it, it was absurd to sell Monotype a design which they could use to compete with me... [14]

The Monotype machine in question was the Super Caster, introduced in 1928 and intended among other things to cast single types in display sizes from matrices that were very often rented from the Corporation. However, in his report Frutiger was reassuring. Although 102 Super Casters were working in France at the time, all but two or three were used by newspaper printers for their own in-house needs. Also, a check of Deberny & Peignot's own sales of display sizes of the Europe family showed that the majority of orders were from small and medium-sized printers, who would not be expected to have their own casting facilities. Frutiger concluded that the Super Caster presented no significant competition to the foundry.

Frutiger's report also shows that Peignot's first proposal to the Monotype Corporation had excluded the right to manufacture Univers for the Monophoto Filmsetter.

> In the context of granting the copyright of Univers, it has been made clear to the Monotype that we could not give them reproduction rights for the Monophoto.[15]

The Monophoto and the Lumitype were coming to the market together; both machines had their first customer installations in 1957. However, Frutiger considered that a printer contemplating the change from metal type to photocomposition would not base the choice of a new system simply on the range of typefaces it made available. On this view the Lumitype and the Monophoto, offering as they did very different facilities to their users, should not be seen as being in competition with one another. On the other hand, some potential customers for the Lumitype (Frutiger mentions *Paris-Match* and the Reader's Digest publication *Sélection*) were insisting on Monotype typefaces for their new machines. Frutiger's opinion was that it would be wiser in the long term to accede to the Corporation's wishes in respect of the Monophoto, hoping for a *quid pro quo* in the form of licences to reproduce Monotype designs on the Lumitype. 'I think it is in our interest to maintain the friendliest relationships, in the spirit of the ATypI, with our larger colleague.'[16]

---

[14] 'A ce moment-là, j'ai joué un jeu très dangereux, qui m'a souvent empêché de dormir : j'ai traité avec la Monotype, qui avait besoin d'une antique, en me disant que si elle ne prenait pas l'Univers, elle en prendrait une autre. Mais c'était très dangereux, car les façonniers fondaient sur machines Monotype des polices de caractères qu'ils vendaient aux imprimeurs typo. A priori, c'était donc absurde de vendre à la Monotype un caractère avec lequel elle me ferait concurrence...' *Caractère*, December 1975, pp. 49–50.

[15] 'Dans le cadre de la cession des droits d'auteur de l'Univers, il a été précisé à la Monotype que nous ne pouvions pas leur donner le droit de reproduction pour la monophoto [sic]'.

[16] 'Je pense que nous avons intérêt de garder des relations tout à fait amicales et

The design of Univers

Peignot took Frutiger's comments on board. On 29 November he wrote to Matson, agreeing to grant reproduction rights to all the variants and sizes of the Univers family for the Monophoto as well as the Monotype. Matson replied on 24 December. At this stage of the negotiations Peignot still wished to restrict the agreement to the Corporation's British [he writes *Anglais* – English] and European markets, citing but not restating reasons that he and Matson had discussed at their earlier meeting. He wrote again on 28 February 1958, thanking Matson for the Corporation's willingness to make a contribution to the launch costs of the ATypI and lifting all the constraints he had earlier placed on its commercialization of the Univers family.[17]

Dreyfus delicately queried the realism of this position on 21 May, shedding light at the same time on the reasons for Peignot's earlier reservations:

> We should very much have liked to have your agreement for the worldwide sale of Univers by The Monotype Corporation Limited: but does not this proposal give you some difficulties in view of your relationships with Garth and the Graphic Arts Foundation?[18]

The Graphic Arts Research Foundation, already referred to in Chapter 8, was the not-for-profit organization that had financed the development of Higonnet and Moyroud's invention in the United States. At the time of Dreyfus's letter its intellectual property was being exploited by Photon Inc, of which W W Garth Jr was chairman. In 1956 Peignot had concluded an agreement with Photon by which Deberny & Peignot would design typefaces for Photon's customers, and Photon would discontinue their practice of copying existing manufacturers' designs.[19] Peignot replied to Dreyfus on 6 June:

> I cannot decide anything about America, since I have not yet had the replies I have once again asked for.[20]

In the margin of Peignot's copy of this letter is an emphatically written note in pencil: 'USA Canada/oui'.

Meanwhile Frutiger was working to resolve the technical problems posed by the collaboration. Dreyfus's letter to Peignot of 21 May 1958 had proposed that in consideration of the sum paid for the rights to the

---

dans l'esprit de l'A.Typ.I. avec ce grand confrère.'

[17] 'Nous levons toutes objections et réserves sur l'utilization que vous pourriez faire de notre série, vous laissant libre de l'exploiter comme vous le désirez.'

[18] 'Nous aurions bien voulu avoir votre accord pour la vente de l'Univers dans le monde entier par The Monotype Corporation Limited: mais est-ce que cette proposition ne vous pose pas des difficultés en raison de vos relations avec Garth et the Graphic Arts Foundation?'

[19] *Du plomb à la lumière*, p. 259. As far as Photon's obligations under it were concerned, this agreement had become a dead letter by the end of the 1960s.

[20] 'Je ne puis rien décider pour l'Amerique tant que je n'ai pas obtenu les réponses que j'ai à nouveau sollicitées.'

design, the Monotype Corporation should be able 'to request without payment any material that might facilitate the manufacture of the Univers design as Monotype or Monophoto matrices'.[21] On 4 June Frutiger wrote to Dreyfus:

> Given that we anticipate cutting the regular versions of Univers (roman and italic in light, medium, semibold and bold) in 1959 and 1960, it could happen that the Monotype were making the same variants at the same time. There would then certainly be some difficulties to overcome in sharing original material between Salfords and Paris... To the extent that our two establishments succeeded in harmonizing their production planning, it ought to be possible for us to lend you original drawings for versions that we have already finished or not yet started if it turns out that you need them.[22]

He enclosed one of Deberny & Peignot's punchcutting patterns as an example, though without great confidence that it would be useful as it was: '... I very much doubt that our dimensions correspond exactly to any of yours'.[23]

Frutiger points out the differences between the Lumitype's width allocation system and that used by the Monotype.

> As far as character widths are concerned, you know that we have on the Lumitype machine a similar system to the Monotype's, but with more values: in addition to Monotype units from 5 to 18, we have half-units as well as units 4 and 17...[24]

He is cautiously optimistic about the possibility of adjusting his designs to work with Monotype's system:

> Reducing the number of widths to suit the Monotype system will certainly mean some work with your technical people at the right moment. I do not think however that many drawings will have to be remade; most of the corrections can be made by changing sidebearings.[25]

---

[21] '... The Monotype Corporation Limited aura le droit de demander sans paiement tout materiel qui pourra aider à la fabrication du dessin Univers en forme de matrices Monotype ou photomatrices Monophoto...'

[22] 'Étant donné que nous envisageons pour l'Univers la gravure des alphabets normaux (romain et italique en maigre, normal, demi-gras et gras) en 1959 et 1960, il se pourrait que la Monotype exécute les mêmes séries pendant la même période. Il y aura donc certainement quelques difficultés à surmonter en ce qui concerne le partage des documents originaux entre Salfords et Paris... Dans la mesure où nos deux ateliers arriveraient à concorder leur planning de fabrication, il devrait nous être possible de vous prêter les dessins originaux de séries déjà terminées ou pas encore commencées chez nous pour le cas où vous en auriez besoin.'

[23] '... je doute forte que notre dimension corresponde exactement à l'une des vôtres.'

[24] 'En ce qui concerne la largeur des caractères, vous savez que nous avons sur la machine Lumitype un système de mesures semblable à celui de la Monotype, mais le nombre d'unités a été étendu: en plus des unités Monotype de 5 à 18, nous avons les demi-unités ainsi que les unités 4 et 17...'

[25] La réduction du nombre des largeurs pour l'adaptation au système Monotype

The design of Univers

In his letter of 21 May 1958 Dreyfus had proposed that Frutiger should check without charge any proofs of the design originating at Salfords, and should also supply modified drawings 'if, because of Monotype units, it was not possible to produce characters identical to those produced by [Deberny & Peignot]'.[26] Peignot wrote in the margin of Dreyfus's letter opposite the second of these proposals '??/principe non': 'No in principle'. On 5 June Frutiger suggested to Peignot that Deberny & Peignot should supply five modified drawings per variant free of charge, and invoice any more at 500 [old] francs apiece. He estimated the cost of each modification at 400 francs, since they would be made by retouching photographic copies of drawings rather than working on the originals. He added that even ten free-of-charge modifications per variant would not be too serious a cost to incur.

Peignot passed this proposal on to Dreyfus in his letter of 6 June:

> ... if the number of letters to be redrawn is too great, and I have at the moment not the slightest idea of what it might be, we should expect that it might take up too much of Frutiger's time and keep him from other work. That being so, we can very well imagine that if the number of modifications did not exceed 5 or 10 characters for each variant there would be no question of asking you for compensation.[27]

Frutiger wrote to Dreyfus again on 25 June, following on a meeting between the two in the previous week. By this time their discussions had moved on to the possibility of the Corporation's making use of the punchcutting patterns that Deberny & Peignot were producing as the first stage of their own manufacture of the Univers family as foundry type. There seems to have been an earlier suggestion that extra sets of patterns might be made for the Corporation. However, since the patterns for three variants – 45, 55 and 56 – had already been cut by 25 June and those for the 46 light oblique were about to be put in hand, this would no longer be a simple matter. The correspondence gives a strong sense of the foundry's 'hands-on', craftsmanlike procedures, implicitly contrasted with the Corporation's strictly regimented industrial processes.

The first stage of pattern-making at Deberny & Peignot was to cut a master from thin cardboard at the same size as the character drawing,

---

demandera certainement une étude en temps opportun avec vos techniciens. Je ne pense d'ailleurs pas qu'il y ait un grand nombre de dessins à refaire; la plupart des modifications pourront se faire en changeant les approches.'

[26] '[Frutiger] fournira des dessins modifiés si, à cause des unités Monotype, il n'était pas possible de graver des caractères parfaitement identiques a ceux sortis par votre maison.'

[27] '... si le nombre de lettres à redessiner est trop grand et je n'ai actuellement pas la moindre idée de ce qu'il pourrait être, il faudrait envisager que cela pourrait absorber une trop grande partie du temps de Frutiger qui serait ainsi soustrait à un autre travail et il faudrait en tenir compte. Ceci étant, nous pouvons très bien imaginer que si le nombre de modifications n'excède pas 5 or 10 signes par série, il ne saurait être question de vous demander une indemnité.'

as a guide for the tracing stylus on the pattern-cutting pantograph.[28]

> ... this procedure [*i.e.* making an extra set of patterns] has another disadvantage: the cardboard from which we make the masters for pattern-cutting is very delicate, and I am concerned that cutting a third pattern would result in appreciable damage.
>
> We have tried copying a pattern in relief by running type-metal into it: this does not give good enough quality, above all because of the way the metal shrinks.
>
> There remains the solution that you are looking into [which was in fact a version of Monotype's standard procedure]: copying our patterns by wax moulding and electroplating.[29]

But even if an effective method of pattern-copying could be worked out it was not clear whether the results would be useful, given the differences between Deberny & Peignot's procedures and the Corporation's:

> – Can you use the same size of pattern for every body size ... ?
> – On our patterns the letters are centred on the backing plate. Does not the Monotype have to have the letter positioned relative to the edges of the pattern according to its sidebearings? or is the pattern positioned in the punchcutting machine by the little notch I can see on the example you sent me?
> – Our manufacturing tolerance is around 7/100ths [*i.e.* 0.07 mm; 0.0028 in]. We wonder if this is enough, given that you are unable to make corrections by hand.
> – Another question that I need to discuss with you and your technical people concerns kerning sorts in the italic alphabets.[30]

---

[28] *cf.* Walter Wilkes's description of pattern-cutting from cardboard in Chapter 3 above.

[29] '... ce procedé présente un autre inconvénient: le carton dans lequel nous découpons notre patron pour la gravure du gabarit est très fragile et il est à craindre que le découpage d'un troisième gabarit aurait pour conséquence des déformations sensibles.

Nous avons essayé d'obtenir une contre-matrice de notre gabarit en relief par coulage de plomb : la qualité obtenue par ce moyen est insuffisante surtout vu le retrait du métal.

Il reste donc la solution que vous rechercez : copie de notre gabarit par moulage cire et bain galvanoplastique.'

[30] '– Est-ce que pour la gravure de tous les corps vous pouvez utiliser la même grandeur de gabarit ... ?

– Sur nos gabarits, les lettres sont centrées par rapport à la plaque de support. Est-ce que pour la Monotype il ne faudrait pas avoir une position de la lettre par rapport aux bords du gabarit compte tenu des approches? – ou, est-ce que la position du gabarit dans la machine à graver est faite chez vous par le petit cran que je vois sur l'échantillon que vous m'avez remis?

– Notre tolérance pour la fabrication est de l'ordre de 7/100ème. Nous nous demandons si cette tolérance est suffisante étant donné que vous n'avez pas la possibilité de la retouche main.

– Une autre question pour laquelle il faudra que je m'entretienne avec vous et vos techniciens est celle des sortes crênantes pour les alphabets italiques.'

The design of Univers

ABCDEFGHIJKLMNOPQRSTUVWXYZ
ABCDEFGHIJKLMNOPQRSTUVWXYZ
ABCDEFGHIJKLMNOPQRSTUVWXYZ
abcdefghijklmnopqrstuvwxyz
abcdefghijklmnopqrstuvwxyz
abcdefghijklmnopqrstuvwxyz

ABCDEFGHIJKLMNOPQRSTUVWXYZ
ABCDEFGHIJKLMNOPQRSTUVWXYZ
ABCDEFGHIJKLMNOPQRSTUVWXYZ
abcdefghijklmnopqrstuvwxyz
abcdefghijklmnopqrstuvwxyz
abcdefghijklmnopqrstuvwxyz

82 *The medium-weight normal-width variants of Univers, in their Lumitype, foundry-type and Monotype versions. In each group the Lumitype version is in the first of the three rows, Deberny & Peignot foundry type in the second and the Monotype version in the third.*

Figure 82 compares the appearance of the Lumitype, foundry-type and Monotype versions of the medium-weight normal-width variants, the 'parents' of the Univers family.[31] The central problem in producing the new version of Univers, the difference in width allocation systems between the Lumitype and Monotype machines, had already been touched on by Frutiger in his letter of 4 June 1958. The machine for which the Univers family had been conceived and developed had a system with 36 units to the em, a minimum character width of 4 units, a maximum width 7/6 of the em square and no limit to the number of characters sharing a single width. The Monotype and Monophoto of the

---

[31] In Figures 82–84 the Lumitype capitals are from the 12-pt showings in the Lumitype specimen book of 1961, enlarged by 137.5%. (In the 11-pt showings the capital alphabet is not complete.) The Lumitype minuscules are from the 11-pt showings, enlarged by 150%. The foundry type is from the 10 Didot showings in the Deberny & Peignot specimen book, also enlarged by 150%. Monotype's version is enlarged by the same amount from the 9D on 10 pt synopsis on a Monotype specimen sheet dated September 1962.

Differences in character image rendering in the three versions illustrated come from the different printing processes used to produce the specimen pages. The Lumitype specimen book is printed by offset lithography, with an ink film through which the paper surface sometimes shows. Both the Deberny & Peignot and Monotype specimen pages are printed letterpress on supercalendered stock. The pale vertical lines sometimes visible on the Deberny & Peignot examples are calibration marks, printed in a light grey at 1-cicero intervals along the line.

period had an 18-unit system for width values, with a 5-unit minimum at the time the work was begun. Although the absolute value of the unit used for a particular design could be altered within wide limits by selecting the set value, the number of different character widths was limited, and some widths could be shared by no more than 16 characters in a matrix-case.[32] These restrictions mean that the overall width structures of all the Monotype series are simpler than those of their Lumitype analogues.

It is difficult to make direct size-for-size comparisons between the different versions of the design. Even if there were a common basis between hot-metal and photographic composition for deciding what 'size' meant, Lumitype SA, Deberny & Peignot and the Monotype Corporation all used different values for their basic unit of measurement. The introduction to the Lumitype specimen book states that the machine works with a 'metric point' of 0.25 mm, and that 15 of these points equal 10 Didot points or 3.75 mm. In fact designs made in the Lumitype studio were drawn to an em quad size of 18 cm at a nominal size of 512 pt, so that the value of the Lumitype point was 18/512 cm or 0.3515625 mm.[33] The Monotype 12-pt quad measured 0.1660 in, giving a value for the Monotype point of 0.1660/12 in or 0.3513667 mm. By comparison, the value of 0.3514598 mm cited by Andrew Boag for the Anglo-American point is the same as the 1/72.27 in used by D E Knuth in his TeX text-formatting language (see Chapter 18). The alphabets used as examples in Figures 82–84 have calibres that are within 0.05 mm of one another, in spite of the differences in their nominal size.

The differences in alphabet length and character shape between the Lumitype and Monotype versions of Univers are due to the exigencies of the Monotype's matrix-case arrangement. In the medium-weight normal-width variants the widest characters, W as well as Æ Œ which are not shown here, have one unit subtracted from their Lumitype widths to bring them down to 15 units.[34] This is the maximum the Monotype matrix-case can accommodate with a 4-unit minimum width. Similarly,

---

[32] 'Unit-shift', which eased this restriction to some extent, was not introduced until 1963.

[33] The 0.25 mm cited in the Lumitype specimen book was the unit of setwise escapement on 200/500-series machines fitted with the so-called 'metric rack' in the escapement mechanism. Machines manufactured by Photon used an 'inch rack' with a unit of 1/100 in (0.254 mm). The value of 0.375 mm cited for the Didot point is smaller than the more generally accepted 0.376 mm. Andrew Boag discusses the subject's vicissitudes in 'Typographic measurement: a chronology': *Typography papers* no. 1 (1996), pp. 105–121.

[34] Information on width values for the Monotype Univers family came from Monotype Hot-Metal in London; for Lumitype Univers from width tables produced by Lumitype SA, in the Lumitype collection at the Musée de l'Imprimerie de Lyon.

The design of Univers 115

m æ œ come down from 14 to 13 units. Most of the Lumitype characters with half-unit width values, including S S, have them rounded down to the unit below. K loses a whole unit, from 11 to 10 units.

The differences in width of K V W X between the Lumitype and Monotype versions mean that the slopes of the diagonal strokes are different. The effect is more noticeable in the oblique than in the upright variant. The change in the widths of S S has altered the shapes of the curves. The feet of Monotype's j j are curiously shaped on the right-hand side, as though their freedom to kern to the left were limited.

ABCDEFGHIJKLMNOPQRSTUVWXYZ
ABCDEFGHIJKLMNOPQRSTUVWXYZ
ABCDEFGHIJKLMNOPQRSTUVWXYZ
abcdefghijklmnopqrstuvwxyz
abcdefghijklmnopqrstuvwxyz
abcdefghijklmnopqrstuvwxyz
ABCDEFGHIJKLMNOPQRSTUVWXYZ
ABCDEFGHIJKLMNOPQRSTUVWXYZ
ABCDEFGHIJKLMNOPQRSTUVWXYZ
abcdefghijklmnopqrstuvwxyz
abcdefghijklmnopqrstuvwxyz
abcdefghijklmnopqrstuvwxyz

83 *The light-weight normal-width variants of Univers, in Lumitype, foundry-type and Monotype versions.*

Figure 83 compares the appearances of the light-weight normal-width variants. The Lumitype versions, 751-45 and 46, have different character width allocations from their medium-weight analogues 751-55 and 56. The corresponding Monotype versions, Series 685 and 689, on the other hand, share the same unit arrangement and hence the same set of widths. The difference is reflected in the alphabet lengths. The length in units of capital A±Z is noticeably larger in the Monotype version, at 277 against 269; that of minuscule a±z less so, at 204 and 201.5 units for Monotype and Lumitype respectively.[35]

---

[35] Comparisons of alphabet lengths are complicated by the differences in set value between the Monotype and Lumitype versions, at $11\frac{1}{4}$ and 11 respectively; also by the difference between point values for the two systems. The physical extent of 204 Monotype units at $11\frac{1}{4}$ set is 44.80 mm; that of 201.5 Lumitype units at 11 set 43.29 mm. A fairer comparison would weight alphabet length by character frequency, producing results that differed between English and French.

The Lumitype and metal-type versions of the light-weight variants are also noticeably different in the extent to which diagonal characters kern to the right of their widths. In his design for the Lumitype Frutiger had had no qualms about letting the images of these characters touch or overlap one another, in both capitals and minuscules and in the upright and the oblique variants. Composing machines of the late 1950s, before the advent of programmable controllers and the 'kerning' and 'tracking' tables that came with them, had no automatic facilities for adjusting the spaces between characters. The designer's problem is to reduce the appearing space following the diagonal character, and this is best achieved by letting the character itself kern a little to the right. In photocomposition, with no mechanical restrictions on the construction of the printing surface, there is no technical obstacle to doing this, even if the following character happens to come all the way to the left of its width. As long as they fit inside the window of uniform illumination in the composing machine's optical system, characters can kern as much or as little as they like. In metal-type composition, on the other hand, the type still has a physical body, and kerns are fragile projections beyond it that are liable to break off in use (and also make the type more difficult and expensive to produce). In Monotype composition the mechanism of the caster also imposes restrictions on the amount of kerning that can be achieved.

Figure 84 compares the appearances of the semibold and bold normal-width variants of Univers. Once again, differences in alphabet length between the Lumitype and Monotype versions arise from the demands of the Monotype's width allocation system. In the Monotype versions of Univers the different normal-width variants use different unit arrangements and hence differing assortments of character widths. The light and medium use arrangement 483, with ten width values in all: 4 and 5 units, 7 to 13 units consecutively, and 15 units. Arrangements 486 and 484, used by the semibold and bold respectively, have eleven values: 5 to 13, 15 and 17 units. In both the semibold and bold the 6-unit width is used only by the exclamation marks ! *!*; in the bold, only Z *Z* use 8 units.

In the semibold minuscule alphabet, all the Monotype characters except a e k m s are wider than their Lumitype analogues. Small f is 1.5 units wider: the largest difference of any character in the normal-width alphabets. Small r t w are one unit wider; the others half a unit. In the capital alphabet there are fewer differences: M N are wider in the Monotype version, and E I J narrower. In the bold minuscules none of the widths differ by more than half a unit. Small f i j l r s t are wider in the Monotype version, and e v y narrower. The bold capitals have many more differences than the semibold.

The design of Univers

ABCDEFGHIJKLMNOPQRSTUVWXYZ
ABCDEFGHIJKLMNOPQRSTUVWXYZ
ABCDEFGHIJKLMNOPQRSTUVWXYZ
abcdefghijklmnopqrstuvwxyz
abcdefghijklmnopqrstuvwxyz
abcdefghijklmnopqrstuvwxyz
ABCDEFGHIJKLMNOPQRSTUVWXYZ
ABCDEFGHIJKLMNOPQRSTUVWXYZ
ABCDEFGHIJKLMNOPQRSTUVWXYZ
abcdefghijklmnopqrstuvwxyz
abcdefghijklmnopqrstuvwxyz
abcdefghijklmnopqrstuvwxyz

ABCDEFGHIJKLMNOPQRSTUVWXYZ
ABCDEFGHIJKLMNOPQRSTUVWXYZ
ABCDEFGHIJKLMNOPQRSTUVWXYZ
abcdefghijklmnopqrstuvwxyz
abcdefghijklmnopqrstuvwxyz
abcdefghijklmnopqrstuvwxyz
ABCDEFGHIJKLMNOPQRSTUVWXYZ
ABCDEFGHIJKLMNOPQRSTUVWXYZ
ABCDEFGHIJKLMNOPQRSTUVWXYZ
abcdefghijklmnopqrstuvwxyz
abcdefghijklmnopqrstuvwxyz
abcdefghijklmnopqrstuvwxyz

84 The semibold and bold normal-width variants of Univers, in Lumitype, foundry-type and Monotype versions.

Although they are not significant for most users, the differences in character width allocation between the Lumitype and Monotype versions of the Univers family make it clear that the two are not identical. Even when, as in Figures 82–84, different nominal sizes are chosen to produce closely similar character-image sizes, the two versions have different rhythms, and the difference in kerning capability between the two composing systems produces noticeable differences in the appearance of diagonal characters. Monotype Univers is not, and cannot be, a copy of Lumitype Univers: it is an adaptation, with its own internal consistencies that reflect the constraints of the system for which it was adapted.

In 1961 John Dreyfus wrote an article, 'Univers in action', for the influential *Penrose Annual*. It contained examples of the family in use (including an elegant railway-timetable design by Herbert Spencer) and a passage, curiously unenthusiastic in its tone in view of Dreyfus's close involvement with the project, about its appeal to 'those *graphikers* who now determine the appearance of so much printed matter.'

> The *graphiker* is greatly interested in the 'colour' of his page. By 'colour' he means, of course, a tone of grey created on a printed sheet by the part which is covered with type. This part he seeks to balance or contrast with other elements in his design, such as drawings, photographs, white space, or areas of true colour. He often becomes very much preoccupied with the tonal effect created by a panel of inked type, sometimes to such a degree that legibility of type becomes to him a matter of subsidiary importance.
>
> The initial appeal of many *graphikers'* designs is made to the emotions, through the eye, and it is assumed that the reader will become sufficiently interested to stomach a congestion of serif-less types. The *graphiker's* choice often falls upon a sans-serif because the simplicity of these letters creates a more uniform colour than seriffed letters.[36]

The first Monotype series of Univers appeared in the autumn of 1962.[37] With the foundry-type version also available, the problem of size designation was still producing confusion in the English metal-type composition market two and a half years after the Monotype version was launched there:

> When Univers was adapted for 'Monotype' matrices, the Corporation determined to adhere to Adrian Frutiger's original design as closely as possible and, *since it was primarily intended for the Continent*,[38] it was made for casting on a Didot point body ... The Didot "design" size of a 'Monotype' face must always be specified both in printers' type lists and on typographers' layouts.[39]

'Ten point', for example, might mean Monotype's casting on a 10-pt body of character images whose dimensions corresponded to the 9 Didot size of foundry type, or images with the dimensions of the 10 Didot size, cast by Monotype on an 11-pt body but by Deberny & Peignot on 10 pt Anglo-American.

---

[36] *Penrose Annual* vol. 55 (1961), pp. 16–17.

[37] The Monotype specimen pages for Series 685, 689, 693 and 696 are dated 9/62 [September 1962]. Each has a note saying that the 9D size will be available in late October 1962, and the 12D size 'later in September 1962'.

[38] My emphasis.

[39] *Monotype Newsletter* no. 75 (March 1965).

The design of Univers

Monotype Univers was a huge success, benefiting from the Corporation's reputation as well as its publicity machine. While 39 000 sets of matrices for Times New Roman were sold between 1933 and 1984, 10 000 sets of Univers Medium had been sold by the same year: more than the total for Monotype Garamond, Bembo and Bodoni taken together, from their launch dates up until that time.[40] The sales of Lumitype machines and matrices were much smaller: so that, paradoxically, the received notion of the design's appearance was formed by a version of it that in some respects at least was extensively modified from the designer's original conception.

Frutiger's position *vis-à-vis* Monotype Univers was in many ways analogous to Jan van Krimpen's *vis-à-vis* Monotype Lutetia. In both cases the technical problem was to adapt a design that was already fully developed for a composing system with a particular set of capabilities to another system with a different, more restricted set. In both cases the designer was closely involved with the work at every stage. Why then was Univers so much more of a success, technically as well as commercially, than Lutetia was?

For one thing, the design of Univers matched the moment of its appearance as that of Lutetia did not. By the late 1950s the modern movement had given rise to an approach to typographic design and a theory of typography that demanded families of related sanserif typefaces. Folio and Futura were only available as foundry type; Helvetica as foundry type or on the Linotype. Fashion had turned away from the classical proportions of Gill Sans. Dwiggins's Metro family, with its single-storied a and pointed capitals, was too idiosyncratic for the time as well as being on the wrong machine for European typographers. As Frutiger wrote in his report of 27 November 1957, 'We know that the Monotype *must* bring out a new sanserif'.[41]

Lutetia's situation was not like this. In a sense, the typeface was a victim of Morison's success. Thanks to his work with the Monotype Corporation, there were enough first-class classical romans already available for machine composition in 1930 to make the extra expense of installing Lutetia and the difficulties involved in using it a formidable obstacle to sales, however good the reviews had been. Also, it was only useful for book printing, which by its nature is a limited market; and then only for certain types of book. It is a measure of Morison's influence in the Corporation of the late 1920s that he could have persuaded it to continue with the project once it had become clear how uneconomical it was going to be.

Frutiger's involvement, too, was different in kind to Van Krimpen's. For Lutetia, Van Krimpen made a single set of drawings. All the work of

---

[40] J Randle, 'The development of the Monotype machine', *Matrix* vol. 4 (1984), pp. 42–53.
[41] 'Nous savons que la Monotype *doit* sortir une nouvelle Antique.'

interpreting them was left to other hands, although he did supervise Rädisch's punchcutting. Whatever the nature of his interactions with the Salfords drawing office, they resulted in a typeface that was, in his own words, unfit for practical use.[42]

What Fred Smeijers calls the 'foggy clouds of admiration' that still surround Van Krimpen and his contemporaries have obscured the fact that this is a quite astonishing admission for a working type designer to make about a project with which he was involved. Even though Van Krimpen disapproved of the drawing office's activities, how could he have been so unfeeling as to allow the efforts it was making on his behalf to go to waste? Like Gill's remark about 'a set of more or less tame employees' for whom 'the local art school has done its poor best',[43] the Lutetia episode speaks volumes about European social structures between the wars.

It is true that Univers was developed in a different technical environment, and for a technology that, in its use of a single set of character shapes to cover the whole range of output image sizes, was simpler to work with than traditional typography as well as being less responsive to some of the reader's needs. Overall, Frutiger's drawings needed much less interpretation than Van Krimpen's did. But where interpretation was needed, as in refitting the light variants to the same widths as the medium, Frutiger was directly involved. He was not too proud to work alongside the people who implemented his design, and share with them the responsibility and the credit for it.

---

[42] *On designing and devising type* (1957), p. 27.
[43] *An essay on typography* (fifth edition, 1988), p. 79.

11 The search for speed

Typesetting machines can never be too fast. This is particularly true in the world of newspapers, where the time taken to set a couple of columns of text may make the difference between scooping the competition and being scooped by them. Rated output speeds were a principal weapon in the specifications wars that were fought out in the mid-1960s between machine manufacturers in the news composition market.

With early direct-photography composing machines, output speed depended above all on the mechanism of the escapement. As long as this contained components that had to be moved and then stopped to position successive character images on the output material, the machine's speed would be limited in one way or another by their inertia. (In machines like the Monophoto Filmsetter and its successors, whose matrices are stationary at the moment of exposure, the inertia of the character selection mechanism has to be taken into account as well as that of the escapement.) Some of the later models in the Photon 200/500 series, for example, had a rated speed of ten characters per second rather than the eight per second of the original design. In the higher-speed machines, however, the time taken for the escapement mechanism to come to rest after steps of more than a certain length meant that a 'no flash' machine cycle had to be programmed before the exposure of a wide character,[1] so that on some types of setting a ten-per-second machine was actually slower in terms of output speed than an eight-per-second one.

A crucial element of Higonnet and Moyroud's original design was the continuously-rotating disc matrix. As the disc rotated, the potential position of successive character images moved in an arc across the output material as they were projected through the optical system. In the 200/500 series the timing slits on the disc periphery that triggered the illuminating flash ensured that each character was photographed in the same position relative to the machine's optical axis, and all the work of locating images in the line of text was left to the escapement. However, with a different layout for the matrix it might be possible to exploit its continuous movement, and thus circumvent at least some of the problems of escapement inertia, by making the images move horizontally along the line of text and locating them in it by varying the timing of the illuminating flash. Higonnet and Moyroud applied for patents covering this idea in 1959.

---

[1] The 200/500 series were 'escape-then-flash' machines: the escapement moved by the width of the next character image to be exposed *before* the matrix was illuminated.

In 1961 the United States National Library of Medicine initiated a study to improve and enlarge the *Index Medicus*, an abstracts journal for the current medical literature. One of the study's objectives was to reduce the preparation time for each monthly number of the *Index* from twenty-two to five days.[2] Each number contained around 12 000 abstracts. Typesetting these within the required period implied a composition speed of around 400 characters per second, which was more than thirty times the speed of the fastest machines available at the time. A machine incorporating Higonnet and Moyroud's moving-character-image approach, however, would be capable in principle of speeds of this order.

Photon Inc were commissioned to produce a photocomposing machine known within the library's project as GRACE (for Graphic Arts Composing Equipment) and by Photon as the Zip 901. The first machine of the series was installed at the library in May 1964. A total of nine were manufactured, of which one was supplied to Computaprint Ltd in London and shown at the TPG exhibition in Paris in 1965.[3]

85 The control unit of the Zip 901. The magnetic-core memory, with a capacity of 2048 22-bit words, is pulled out on its slides. Below it is the backplane wiring for the transistorized logic modules.

---

[2] E R Lannon, 'Computers and composition in the United States government', *Advances in computer typesetting: proceedings of the 1966 International Computer Typesetting Conference* (1967), p. 82.

[3] *Du plomb à la lumière*, pp. 295–300. The Computaprint machine ended its days at Guildford Technical College. The photographs in Figures 85–91 were taken when the machine was dismantled there in June 1978.

The search for speed 123

86 *Interior view of the 901's photographic unit. The film magazine is in the foreground. On its left are the tensioning and spooling motors of the film transport mechanism; on the right the two stepping motors that provided line-by-line movement of the film. At the other end of the machine's bedplate is the array of 264 flash tubes and condenser lenses, normally hidden by the three glass plates of the matrix assembly.*

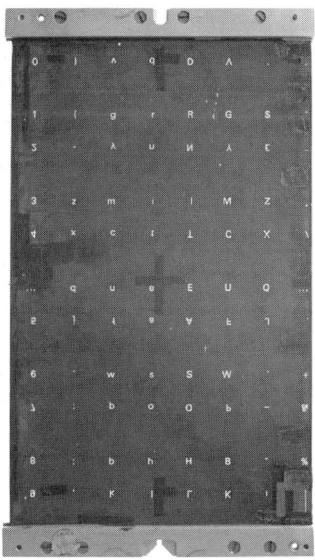

87 *One of a set of three matrix plates for the 901. One-fifth actual size. The illustration shows the emulsion side of the matrix. The crosses of photo-opaque adhesive tape suggest that it was photographed from four intermediate plaques.*

88 Another view of the 901's interior, looking from above and to the left of the film magazine towards the flash-tube array. In the foreground is the film-tensioning motor with its friction clutch. The moving lens, at the extreme left-hand end of its travel, is just visible through the slot in the lens carriage mounting. The left-hand end of the mirror tunnel housing is visible between the film magazine and the lens mounting. The dark strip at the upper part of the lens carriage is the optical grating which forms part of the lens position sensing mechanism.

89 The lens carriage and its mounting, seen from the direction of the flash-tube array. The carriage is driven by the motor at the lower left via a toothed rubber belt. It has been moved towards the centre of its travel from its position in Figure 88.

90 Another view of the lens carriage. The mirror tunnel housing is visible beyond the carriage slides, with the film magazine in the background.

91 A side view of the flash-tube array. The matrix-plate mountings are to the right, between the brackets holding the condenser-lens array to the bedplate.

Instead of the continuously rotating matrix, fixed optical system and stepping escapement of the Photon 200/500 machines, the Zip had a fixed matrix and an optical system with a single continuously moving lens. Its matrix was made up of three large plates, each carrying 88 character images (Figure 87). Every character position on the matrix had its own flash tube (Figure 91).

The first element of the optical system was the moving lens, which was driven to and fro across the full width of the output material.

This was followed by a 'mirror tunnel' that aligned the baselines of character images from different rows of the matrix plates by successive reflections. Alternate rows of character images on the matrix are right or wrong reading and upright or inverted, depending on the number of reflections the images would undergo in their passage through the tunnel.

The character images on the matrix were larger than those on the matrix discs of the 200/500 machines, and were imaged on to the output material at a fixed reduction ratio of 4:1. This meant that changes of image size in the output had to be accommodated by incorporating differently sized images on the matrix, so that the typographic flexibility of the machine was severely limited.

The Zip was the fastest-ever direct-photography machine, with a composition speed at its debut of 300 characters per second; this was raised to around 500 per second with later modifications. These speeds, though, were achieved at the cost of typographic capability, as can be seen by the kinds of output the machines were used to produce: telephone directories, airline timetables and and vehicle parts lists, as well as the simple typography of the *Index Medicus*.

Rather than being a general-purpose photocomposing machine, the Zip was a special-purpose output device for precisely specified material that had already been completely formatted by computer programs. It was very expensive (around £120000 in 1964), and needed a good deal of attention in daily use.[4]

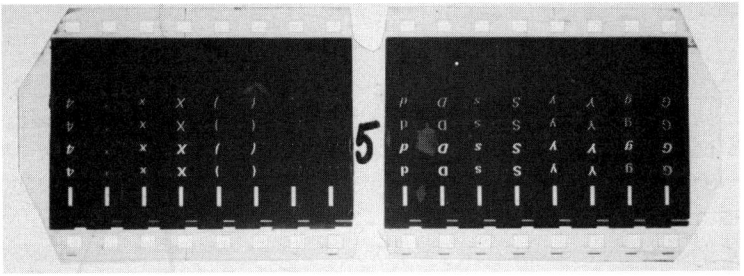

92 One of the set of eight filmstrips that made up a matrix for the Photon 713.

The Photon 713 series of machines, announced in June 1964 and aimed squarely at the newspaper market, implemented another version of Higonnet and Moyroud's moving-character-image approach in which a simple lens-and-mirror assembly moved in steps corresponding to the accumulated widths of several characters in the line. The 713's matrix assembly was a drum rotating on a vertical axis, dressed with filmstrip matrices (Figure 92) carrying 96 characters each of four typeface variants. The character baselines on the filmstrips were horizontal, so that the potential position of each character image in the matrix row was swept

---

[4] Balancing the intensities of the 264 individual flash tubes to achieve uniform character image density on the output material was a particular problem.

across the escapement step as the drum rotated. Within each step, character images were selected and positioned on the output material by firing the flash at an appropriate moment.

The 713-10, the first machine in the series, had a matrix drum with two sets of filmstrips, giving it a repertory of eight typeface variants, and a turret of eight sizing lenses on the model of the 200/500 series' twelve-lens turret.[5] Each pair of variants on the filmstrip were duplexed: that is, the characters in the two variants shared the same widths. The upright and oblique variants of Univers, such as those shown in Figure 92, had been designed with duplexed widths and hence could be used without problems. Adapting other designs for use with the 713 series gave rise to the same kind of difficulties that had been faced in designing for linecasting machines, but without the impossibility of kerning that had existed in the earlier technology.

The basic platform of the 713 series served as the foundation for a long series of developments, both photomechanical and electronic. In 1966 the 713-20 appeared, the first photocomposing machine to be fitted with hard-wired logic allowing the use of input tapes that had been keyboarded without line-end instructions.[6] The 713-5 that followed it in 1967 had a single set of filmstrips, two sizing lenses and a simple swing-axis mechanism instead of a rotating turret for selecting them. Its control circuitry used integrated circuits instead of the discrete-component logic modules of the 713-10, allowing a substantial reduction in size as well as price.

The 713 machines had the mechanical simplicity, typographic flexibility and (for the period) the low prices that their target market demanded. Fed with punched paper tape produced at separate keyboards, their output speed of around 20 characters per second was much faster than that of the 200/500 series, and better than the 14 per second of their immediate rival the Linofilm Quick. In addition, the Quick had a fixed-magnification optical system, so that the matrix grid had to be changed to change the output character image size.[7] The 713-30 of

---

[5] *Du plomb à la lumière*, pp. 301–307. The layout of the 713 machines is illustrated in A H Phillips's *Computer peripherals and typesetting* (1968); their escapement mechanism is described in detail in 'Electronics in typesetting', *Wireless World* vol. 74 no. 1389 (1968). Consistency in the vertical alignment of character images on the output depended crucially on the manufacturing accuracies of the matrix drum and its rotating pedestal and the positioning accuracy of the filmstrips on the drum. Photon's original notion, that a single drum could be dressed with interchangeable sets of filmstrips, was never practical in the European market for this reason.

[6] In English these were often misleadingly referred to as 'endless' tapes. The French 'bandes perforées au kilometre' is more vividly descriptive of the labour involved in producing them, which in France was often performed by non-unionized women operators.

[7] *Computer peripherals and typesetting*, p. 510.

1967 increased its output speed by repeating frequently used characters around the matrix, so that more than one exposure could be made for each revolution of the matrix drum. In 1969 the 713-100 series produced a further increase in speed by exposing characters during the reverse as well as the forward movement of the escapement mechanism – a *tour de force* of their hard-wired control logic.

12 Scanned-matrix photocomposition

The upheaval in the American military and scientific establishments that resulted from the launch by the USSR in 1957 of the first earth-orbiting satellite had produced a steep rise in the amount of information handled and output by computers. Intended mainly for numerical calculations, the large machines of the early 1960s had very poor facilities for producing alphanumeric output, often limited to high-speed line printers with repertories of 64 single-width ('monospaced') characters.

In 1962, shortly after the study was begun at the National Library of Medicine that resulted in the development of the Photon Zip 901, the United States Congress instituted a programme to overcome the problems of printing from computer-generated copy (which, in the context, means 64-character line-printer output). This resulted in a commission to the Mergenthaler Linotype Company and CBS Laboratories Inc in 1964, to produce a versatile high-speed composing machine. The result, technically much more ambitious than the Zip, was the Linotron 1010. Five examples of the machine were built, of which the first was delivered to the Government Printing Office in September 1967. Two machines went to the Wright-Patterson Air Force Base as part of the United States Air Force's Lexical Graphical Composer project, whose objective was to typeset and incorporate illustrations into material that had formerly been produced on line printers.

> The U S Air Force prints something like a billion and a half pages from computer print-out just in the one area of its stock list catalogues... We have found that we can pack three times as much information on a page if we use Linotron typography, which gives quite a saving: more than the cost of the machine.[1]

The 1010 took the radical step, essential for a truly high-speed composing machine, of eliminating moving parts both in the selection of character images and in their positioning on the output material. It used 255-character photographic matrices scanned by special-purpose electro-optics,[2] and produced full-page output on a high-resolution flat-face cathode-ray tube (CRT). Phillips quotes the machine's speed as 'up to 6000 characters a second',[3] though since character images

---

[1] V M Corrado, manager of graphic systems engineering, Mergenthaler Linotype Company, in *Report of proceedings, Computer Typesetting Conference, London University 1964*, p. 221.

[2] It is not quite true that the character-selection part of the 1010 had no moving parts. The machine had four matrices mounted on a rotating carrier that positioned them one at a time in front of the scanning tube. Character images from different matrices could be mixed on the same output page, though at a considerable cost in output speed.

[3] *Computer peripherals and typesetting*, p. 562. In *Electronic typesetting* (1984) Wallis

were drawn at constant resolution on the output material its speed in characters per second varied with output image size. A price of 'about $400 000' was quoted for the Linotron 1010 in 1969, with a delivery time of 12–15 months, but none was ever sold to the private sector.[4]

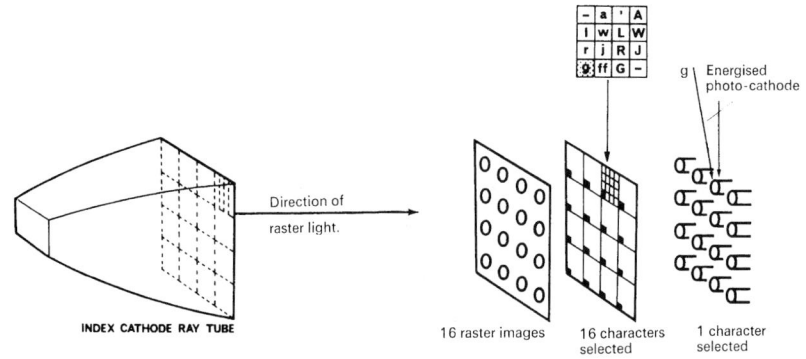

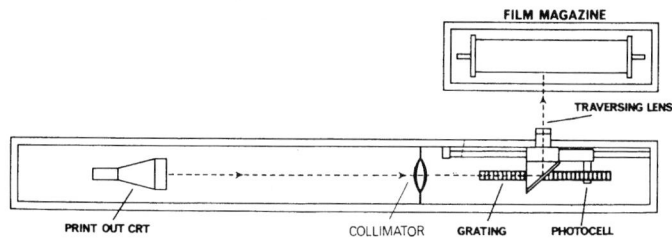

93 *Schematic layout of the Linotron 505: from* Computer peripherals and typesetting.

The same idea of an electronically scanned photographic matrix, though very differently implemented, was used in the Purdy-McIntosh Filmsetter, developed by Peter Purdy and Ronald McIntosh in England. Announced in 1966, the machine appeared in prototype in 1967 and was rechristened the Linotron 505 when its development was taken over by Linotype in 1968. As with Photon's 713 direct-photography machines, its target market was newspaper composition.

The 505 used large glass matrices, carrying sixteen groups of fifteen characters each. (Each group was a 4×4 array of character images of which one was blank.) Four of these matrices were fitted in the machine,

---

quotes a more conservative figure of 'up to 1 090 characters per second': still more than twice the speed of the Zip 901.

[4] J W Seybold, *Report on cathode ray tube character generation devices* (1969), p. 59. In his 1966 paper, E R Lannon mentions that the Linotron 1010 developed 'from work performed by the Mergenthaler Company on a project dealing with electronic translation of foreign language documents'. The cold war was clearly no hindrance to the development of such large, expensive, capable but ultimately uncommercial systems.

Scanned-matrix photocomposition

interchanged by a windmill arrangement somewhat like that of the 1010. One of the character-image groups on the matrix was illuminated by a raster pattern generated in one of 16 positions on a scanning CRT; one of an array of 16 photomultiplier tubes was activated to pick up the light passing through a single image in the group. Impulses from the photomultiplier were used to switch a single scan-line on the output CRT.

The images of successive scan lines were positioned on the output material by a continuously moving lens-and-mirror assembly, in effect producing a synthetic image of a very wide CRT. A grating and photocell in the lens transport mechanism generated clock pulses which triggered the deflection electronics on the scanning and output CRTs (Figure 93). In later models the moving lens and mirror were replaced by a small travelling CRT, allowing the machine's maximum linelength to be extended to 100 picas (422 mm; 16.6 in). (A similar increase in capability had not been available to the 1010, whose fixed relay lens limited the linelength the machine could produce.) Register marks below and on either side of each character were used to position the scan-lines on the output CRT; the marks themselves were suppressed by the imaging electronics.

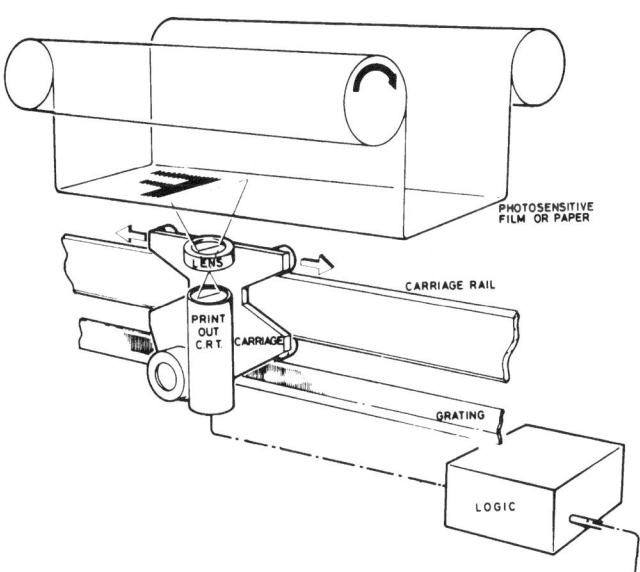

94 *Schematic layout of the Linotron 303's output end. The input end operates in a similar way to that of the 505, though it has fewer components.*

The 505's successor machine, the Linotron 303, used a similar but simpler arrangement at the scanning end, and the same travelling CRT at the output end that had been used in the 100-pica 505 (Figure 94). Instead of the 505's four large matrices, the Linotron 303 used 11 or 24 smaller ones, each carrying 144 character images photographed on film and mounted in a plastics holder (Figure 95).

95 A matrix for the Linotron 303. Actual size.

Matrices for the 505 were made by two-stage reduction via a 16-character intermediate glass plaque, with Linotype's usual reversal-processing technique. For the 303, with smaller images on the matrix, three stages of reduction and a second 144-character film intermediate were used.

Crosfield Electronics Ltd, who had been agents for Lumitype-Photon machines in Great Britain, Scandinavia, eastern Europe and some Commonwealth countries, embarked on the development of their own photocomposing machine in the late 1960s. The Magnaset 226, like its contemporary the Linotron 505, had photographic matrices and CRT output. The approaches adopted by Crosfields to the capture and display of character images, however, were radically different from Linotype's.

The Magnaset's matrix assembly was a horizontally mounted drum that carried eight rows of matrices in removable holders. There were eight holders in each row: each holder was fitted with a filmstrip carrying 22 images with a capital-letter height of 3 mm (Figures 97–98). This meant that the complete matrix assembly was very large.

Each row of matrices was associated with a flash tube inside the drum and a simple lens outside it, which imaged characters from the matrix at constant size on the photocathode of a television camera. The image in the camera was scanned at variable resolution, and written at constant resolution on the output CRT. Thus the size of the output image depended on the resolution of the camera scan, with low-resolution scans producing small images.

Scanned-matrix photocomposition

The matrices themselves were made by a procedure that, in its emphasis on flexibility and compactness, owed a good deal to its designer's experience of Photon's large matrix-making cameras (*cf.* Chapter 8). The starting point was precisely sized negative character images on 35-mm film. These were produced from phototypes of the Lumitype typeface range, used under licence from International Photon Corporation (the successors to Lumitype SA). The negatives were further reduced in an optical assembly mounted on a one-metre-square surface plate, to produce positive intermediates photographed on high-resolution film (Figure 96). The 'register bar' at the left of the character image was added at the same time.

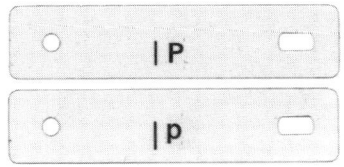

96 *Two of the positive intermediate characters from which the Magnaset's matrices were made. Actual size. The register bars control the size of the scanning raster in the composing machine's television camera.*

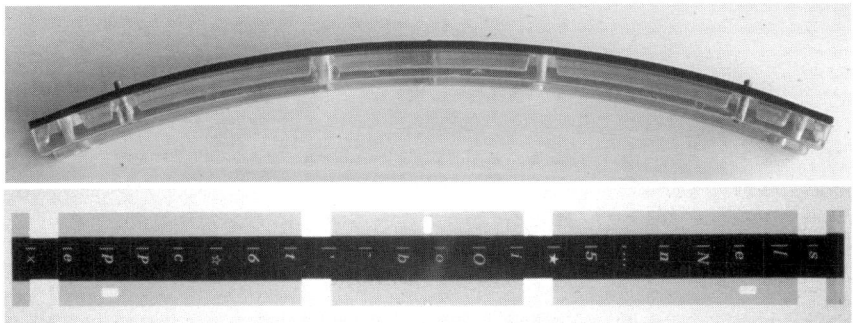

97 *Above: side view of a matrix holder for the Magnaset 226. Half actual size. The matrix strip is sandwiched between the holder's two elements. The projecting pins locate the holder in the matrix drum.*
Below: the matrix strip removed from the holder. The large cutouts are to accommodate the screws that hold the matrix holder's two elements together. The three slotted holes in the strip fit over the holder's locating pins.

Sets of 22 positives were mounted in a vacuum jig under clean conditions and contact-printed on high-resolution film to produce the matrix strips, which were mounted in plastics holders for fitting to the matrix drum (Figure 97).

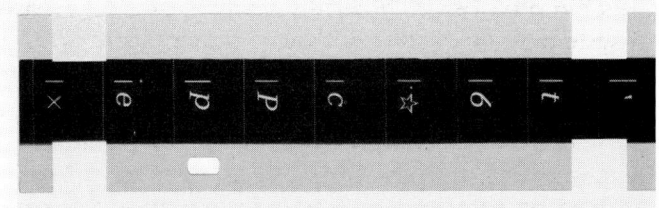

98 *Close-up view of the left-hand end of the matrix strip in Figure 97. Actual size. Frequently occurring alphabetic characters are repeated next to the capital-minuscule pairs (P p in this illustration) on the matrix.*

As with the Linotron 1010, the face of the Magnaset's output CRT was imaged on the photosensitive material by a fixed relay lens. The output display was a compromise between the single scan-line of the 505 and 303 and the full-page output of the Linotron 1010. Character images were written in a letterbox-shaped rectangular 'window' on the tube face, with areas of text being composed rather than individual lines. Each character image was retained on the camera's photocathode until all the instances of that character in the window had been written; so that in effect the camera acted as a fast-access digital storage device. The machine was controlled by a Digital Equipment PDP8 computer.

While the Magnaset was a commercial failure in spite of its innovations, the Linotrons were not the only scanned-matrix machines to succeed. The Compugraphic Corporation, which had revolutionized the photocomposing market in 1968 with a range of simple low-cost direct-photography machines, followed the same tradition in 1973 with the Videosetter. This was a budget-priced reworking of the principles behind the Linotron 1010, with interchangeable photographic matrices scanned by an image-dissector tube. Unlike the 1010, though, which produced full-page output on a large and expensive high-resolution CRT, the Videosetter wrote successive single lines of text on a tube with a fibre-optic faceplate. The machine was aimed primarily at the American newspaper market.

The Linotrons, Crosfield's Magnaset and Compugraphic's Videosetter are all examples of a class of devices that we can call *scanned-matrix* photocomposing machines. As with direct-photography machines, the data used to construct character images on the output material is stored in the form of photographic images on a matrix. Instead of being reproduced directly, though, as they were in the earlier technology, the matrix images are scanned electronically to provide switching pulses for the beam on a CRT whose faceplate is imaged on the output material.

Linotype's scanned-matrix machines changed the size of the output image by changing the vertical amplitude of the line on the output tube and the horizontal pitch of the pattern with which the matrix was scanned. The horizontal resolution on the output material remained constant at 1296 lines per inch or 18 lines per point,[5] so that with an 18-unit system for character widths the nominal size of the output image could be set in 1-point increments. (In fact the 505 in its basic configuration offered nine sizes from 4 to 12 pt in 1-point steps, and five more from 14 to 28 pt.) In effect, a different amount of information was sent to the output electronics for each output image size. The scanning pitch on the matrix and the amplitude of the writing line could be changed independently, so that condensed and expanded images could be produced on the output from a single image on the matrix. Similarly, the writing line could be slanted to produce an obliqued pseudo-italic.

Because the scan of each character had to be completed before that of the next one could begin, the character images on the output in straightforward setting had to fit inside a contiguous series of upright rectangles (or sloping parallelograms, if the writing line was slanted). This imposed a restriction on kerning which was very much like that placed on the original Linotype by the physical exigencies of the brass matrix. In the 505 and 303, though, as in all photocomposing machines, there was no array of actual objects that correlated directly with the row of character images on the output material, and hence no material reason why one character image should not overlap another. Kerning could be achieved, at some cost in output speed, by composing a line of text with several passes of the imaging lens so that kerning characters in the line were correctly positioned relative to their neighbours.

The Linotron 505 and 303 achieved their high output speeds[6] in the same way that the Photon Zip had, by replacing the stop-start movements of a stepping escapement by the uninterrupted sweep across the output material of a single imaging lens. The Linotron 1010, the Magnaset and the Compugraphic Videosetter went a stage further, by eliminating physical mechanisms altogether from the setwise positioning of character images within the line of text. The first two went further yet by setting several lines, or for the Linotron a whole page, between successive vertical movements of the output material. This progressive dematerialization of the systems at the output end of the machine was a prefiguring of things to come. At the input end, however, the means for storing character images were still physical – aggressively so in the Magnaset's case – even if the character selection and sizing mechanisms that followed them were mostly electronic rather than optical. It was with the next generation of machines, evolving simultaneously with scanned-matrix machines but starting from a different point and initially addressed to different markets, that the systems at this end of the machine would dematerialize as well.

---

[5] The machines also had a high-speed mode in which the output resolution was 648 lines per inch.

[6] Arthur Phillips quotes a composition speed for the Linotron 505 in its original form of 90 characters a second at its higher writing resolution: *Computer peripherals and typesetting*, p. 549.

13 Fonts and typefaces in photomatrix manufacture

Photocomposing machines of the first generation had to be shut down to change the output image size.[1] While the machine's optical system was being reconfigured the matrix assembly could be changed as well. This meant that it was practicable for manufacturers to offer two or three sets of matrices for the same design, differently proportioned according to the sizes for which they were intended to be used. Monophoto Bembo, for example, had three sets of matrices: 'A' for 6 and 7 pt, 'B' for 8 to 12 pt, and 'C' for 14 to 24 pt. Most Monophoto faces had two, with the 'B' set covering the range from 8 to 24 pt. With this approach, photocomposed output could be made to emulate reasonably closely both the appearance and the metrics of a design that had been originated for hot-metal composition.

In this situation the relationship between fonts and typefaces is very similar to what it was in the earlier technology. The set of matrices is the font; the typeface is realized by the two or three fonts that cover the size range. The change of character image size between matrix drawing and output material, though, is handled in only two stages, by the matrix-making camera and the composing machine's optical system, rather than in the multiple processes of pattern-making and mechanical punchcutting.

In 'second-generation' machines like the Lumitype-Photon 200/500 series the whole range of character image sizes on the output material is derived from a single set of images on the matrix.[2] This raises in a more acute form the same issue that had worried purist typographers at the end of the nineteenth century with the introduction of variable scaling on the punchcutting pantograph (see Chapter 3). The facility is now no longer a *faute de mieux* for lazy or hurried typefounders, but an inherent and effectively inescapable part of the composing system. Very few customers indeed will be ready to sacrifice valuable space on an expensive unitary matrix by specifying more than one font for a single typeface in the interests of typographic quality alone.

The designs made in the Lumitype studio, based as they were on their

---

[1] Matrices for the Intertype Fotosetter were made for one of four different character image sizes: 6, 8, 12 and 18 pt. The machine could set two sizes in the line by mixing matrices from two magazines carrying images of different sizes.

[2] The Linotype VIP, like its Linofilm predecessors, used matrices with different character image sizes to cover the whole of the output size range. This was necessary because of the limited magnification range of the machines' zoom-lens optical systems. As Figure 65 suggests, however, matrices for the VIP's two size ranges were made from the same intermediate plaque, so that the design of the matrix characters did not vary from one type of matrix to the other.

own dimensional standards and a novel system for allocating character widths, were different enough from their metal-type predecessors to be considered as typefaces in their own right.[3] In the simple case, each of the 90-character 'alphabets' on a Lumitype disc was a font for one variant of a typeface. (In real discs made for the European market the accented characters that the 90-character set would not accommodate were fitted in elsewhere on the disc or synthesized with the machine's 'floating accent' facility.) Apart from Univers with its 21 variants, fonts for three or four typeface families – made up of roman, italic and bold variants, and perhaps bold italic as well – could thus be carried on a single disc.

The relationship between typeface and font in these circumstances is simpler than it was in hot-metal composition or first-generation photocomposition. Instead of being realized by different sets of patterns or drawings from which fonts are made for different parts of the output size range, typefaces are now embodied in single sets of character masters from which fonts are made for the complete range of sizes. As with metal-type designs, though, the definitive reference for both their appearance and their technical characteristics remains the manufacturer's specimen book.

The rush of new photocomposing machines to the market that began in the late 1960s and is vividly described by Lawrence Wallis[4] brought these simplicities to an end. There was more than one machine of which the output image quality could reasonably be described, in Wallis's words, as 'awful'. On the technical front, some of the new manufacturers underestimated the difficulty of producing good-quality character masters for matrix photography, and also the importance of controlling photographic variables in the matrix-making process. On the aesthetic front, they took advantage of the lack of restriction on the copying of existing designs that existed in the American market at the time. (The names of typefaces were protected as trademarks, but the design of their characters had no corresponding protection.) On the economic front, they were reluctant to invest the considerable resources demanded by the production of useful type-specimen books. Suddenly there were many new versions of a few familiar or hackneyed designs. Many had unaccustomed names: Ballardvale, Humanist. Their appearance – in both senses of the word – raised questions that had never needed to be considered in the days of metal-type manufacture. If all the variants of Emmenthal (say) are rendered by character images that are identical in every respect to the corresponding images in Helvetica, are the two

---

[3] Some traditionally minded English customers found it hard to accept that Lumitype Baskerville 401, closely based on punches descended from Baskerville's foundry to Deberny & Peignot, had anything to do with 'real Baskerville', incarnated for them in Monotype's hot-metal Series 169.

[4] *Electronic typesetting* (1984).

typefaces different just because they have different names and the fonts that produce the images come from different manufacturers? If the hot-metal and photocomposed versions of a well-known design from a famous manufacturer have different x-heights at the same nominal size, and the italic of one is irregular in weight while the other is uniform, to what extent do the two versions realize the same typeface?

In these circumstances the abstract notion of a typeface as something defined by a particular collection of appearance characteristics, rather than by a single set of physical objects such as drawings or patterns, begins to make sense. There are no longer, as there were with metal type or early photocomposition, a few well-characterized renderings of particular designs whose appearance is fully defined by their manufacturers' specimens. Instead, multiple versions of the same design cluster around each other in a space that embraces the whole range of possible appearances of a particular mechanically written script. A group of close neighbours in this multidimensional *script appearance space* constitutes a typeface, because the appearance of each member of the group is more like that of the designs adjacent to it than it is like that of others further away. Emmenthal and Helvetica are indeed the same typeface, because their appearance characteristics situate them at identical points in the space. Both versions of the famous manufacturer's well-known design realize the same typeface in spite of their differences in appearance, because these are not large enough to separate them very far. The many versions of Times Roman that were produced at the time, although they were far apart along some of the dimensions of script appearance space, still formed a group whose members resembled one another more than they did any other typeface.

The appearance-space model is also useful for characterizing the task faced by Adrian Frutiger and the Monotype drawing office at Salfords earlier in the decade, in adapting the Lumitype Univers family for the Monotype system. In its terms, the task was to make a cluster of new designs whose internal structure was as similar as possible to the cluster formed by the existing Lumitype family and whose centre of gravity was located as near as possible to it in the space. The new designs, for example, like the existing ones, should have identical stroke thicknesses between condensed, normal-width and expanded variants at a given nominal weight. This identity of strokeweight from one variant to another gives rise to differences in appearing weight between variants; but the relationships between the differing weights, and hence the relative positions of the variants within the cluster, should remain the same between the two versions. Identity of appearance of diagonal characters between the two versions, on the other hand, is impossible to achieve, because of the variations in slope that follow from the differences in width allocation and kerning capability between the systems for which they were intended.

99 *The Photo Typositor: from publicity material produced by the Visual Graphics Corporation. Characters are projected from a filmstrip matrix on to a strip of photosensitive material via a variable-magnification optical system. Additional anamorphic lenses allow the slant and aspect ratio of character images to be altered. The output material unrolls from the right of the machine into a liquid-tight processing cell in front of the operator, who can position each character image and monitor its development visually.*

The facilities offered by some hand-operated photolettering machines such as the Visual Graphics Corporation's Photo Typositor (Figure 99) also began to cast doubt in the latter part of the 1960s on the traditional notion of what constituted a typeface. If an operator could condense, expand, slant or backslant successive images in a single piece of composition, what was the relationship of the results to the realization of the unmodified typeface that was shown in the font manufacturer's specimen book? Every new setting of the machine changed some of the metric properties of the images that were produced, altering their appearance as a result and hence, perhaps, realizing a different typeface on the output material. Since the machine's settings could be widely varied between limits and there were two axes of variation to choose from, the number of variants (and hence of potential typefaces) that could be produced was very large.[5] On the other hand, though, all the variant images on the output material were derived by simple

---

[5] Publicity for the Photo Typositor speaks of '2800 sizes, slants and proportions from a single film font'.

geometrical transformations from the single set of images in the font. Very many of the images' metric properties, such as the ratios of vertical to horizontal strokeweight or of x-height to cap height, remained unchanged. Equating the multiplicity of variants on the output material with the unmodified version of the design shown in the specimen book was thus simply a question of choosing which aspects of the variants' descriptions, and hence which dimensions in their appearance spaces, to ignore.[6]

Scanned-matrix photocomposing machines, when they arrived at the end of the 1960s, reproduced electronically and at high speed most of the character-image manipulations that had been possible manually with photolettering machines. Variations in clock-pulse timings and CRT deflection voltages replaced the adjustable cylindrical lenses of the earlier technology. In the abstract, though, these differences simply reflected a difference in approach to the problem of transferring character images from the matrix to the output material. The relationship between the single image on the matrix and the variant images on the output was exactly the same as it had been in the earlier technology.

The climate of typographical uncertainty that prevailed in the latter half of the 1960s was the consequence of a profound technological shift: the change from direct to indirect imaging of typeset characters that photocomposition gave rise to. In metal-type manufacture and letterpress printing the whole series of image transfers, from the punch via matrix and type to the character image on the output material, was performed by straightforward mechanical processes that offered no scope for transformation of the image itself. In photocomposition, by contrast, image transfer from character master to matrix and from matrix to output material was indirect, performed by bundles of light-rays and mediated by optical or electro-optical systems that at the very least allowed output images in a range of sizes to be produced from a single image on the matrix. This breakdown of the mechanical link between type and image, coupled with the shift from relief to planographic printing surfaces that came with the rise of offset lithography, called into question all the conceptual and dimensional frameworks on which five hundred years of received wisdom about type and typography had been built.

---

[6] This is a *post hoc* resolution of a situation which at the time gave rise to a good deal of harrumphing in typographically conservative circles.

Part 3: Digital and numerical techniques

14 Digital and numerical photocomposition

In 1964, the same year that the development of the Linotron 1010 was begun, the firm of Dr.-Ing. Rudolf Hell GmbH in Keil was approached by a group of European telephone service providers to explore the possibility of composing directory listings on 70-mm photographic film.[1]

100 The Digiset 50T1: from Computer peripherals and typesetting. *The output CRT is in the left-hand open cabinet, housed in an antimagnetic shield. The unit with the meter is its power supply. The fixed relay lens is at the right-hand side of the next cabinet, behind a light-tight cover. The film transport mechanism is in the rightmost cabinet, with an automatic processor below it.*

The resulting machine, the Digiset 50T1 (Figure 100), was announced at the TPG exhibition in Paris in 1965, and a prototype was shown in 1966. Two machines were operational in 1967: one at Lux Bildstudio GmbH in Neu-Isenburg, and one at the Copenhagen telephone company KTAS.[2]

The principles on which digital photocomposing machines like the Digiset operate are appealingly simple. The electron beam of a high-resolution flat-faced CRT scans out a small raster pattern on the tube

---

[1] J W Seybold, *The world of digital typesetting* (1984), p. 127. This work and its predecessor *Fundamentals of modern photocomposition* (1979) provide an excellent introduction to electronic typesetting techniques as well as comprehensive descriptions of most of the machines mentioned here.

[2] A H Phillips, *Computer peripherals and typesetting* (1968), p. 566.

face. Unlike the familiar fixed horizontal raster of a television display, this one is a variable-width rectangle made up of successive vertical lines. As the pattern is scanned out the beam is switched on and off, under the control of data stored in the machine, to build up a character image. The face of the writing tube is imaged on the photosensitive output material by a simple optical system consisting of a single fixed relay lens. This transfers to the output material a succession of character images written across the width of the tube face.

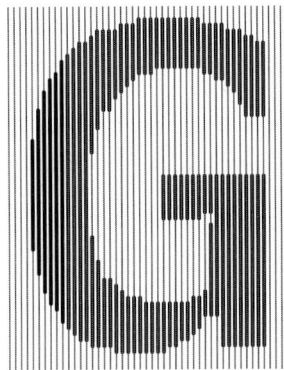

101 *Drawing character images with a vertical raster scan. Left: the pattern traced out by the writing spot of the CRT. The pattern is written from right to left; the spot travels upwards along successive lines at a constant rate, and flies back quickly to the start of the next line. Right: images are drawn by brightening up the writing spot at the correct moment during the scan of each line. The data for the character image is taken from the illustration on p.[23] of* Matthew Carter: Bell Centennial *(1982).*

Writing character images on the output material of a digital photo-composing machine is a binary process. The intensity of the electron beam that excites the CRT's phosphor to produce light may vary from point to point on the tube face, to compensate for characteristics of the machine's optical system, or it may change with output image size; but the image itself is written on the output material with dots or lines of uniform blackness, not with shades of grey. The problem that always has to be solved in photocomposing machines using CRT output is how to handle the data from which the character images on the output material are constructed.

Scanned-matrix machines like the Linotron 505 extracted binary data from photographic character images with scanning CRTs and photomultiplier tubes. The Digiset, by contrast, stored image data directly in computer memory.[3] The 1965 laboratory model of the machine stored

---

[3] Lawrence Wallis, working for the Monotype Corporation at the time, describes himself as 'wandering round the Paris exhibition [*i.e.* the TPG of 1965, where the Digiset was announced] thoroughly bemused by the notion of digitised

Digital and numerical photocomposition 145

one binary digit (one bit) for each individual element (picture element or pixel) of the image, and an average character required around one kilobit (1024 bits) of storage.[4] Data from the store has to be accessible at speeds corresponding with the writing speed of the machine. The maximum speed of the Digiset 50T1 was 600 characters a second, so that the image data rate had to be 600 kilobits/sec or more.

In the mid-1960s digital storage that would work at this speed was mainly implemented with magnetic-core memories, in which arrays of small ferrite toroids were threaded with fine wires. Data bits were stored and read by currents passed through the wires. Memories of this type were very expensive, at around 20 cents/bit in 1965, and their capacities extremely small by present-day standards.[5]

102 *Enlarged printout from Digiset image data. The image is 57 dots high and 44 wide, four times as large as the 6 pt images of the prototype machine.*

The prototype Digiset used a module of 196 kilobits (24.5 kilobytes) to store the data for 180 characters at a maximum size of 14 pt. While Dr Hell himself could remark in 1965 that 'using two or three magnetic-core memories instead of one is only a question of price',[6] the cost of emulating the 1440-character repertory of the Photon-Lumitype 200/500 series machines, for example, exclusively in high-speed storage would clearly have been prohibitive. The solution, which inevitably affected the output speed of the machine to some extent, was to store image data 'off-line', normally in compressed form, on a slower but still

---

founts or a filmsetting machine bereft of a photo-matrix': *Electronic typesetting* (1984), p. 43.

[4] In his 1965 article describing the machine, Dr Hell says that a 6 pt character is 48 pixels high: 'Le Digiset, composeuse binaire électronique', *Caractère* November 1965, p. 11. A character that filled the em square would require 2304 (48 × 48) pixels, but most characters are not as large as this.

[5] A memory expansion module for the Digital Equipment Corporation's PDP8 computer, with a capacity of 4000 12-bit words, cost $10000 in 1965.

[6] 'Utiliser deux ou trois mémoires à microtores au lieu d'une n'est qu'une question de prix': *Caractère*, p. 11

reasonably fast medium. From here it could be loaded and expanded into high-speed memory by the machine's electronics when it was needed. The prototype Digiset used punched paper tape for off-line storage. Production versions of the machine used magnetic tape, and later machines from other manufacturers magnetic drums or disks. We can describe as *digital-font* photocomposing machines those machines that store data in electronic form and use it directly to construct binary character images.

The Digiset was the ancestor of several families of digital-font machines: the Autologic APS series, Dr Hell's own 50T and 40T series, the Harris-Intertype Fototronic CRT and the Linotron 404 and 606. All of them shared a similar schematic layout, with the faceplate of a fixed high-resolution CRT imaged on the output material by a fixed optical system. (The APS 5 and Micro-5 used a vertically-mounted CRT and an optical path folded with mirrors to produce a more compact enclosure.) All of them had high output speeds (from 275 to 2000 characters per second for the Fototronic CRT, for example, depending on image size) and were correspondingly expensive (a Fototronic with a 512-character memory cost \$350000 in 1969).[7] All of them used binary character image data, stored in compressed form on magnetic tapes or disks and expanded into the machine's high-speed memory to specify exactly the dots and lines of light that made up the output image.[8]

The high price per unit of display resolution of electronic storage in the 1960s and early 1970s meant that most digital-font machines could not afford to keep a different set of image data in high-speed memory for each output size.[9] Loading new data from magnetic tape or disk into memory for each change of size in a typesetting job was slow by comparison with the machines' output speed. Instead, the resolution of the patterns written on the output CRT was varied so that a single data set could be used to produce output images in a range of sizes. Early production models of the Digiset 50T series, for example, used two sets of data: the smaller to produce output images in the range from 4 to 12 pt, and the larger from 8 to 24 pt.[10] The output images could be condensed, expanded or slanted, in much the same way as those

---

[7] J W Seybold, *Report on CRT character generation devices* (1969).

[8] The Fototronic had a proprietary image format in which the electron beam wrote successive 'patches' of uniformly-spaced dots, rather than switching a spot at intervals in the scan-lines of a regular raster pattern.

[9] Alphanumeric Inc, the parent company of Autologic, owned patents on image data compression that allowed the Autologic APS3 to use a separate set of data for each output image size (*The world of digital typesetting*, p. 129).

[10] *Ibid.*, p. 128. The Digiset 50T machines were marketed in the United States by RCA as the Videocomp 820 series, with 32 kilobytes of high-speed memory. This held four sets of image data for the smaller size range; reloading it from magnetic tape took around one second.

in scanned-matrix machines, by altering the parameters of the raster pattern on the CRT.

In the first half of the 1970s digital-font machines were at the upper end of the photocomposing market, with scanned-matrix machines below them and direct-photography machines at the lower end. Even though the cost of computing power and digital storage were falling all the time, the expensive microspot CRTs and high-performance optical systems of digital-font machines, and the problems of storing and handling binary-mode character image data, still confined them to applications such as telephone directory or newspaper text setting where typographical variation in the output was restricted and composition speed was at a premium. The machines were too costly and insufficiently flexible for the more variable demands of general typesetting work.

Keeping character image data in electronic form, though, was a very attractive prospect for type manufacturers. However expensive it was to produce the first copy of a given set of data, the cost of the second and subsequent copies was negligible. The copying process was error-free, and the time it took insignificant. Two things were needed if high-speed electronic typesetting was to come within the reach of the ordinary printing trade: a format for image data that, like a photographic matrix, would allow output images in a wide range of sizes to be produced from a single data set, and a less expensive way of getting the images themselves on to the output material.

103 Character images at three different sizes, derived from an outline made up of straight-line segments; adapted from Linotype Century Old Style. The outer and inner contours have 50 and 25 data points respectively. The 'flats' in the bowl are easily visible in the larger sizes.

The first of these arrived in 1971, with the Seaco 1600 CRT photocomposing machine. The layout of the Seaco machine was the same as that of its digital-font contemporaries, but the fonts it used specified character shapes in numerical rather than digital terms. The specifications in the fonts were sequences of coordinate pairs, each of which defined a point on the character outline. The points in the sequence were joined by straight-line segments to produce a specification for the outline. This was scaled by the machine's software to provide output character images at different sizes (Figure 103).

The Seaco machine was unsuccessful in spite of the technical advance that its approach to character image generation represented. The simplified imaging technique that was the second requirement for electronic typesetting's move into the general market arrived with MGD Graphic Systems' Metro-Set machine in 1972. Instead of the familiar high-resolution flat-face CRT imaged on the output material by a fixed relay lens, the Metro-Set had a new type of output imaging device: a CRT with a fibre-optic faceplate. This was a slot-shaped bundle, 11 in (28 cm) wide by 1 in (2.5 cm) deep, of single-strand fibre light-guides. The inner ends of the fibres, inside the tube, were coated with light-emitting phosphor, and their outer ends were in direct contact with the output material. In effect this arrangement did away with the output optical system altogether, relying on irradiation in the photosensitive emulsion of the output material to fill in the minute unilluminated interstices between the fibres.

Like the Seaco machine, the Metro-Set used numerical fonts; but instead of being sequences of straight lines, data in the Metro-Set fonts was made up of specifications for straight lines and arcs of circles. The beam on the output CRT wrote a raster pattern for each character in the usual way; the binary instructions that switched it on and off were derived from the outline specifications by special-purpose hardware, giving the machine its high output speed of 1000 12-pica lines per minute at an output resolution of 744 lines/in (29.3 lines/mm).[11] The machine was controlled by a minicomputer with 24 kilobytes of memory and an 8-megabyte hard disc for font storage.

The Metro-Set was several years ahead of its time. The next machine to use numerical character outline specifications was the Linotron 202, introduced in 1978 and intended as a replacement for Linotype's VIP direct-photography photocomposing machine in the trade typesetting market. (MGD Graphic Systems, oddly enough, chose to abandon typesetting in the same year, in spite of their machine's technical success.)

The 202, like the Metro-Set, had a tube with a fibre-optic faceplate; but the character outline specifications it originally used, like the Seaco machine's, were sequences of straight-line vectors. As with the Seaco, these were converted into binary image data by software in the machine's controlling computer.[12] Outline data for two variants could be held in high-speed memory for immediate use; more fonts were stored on interchangeable floppy discs. Alert to the demands of its market, the 202 traded away output speed in favour of versatility and cheapness.[13]

---

[11] The machine had two other resolution modes: 496 and 1488 lines/in (19.5 and 58.6 lines/mm).

[12] The 202's software was upgraded in 1980 to use 'Superfonts', which specified character shapes in terms of curves as well as straight lines.

[13] It was far from cheap, however, in present-day terms: Lawrence Wallis (*Electronic typesetting*, p. 46) quotes a basic price for it in 1982 of £32000.

Digital and numerical photocomposition

A feature of the numerical approach to character image generation is that images in the whole range of output sizes are written on the output material with the same resolution: that is, with the same number of writing lines per inch. This means that certain aspects of output image quality, such as edge-sharpness, are consistent across the size range. This is not the case with digital-font machines, where within the range covered by a particular font the size of the images on the output material is changed by changing the writing resolution and perhaps also the size and brightness of the writing spot on the output CRT. The changes are made by altering the tube's beam current and focus, with consequent effects on the sharpness of the output image.

With the direct-photography photocomposing machines of the mid-1970s the trend of development had moved away from standalone machines driven by punched paper tape, exemplified by the Linotype VIP or the Monophoto 400 series, and towards smaller and cheaper direct-entry machines in which the keyboard and the photographic unit were combined in a single unit. (In one sense this was a return to the technology's roots: Higonnet and Moyroud's Photon 200 had been a direct-entry machine.) In 1979, the year after the appearance of the Linotron 202, Mergenthaler Linotype GmbH moved numerical photocomposition in the same direction with the introduction of the Linotype CRTronic. This was a direct-entry machine, small enough to fit on a tabletop if not a desktop, using outline fonts similar to the Linotron 202's. Output was by means of a small travelling CRT like that in the Linotronic 303. The machine had two microprocessors and two floppy-disc drives: one for font storage and one for text handling. Its visual display allowed simple editing of the input text and the commands embedded in it. Wallis said of the CRTronic in 1982 that 'it sounds the unmistakeable death knell of the photo-matrix'.[14] At the time the price of a machine was between £13 000 and £18 000, depending on the range of options available.

---

[14] *Electronic typesetting*, p. 32.

15 Digital and numerical fonts

Scanned-matrix, digital-font and numerical-font photocomposing machines are sometimes grouped together as 'third-generation' devices, on the basis that all three types of machine use cathode-ray tubes to generate character images on the output material.[1] I prefer to place them in separate categories, on the basis that the fonts they use – the means by which they store the specifications for the images they produce – are fundamentally different.

The difference relates to the mode in which the specifications in the font are stored. The fonts in scanned-matrix machines store their specifications in graphic mode. The objects on the matrices of a scanned-matrix machine from which the output character image specifications are derived are themselves images: visible entities, replicating at a smaller size the images on the camera masters from which the matrix was made. The specifications in digital and numerical fonts, on the other hand, depend for their concrete existence only on the data medium that carries them. In digital fonts, character image specifications are stored in a compressed representation of binary mode.[2] The groups of numbers in the font are expanded inside the composing machine into the sequences of binary digits that in turn specify the voltage pulses that control the construction of character images on the output CRT. With numerical fonts, the data in the font specifies character outlines, and using it involves an additional step: the binary data for an image of a particular nominal size has to be extracted from the numerical specification in the font. This part of the process is known as *scan conversion* or *rasterization*, and normally takes place in the composing machine's controlling computer.[3]

The 'third-generation' classification recognizes the fact that in all three types of machine character images are written on the output CRT, and hence on the photosensitive material, by a binary process. It is true that in scanned-matrix photocomposition the character image on the matrix is dissected electronically to produce the information from which the output image is constructed, and the pulses of voltage produced when the matrix is scanned are shaped in the machine's internal circuitry so that the spot of light on the writing CRT is either

---

[1] *cf.* J W Seybold, *The world of digital typesetting* (1984), ch. 9.

[2] The data in the fonts for the original Digiset was not compressed, because the electronics of the time could not expand it fast enough to match the machine's target composing speed.

[3] For a technical overview of scan conversion methods, see Roger Hersch's survey 'Font rasterization: the state of the art', in *Visual and technical aspects of type* (1993).

on or off. However, this is not a translation from a graphic-mode to a binary-mode *representation* of the image, because the sequence of shaped pulses is not stored inside the machine for later use as a specification for the image's configuration. It is also true that the output character images will normally differ in size, and perhaps in aspect ratio and slant as well, from the matrix images that served as their originals. Once again, though, these differences result from simple electronic manipulation of the signals generated when the matrix is scanned, rather than from varying interpretations of a single explicit specification held inside the machine in electronic form.

Digital-font photocomposition, by contrast, normally involves two transitions between representational modes. In conventional digital fontmaking, the graphic-mode character shape specifications on existing character masters are translated by scanning and editing into the binary-mode specifications for character image configuration that (after compression to reduce their extent) go to make up the font. In composition, the compressed binary-mode specifications in the font are expanded and interpreted in the composing machine to produce graphic-mode character images on the faceplate of the output CRT.[4] As with scanned-matrix machines, the images produced from a single digital font may differ in size, aspect ratio and slant from one another; but this is because the specification in the font is being differently interpreted to produce the different variants. In numerical-font composition there is a third mode of representation: the numerical specification of the character outline in the font, which is rasterized to produce the binary-mode specification from which the character image itself is produced.

From the type-designer's point of view, CRT machines using digital fonts had two great advantages over both scanned-matrix machines and those using numerical fonts. Scanned-matrix machines, like most direct-photography photocomposing machines, used a single set of matrix character images to cover the whole range of output image sizes. This was rarely less than 8:1 (from 6 to 48 pt, for example), and it was extremely hard to make a design that did not look cramped at one end of the range or gappy at the other, particularly with the 18-unit width allocation system used by the Linotype machines. Numerical-font machines also use a single font for the whole size range, although their width allocation systems are normally less restrictive. Digital-font machines, on the other hand, seldom covered a size range of more than 3:1 with a single set of image data, so that designs could be optimized for the ranges in which they were used. Because positioning the raster on the face of the output CRT and writing the character image itself

---

[4] We assume here what is normally the case: that the optical system of a digital-font photocomposing machine does nothing more than project an image of the CRT's faceplate on to the output material.

were independent operations, there were no inherent restrictions on kerning.

The other great advantage of digital-font technology was the degree of control that could be exerted over the configuration of the output image. Image data for existing designs was normally acquired by scanning character artwork on a drum scanner at high resolution and scaling the resulting pixel arrays algorithmically. This was particularly easy for Linotype, since their camera masters, cut from two-layer laminated film with high-contrast edges to the character shapes, were already perfectly suited for scanning (*cf.* Figure 64 above). However, the scanning process itself was apt to generate errors at the pixel level, particularly where the scanning spot ran along a straight edge parallel to the scanning direction (Figure 104). Errors of this type tended to survive straightforward arithmetic scaling, so that it was necessary for the scaled data to be edited by hand. This gave both manufacturers and designers the opportunity to make modifications to the image data, with the certainty that they would be carried over into the output image.

104 *Printout from an uncorrected scan. The character image is 126 pixels high. The scanning spot has dithered along the vertical edges of the descending stroke, and failed to render the curve at the outer left-hand edge of the bowl. The notches at the junctions of bowl and stem suggest that the scan was made from an unmodified character master originally intended for direct-photography photocomposition. From* Ikarus for typefaces in digital form *(URW, Hamburg, 1983).*

Equally, though, there was no absolute requirement to prepare new designs intended for digital-font manufacture as large character masters in the way that there had been for photomatrix production. Drawings could be prepared directly as pixel diagrams, on a grid whose dimensions corresponded to the base size of the image data set for which they were

Digital and numerical fonts 153

intended. Two families of designs made in the 1970s for telephone directories, Bell Centennial by Matthew Carter and Galfra by Ladislas Mandel, illustrate variations on this approach.

In both cases the designers began work using methods with which they were familiar from earlier technologies. Carter's brief was to make a set of designs analogous to Linotype's Bell Gothic, but more robust against the effects of composition on the CRT typesetters of the period as well as those of offset printing with thin inks at high web speeds.[5] He worked out the parameters for the new designs before digitization was begun, by making matrices for the Linotype VIP direct-photography composing machine from conventional analogue drawings and using them to set specimen directory pages. Once these had been approved by the client Carter went on to construct pixel diagrams on the basis of the matrix drawings, making reduced photographic pasteups of the diagrams to check their appearance at final size. In the latter stages of the work Carter wrote out by hand the start and finish coordinates of character elements for each vertical line of the raster. This data was plotted on a hard-copy printer and final corrections made on the printout. The fonts were first used on a Linotron 606 digital photocomposing machine.

105 Above: mechanical digitizations of drawings by Ladislas Mandel for three characters of his Galfra Regular design. Below: Mandel's pre-digitized drawings for the same characters. Adapted from material in the designer's collection; one-fifth actual size.

Mandel began the development of the Galfra family by making analogue drawings on a grid whose asymmetrical unit, wider than it was high,

---

[5] The story is illustrated in *Matthew Carter: Bell Centennial* (1982).

represented the resolution of the Digiset image data set for which the design was originally intended. This allowed him to define strokeweights and counter widths directly in terms of pixel counts, and thus to establish the finely judged relationships between the typographic colour of different family members by which he set great store. However, he was not satisfied with the configuration of the pixel diagrams that resulted when his drawings were scanned and digitized by conventional methods. His response, like Carter's but with a different motivation, was to make pixel diagrams (which he called 'pre-digitized drawings') directly (Figure 105).

The direct control over character image configuration that digital font-making afforded could also be used to exploit the imaging characteristics of the composing machine itself. The combination of light-emitting phosphor, relay lens and photosensitive emulsion by which digital photocomposing machines produced character images was not capable of fully resolving isolated pixels in the character image specification. However, discontinuous patterns of pixels could expose the output material enough to produce curves at character edges that appeared to be drawn with a higher writing resolution than that of the composing machine itself. This technique, known as dentation or 'half-bitting', was effective in rendering slow curves and dished terminals in a character shape (Figure 106).⁶

 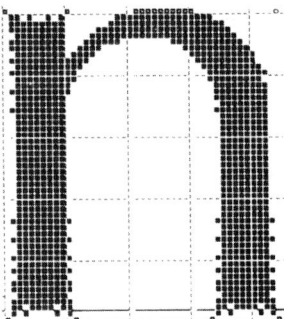

106 Left: a 10-pt character from Autologic Inc's Athena design, imitated from Hermann Zapf's Optima. Right: the pixel pattern that generated the image on the left. The pattern is 49 pixels high from the baseline to the top of the arch. From an Autologic type specimen book of around 1984.

Early digital-font technology was in many ways an ideal environment for type design. The designer had a choice of methods: to make large drawings and let the manufacturer derive fonts from them by scanning and scaling, or to specify the image data directly by making pixel

⁶The technique is described, in the context of 300-dpi laser-printer setting, by Richard Rubinstein in his *Digital typography* (1988), pp. 80–81.

diagrams. In the first case it was possible to correct the appearance of the typeset character images by modifying the image data after the scanning stage. In the second, the designer was in much the same position *vis-à-vis* the output character images as the hand punchcutter, but with the huge advantage that mistakes in their construction could easily be corrected. Designs for applications such as telephone directory or newspaper text composition could be optimized, even to the extent of adding or removing individual pixels, for the sizes in which they would be mostly used (Figure 107).

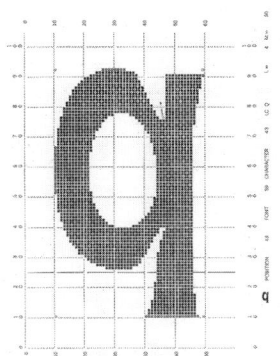 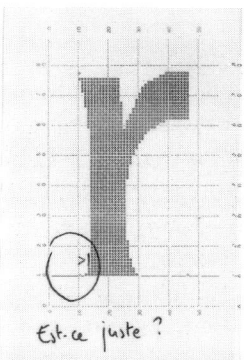

107 Corrections by Ladislas Mandel to Autologic image data for one of his Galfra family. In the upper crotch of q *a single pixel has been marked for deletion. To the lower left of* r *a column of five pixels is marked on a tracing-paper overlay with the query 'Is this correct?'. From material in the designer's collection; half actual size.*

The designer could be confident that pixel configurations defined for the base size of a font would be maintained over the whole range of sizes for which the font was intended, and could make allowances in the design for the changes in CRT spot size and writing resolution involved in going from one size to another within the range.

The relationship between fonts and typefaces in digital-font photocomposition is very much like that in hot-metal composition. In that technology punches had to be cut and matrices struck for each output image size, and because of the limited reduction range of the punchcutting pantograph several sets of patterns were needed to cover the whole range of sizes.[7] Equally, though, patterns derived from a single set of drawings could be used for every size, though at some cost in typographic quality.

In digital-font photocomposition a single font is normally usable over a size range of about 3:1; from 4 to 12 pt, for example, or from 12 to 36 pt. Because the font specifies output images explicitly in terms of their

---

[7] *cf.* Chapter 5.

pixel configurations it would be unwise to go outside this range at the high end, because of the deterioration in image quality that would result from writing a character image with too few pixels too far apart on the output material. It would also be difficult to use a font at less than its smallest recommended size, because the pixel separations in the image specification would be smaller than the machine could produce at its maximum writing resolution. Thus the need to use different fonts for different parts of the size range is an inherent feature of the technology, rather than being a matter of choice for the type manufacturer.

In these circumstances, the amount of effort that the optimization of a typeface's rendering at different parts of the machine's overall size range should absorb becomes a decision for the manufacturer; influenced, like all such decisions, both by economic factors and by deadlines. Technical factors present no obstacles, since the different fonts have to be made and corrected in any case. Economically the question may not be so simple. The complete controllability of the fontmaking process makes it very tempting to change 'just one more pixel' time after time, in search of a better rendering.

In digital and numerical font manufacture, as with other kinds of computerization, the hardware requirements of the process move away from purpose-built precision devices towards general-purpose digital computers supported by non-task-specific peripherals. For fontmaking these are digitizing tables, high-resolution visual displays and plotting devices. The complexity is now in the fontmaking software: vastly more elaborate than the mechanisms of a matrix-making camera, and just as difficult to build, but calling on different kinds of skill.

The information generated in the first stages of fontmaking can be organized in many different ways, depending on the design objectives of the composing machine in which a particular font is to be used.

A machine intended primarily for setting text sizes, for example, may use fonts that represent character outlines as relatively small numbers of straight-line segments. This makes scan conversion simple and consequently fast. Fonts like this, though, are unsuitable for large output image sizes, where, as Figure 103 suggests, the absence of curves in the image's edges becomes obtrusive. Not surprisingly, schemes for organizing numerical character shape specifications, *font formats*, have become progressively more complex as the computing power and high-speed data storage available to composing machine manufacturers for a given cost have increased.

One way of dealing with the variety of numerical font formats, both existing and anticipated, is to build a database of character outline specifications whose format is not specific to any particular composing machine, but from which different machine-specific formats can easily be derived. This so-called *device-independent* approach was pioneered in

Digital and numerical fonts 157

the Ikarus system, developed in the second half of the 1970s by URW in Hamburg.[8]

The input side of Ikarus uses large outline character drawings, similar to the pattern drawings used in mechanical punchcutting. Points on the outline are marked and their coordinates captured with a digitizing tablet and a magnifying cross-hair cursor. There are four categories of points: *start points* which begin a contour; *corner points* which mark sharp corners; *tangent points* at the ends of straight lines; and *curve points* which lie on curves. Curves are represented in the database as arcs of circles.

The accuracy of the data capture is checked by redrawing the character outline on a computer-driven plotter and comparing it with the original. A good deal of skill is needed to choose locations for curve points that will cause the original shape of the curve to be rendered correctly. The system lays great emphasis on precision:

> ...in hand-digitizing, a body size of about 15 cm is the easiest to work with and...a precision of at least ±0.03 mm must be attained. Thus [in the development of the system] we chose to achieve a technical resolution of ±0.01 mm, or 15 000 × 15 000 units per em square.[9]

Ikarus was originally developed to drive a drafting machine that cut masters for photographic matrix-making from 'Rubylith' two-layer laminated film.[10] In this role the system functioned as a translator, from a graphical mode of character shape specification to a numerical mode and back again. Work could not begin unless a character shape already existed to provide a source of data. Although corrections to the captured data could be made by editing the coordinates of points on a display terminal, the system in its original conception was not interactive: the operator could not see the results of changes to the data, either as they were made or immediately afterwards.

A more responsive system was developed by Bitstream Inc in Boston in the early 1980s. It used vector display terminals that had originally been produced by the Camex Corporation for the interactive makeup of newspaper advertisements (Figure 108).[11] Like Ikarus, input to the Bitstream system was from a digitizing tablet and cursor, with the same categories of start, corner, tangent and curve points. Unlike Ikarus, though, an outline could be displayed on the terminal as soon as enough data had been entered, so that the operator could see at once if there were mistakes in the numerical description that was being produced.

---

[8] The system is described in two books by Peter Karow, its progenitor: *Digital formats for typefaces* (1987) and *Font technology* (1994).

[9] *Font technology*, p. 98.

[10] The transfer-lettering manufacturers Letraset also used an Ikarus system to cut character masters in Rubylith (Paul Luna, personal communication).

[11] Bitstream's use of the Camex terminal is briefly described by Lynn Ruggles in *Letterform design systems* (1983).

The system could also display the outlines of other characters (H or O, for example) on either side of the character being worked on, so that the operator could position it correctly within its width.

108 *A Camex LetterIP input terminal, photographed at Bitstream Inc in 1983.*

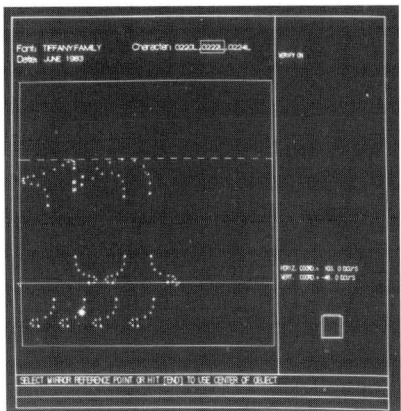
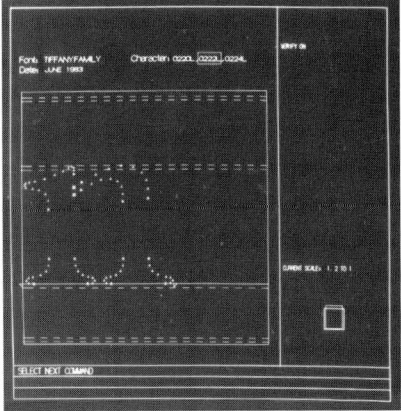

109 *Two stages in the construction of a Tiffany Roman* n *on the Camex LetterIP; from photographs by Wendy Richmond. In the first picture the operator has selected one of four identical instances of the group of points that defines a left-hand foot serif, prior to moving it into position. In the second the points defining the outline are all in place, with alignment references shown for the cap line, x-line, baseline and footline and their top and bottom overshoots.*

In both the Ikarus and the Bitstream systems, the numerical data the system collects is more than simply a description of an existing set of outlines. It is a set of specifications for character shapes. The distinction is clearer in the Bitstream system, where the criterion for the correctness of the captured data is whether it gives rise to a character shape on the display that the operator finds satisfactory. In the Ikarus system the data is correct when it exactly regenerates the character shape on the digitizing tablet. But the fact that Ikarus's outlines as well as Bitstream's are specifications rather than descriptions can be seen from what can be done with them.

Hamburgefonts
Hamburgefonts
Hamburgefonts
Hamburgefonts
Hamburgefonts

110 Variations on Letraset Aachen medium, automatically generated by the Ikarus system. From top to bottom: outline, inline, relief, drop-shadow and 'round'. Adapted from URW Typeworks Library *(1992).*

Figure 110 shows a group of variant designs, produced from a single set of numerical outline specifications by changing the rules by which the specifications are interpreted as the character shapes are drawn. 'Outline' draws a line of specified thickness round the inner edge of the character outline. 'Inline' fills the character shape and draws a white line inside it. 'Relief' and 'drop-shadow' draw round the outside of the character shape, with added rules about how the line round the shape is drawn and what to do when line and shape overlap. 'Round' reproduces sharp corners in the outline as arcs of circles.

Because they are mathematical abstractions, the outline specifications in a numerical font can themselves be transformed mathematically. This means that it is easy to produce condensed, expanded and slanted variants of a basic design. It is also possible to produce variants whose graphic characteristics lie along a range defined at two points by sets of data derived from drawings. This technique was first used commercially in 1977, in Matthew Carter's design for Linotype of his Galliard typeface family. Carter drew the medium and extrabold ('black') weights of the roman; the bold was interpolated between the two, and the ultrabold extrapolated from the extrabold. A similar approach was tried with the italic variants, although in the event Carter drew them himself.[12]

The development of satisfactory mathematical techniques for defining character shapes led, understandably enough, to the doctrine of the 'definitive outline' in font manufacture. As its name implies, this is the

---

[12] Matthew Carter, 'Galliard: a modern revival', *Journal of typographic research* vol. 19 no. 1 (1985), pp. 77–97.

notion that each character in a typeface needs only a single outline to specify its shape completely. The specification can be interpreted in different ways to provide data for different composing technologies, but its contents themselves do not need to be modified, either according to the particular technology envisaged or as a function of the size at which the character images derived from it are to be displayed. While the idea reflects common practice in direct-photography photocomposition, it ignores the precedents set in matrix manufacture for hot-metal composition as well as the traditions of hand punchcutting.[13] Economic and logistical factors, however, combined to make it the prevailing orthodoxy in computer-based font manufacture for CRT machines, and it was adopted uncritically by the developers of the composing technology that followed.

---

[13] Updike's remarks about the range of type sizes that could be cut pantographically from a single pattern were quoted in Chapter 3 above. They were clearly intended to serve as a criticism of the new technology rather than as an endorsement of it.

16 Laser imagesetters and the PostScript revolution

Lasers appeared at the beginning of the 1960s, drawing on the previous decade's developments in low-noise microwave amplification. The fundamental theoretical paper by Schawlow and Townes was published in 1958. It was followed in 1960 by Maiman's report of laser action in an optically pumped ruby crystal, and in 1961 by a paper from a group at Bell Telephone Laboratories announcing the continuous emission of visible laser light from a gas-discharge tube containing a mixture of helium and neon.[1] These papers, together with the underlying simplicity of the technology, prompted a huge surge of research and development work, to the extent that only three years later the *Scientific American* could publish a recipe for a home-built helium-neon laser.[2]

In the early 1960s, however, photocomposing-machine manufacturers had other preoccupations. It was not until 1972 that a laser was first used in photocomposition; and then simply to provide an extra-bright light source that enabled a Photon 560 disc-matrix machine to be adapted (as the Photon 561) to use dry-process photosensitive material. The first true laser photocomposing machines appeared in 1976. One, the Dymo DLC-1000, used a laser light source and electro-optical beam deflectors to emulate the repositionable raster patterns of a conventional CRT machine. The other, the Monophoto Lasercomp, was an imagesetter in the modern sense of the term.

The characteristic of an imagesetter that distinguishes it from earlier kinds of photocomposing machine is that its unit of output is an entire page rather than a single character. At the output end of the machine a spot of laser light, much brighter and sharper than the writing spot of a CRT composing machine, makes successive scans of a single line across the whole width of the output material. The material itself moves at right angles to the scanning direction of the light spot. This combination of horizontal scan and vertical movement generates a single raster pattern covering the whole area of the page. The laser runs continuously: the writing spot is switched by a modulator which deflects the laser beam away from the scanning optics to turn the spot off.

Depending on the particular components used, the modulator will have a maximum rate at which it can switch the laser spot, and the

---

[1] A Schawlow and C H Townes, *Physical review* vol. 112 (1958), pp. 1940–1949; T H Maiman, *Nature* vol. 187 (1960), pp. 493–494; A Javan, W R Bennett & D R Herriott, *Physical review letters* vol. 6 (1961), pp. 106–110. The early history is summarized by J H Sanders in D Fishlock (ed.), *A guide to the laser* (1967).

[2] C L Stong, 'How a persevering amateur can build a gas laser in the home', *Scientific American* vol. 211 no. 3 (1964), pp. 227–241.

output-material transport a minimum increment by which it can move the photosensitive film or (more often) paper. These two factors together give the imagesetter its *writing* or *output resolution*. The Lasercomp, for example, had an output resolution of 1000 dpi (dots per inch; 39.37 dots per mm) in both directions; horizontally corresponding to the scan velocity and the modulator switching speed, and vertically corresponding to the movement of the output material.

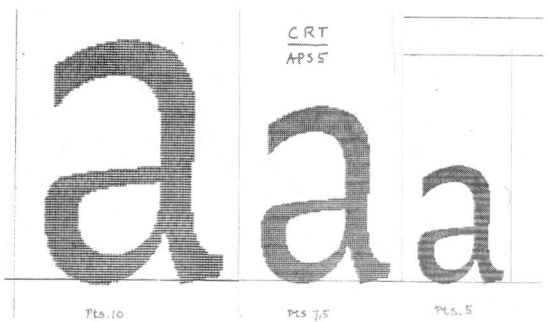

111 *Character images at three sizes, with an overall range of 2:1, derived from the same raster pattern by changing the output resolution. This and Figure 112 are taken from material in Ladislas Mandel's collection; one-third actual size.*

112 *Different raster patterns for a size range of 5.9:1 at constant output resolution. The ascender height of the largest character is 89 pixels, or 6.43 pt at 1000 dpi.*

Although both laser imagesetters and CRT photocomposing machines write images in a raster pattern with a moving spot of light, the fact that the imagesetter's raster covers a complete page at constant resolution means that a different approach has to be adopted to the problem of sizing character images on the output material. Within the size

Laser imagesetters and PostScript 163

range covered by a particular font, digital-font CRT machines change image size by changing the resolution at which the output raster pattern is written, without altering the number of elements it contains. Numerical-font CRT machines do not do this, and laser imagesetters cannot. Because the writing resolution is fixed, each output image size demands a raster pattern with a different number of elements. Figures 111 and 112 show Ladislas Mandel, beginning a design for the Lasercomp, exploring the consequences of this difference.

In fact it was only at the beginning of the technology that laser imagesetters used discrete bitmap fonts. A description of the Lasercomp published in January 1978 mentions that several prototypes were in field test at that time, and states that bitmap fonts in quarter-point increments of size from 4 to 256 Didot could be supplied by Monotype.[3] Writing in 1984, Lawrence Wallis suggests that it was also possible to rasterize outline fonts off-line in the machine's controlling computer during setup for particular jobs, with the results being stored as run-length encoded bitmaps on the computer's 80 Mb hard disk.[4]

The technology used in the Lasercomp had also been explored at the Xerox Palo Alto Research Center (Xerox PARC). A group at PARC headed by Gary Starkweather produced an experimental laser printer that was already in use in 1973.[5] The Dover printer followed in 1974. This combined a scanned-laser imaging system with the paper-handling mechanism of the 7000-series high-volume photocopier to produce a fast page printer with a resolution of 384 dots per inch. The Dover was extremely influential in the computer-science world, since Xerox donated machines to several universities including Stanford.

In 1977, the year after the Lasercomp was announced, Xerox introduced its 9700 Electronic Printing System. In a sense this was a commercial version of the Dover's approach: a large, fast, expensive printer for office and print-room applications, based on the mechanics of the 9200 high-volume copier and with a Digital Equipment PDP11/34 minicomputer controller instead of the Xerox Alto personal workstation the Dover used. Its resolution was 300 dots per inch in both directions, and its output speed two 8.5×11-inch pages per second.[6]

---

[3] *The Seybold report* vol. 7 no. 9 (1978), p. 24.

[4] 'Lasercomp cannot size type dynamically and Monotype International supplies the digital founts as individual masters for every size or as a single master for all sizes. In the latter case the generation of discretely sized characters occurs during the fount loading operation. Corollary of the last statement is that the machine must be dressed in anticipation of precise job requirements' (*Electronic typesetting*, p. 49).

[5] US Patent 4040096 of 1977. Starkweather's first patent application for a laser scanner using a rotating polygonal mirror was filed in November 1972.

[6] The 9700's imaging system is discussed by Starkweather in his contribution to *Laser applications* vol. 4 (1980). The printer would accept input on-line from

Machines like the Lasercomp or the 9700, that write a whole page of output as a single raster pattern, have no built-in obstacles to mixing graphic material with text, as long as their writing resolution is high enough to handle half-toned images adequately. Indeed this was a selling point in the 9700's market: the machine did not have to be kept supplied with stocks of preprinted forms. In this respect laser imagesetters are very different from earlier photocomposing devices, whose primary purpose was to produce assemblies of character images and which generally speaking had only the most rudimentary facilities for producing non-textual graphics.[7]

Equally, the problem of specifying whole-page output for an imagesetter is quite different from that of specifying the output from a conventional photocomposing machine. Control languages for the CRT machines of the 1970s followed the same paradigm as the Teletypesetter (TTS) code that had preceded them, seeing the output page as made up of sequences of character image rows, perhaps with changes of style or size from one row to another or within the row. Where non-textual graphic elements were called for, areas were reserved for them on the page; the graphics themselves were to be inserted in a separate operation, after the type on the page had been composed. Interactive page make-up terminals could be used to specify the sizes and relative positions of text and graphics, but the two were still handled separately at the typesetting stage.[8]

A system whose unit of output is a complete page, by contrast, needs a method of specifying page content that can handle text and graphics together. It also has to be capable of dealing on an equal basis with pictorial graphics and non-pictorial graphic elements – the rules, borders and ornaments of earlier technologies. The logic of whole-page output led Xerox and others towards the first developments in *page specification languages*, which could handle all the graphic elements, both textual and non-textual, that might appear on a page.[9] The development of

---

IBM System/360 and 370 computers, or off-line from 9-track magnetic tape in several formats. It rented for $5 300/month on a one-year lease, with an additional charge of 0.35 cents for each page printed.

[7] Some CRT machines could be coerced into producing pictorial images as assemblies of large specially-programmed character rasters.

[8] See *The world of digital typesetting* (1984), ch. 17.

[9] Page specification languages are normally referred to in the literature as *page description languages* (PDLs). This usage seems to me to reflect a confusion, not unknown in the computer-science world, between the ideal characteristics of an object and those of its real-world instantiations. The specification for a page to be produced can only be interpreted exactly, and thus constitute a description of the page, by an output device with ideal performance characteristics: infinite writing resolution, perfect linearity and so on. No such devices exist. That they may be more or less closely emulated by high-end laser imagesetters does not alter the essential point.

Laser imagesetters and PostScript 165

these languages led in turn to the development of the crucial element of laser imagesetters as they evolved at the turn of the 1980s: the *raster image processor* or RIP.

The output end of a laser imagesetter does not draw individual images of the characters or graphic elements it produces. All it can do is to produce patterns of dots and lines that cover the area of the output material. The RIP's function is to take the specification for the page to be produced, and interpret it into a sequence of instructions for the imagesetter's output end to follow. If a single RIP were programmed with the differing characteristics of different imagesetters, it could produce output for any of them from a single page specification. This is the notion of *device independence* in imagesetting: the specification of a page to be produced does not have to be adapted to take account of the special characteristics of any particular output device.[10] Thus, for example, corrections to a print job can be made from a marked-up proof produced on a low-resolution laser printer, and the job itself subsequently output on a high-resolution imagesetter, with the reasonable certainty that there will be no unintended changes in the makeup of its pages between proofing and output.

The first commercial system to realize these ideas more or less completely in the typesetting field seems to have been the SuperSetter of 1983, produced by the Camex Corporation. Aimed at the American newspaper market, this used a Camex-designed RIP (the 'BitCaster') to drive devices with three different output resolutions. Interactive page makeup was done on Camex Breeze raster-scan displays with a screen resolution of 1024×800 pixels. A 480-dpi laser printer made by Canon was used for proofing, and an imagesetter using the hardware of Monotype's Lasercomp for high-resolution output.[11]

The PostScript page specification language was launched by Adobe Systems Inc in 1984.[12] The company had been formed in 1982 by John Warnock and Charles Geschke. Both had come from PARC, where they had been involved in the development of Interpress, Xerox's specification language for its range of office laser printers.

PostScript was devised as a page specification language with a simple imaging model and a single formalism for describing the outlines of objects of all kinds on the page. The imaging model constructs the

---

[10] There is, though, an implicit assumption that all the devices to which the specification will be presented produce as their output whole-page images expressed as raster patterns, and do so in broadly similar ways.

[11] The SuperSetter system is described in *The world of digital typesetting*, ch. 23, and also by W J Solimeno in the *Seybold report on publishing systems* vol. 14 no. 12 (1985).

[12] Brian Reid, in a note written in March 1985 for the LaserLovers internet newsgroup, gives 15 March 1984 as the date on which the first PostScript language manual was shipped to a potential customer.

specifications for graphic objects on the output material as if they were made up of layers of opaque ink successively applied to a white page.[13] The outlines of objects are specified as sequences of straight lines and Bézier cubic splines; this makes scaling easy and scan conversion relatively straightforward. Outlines can be filled with solid colours, tints or patterns. Continuous-tone images are treated as arrays of pixels with specified intensities.

In the original conception of the language, text characters were treated in just the same way as other computationally defined graphic objects on the page that was being specified.[14] This approach had the great advantage that no special mechanisms were needed in the language to handle character shapes. As the first edition of the reference manual states:

> In the PostScript graphics model, text characters (in both standard and user-defined fonts) are treated as graphical shapes that may be operated on by any of the PostScript graphics operators.[15]

This had not been true of the bitmap fonts used by earlier page specification languages.[16]

Warnock and Geschke had originally intended to use PostScript as a graphics specification language for engineering workstations that Adobe would manufacture.[17] However, the company was approached by Apple Computer early in 1983 to develop a RIP for Apple's 300-dpi desktop laser printer, the LaserWriter (Figure 113).

Apple were working on their Macintosh personal computer, whose graphic interface commercialized ideas that had been originated by Xerox in the 1970s with the Alto machine. They had also reached an agreement with Canon Inc in Japan to develop a printer based on Canon's LBP-CX xerographic marking engine. The target price of this device was much less than that of its equivalents in the graphic-arts

---

[13] *cf.* J Warnock & D Wyatt, 'A device-independent graphics imaging model for use with raster-scan devices', *Computer Graphics* vol. 16 no. 3 (1982).

[14] Computationally defined objects, in this sense, have outlines that can be completely described by mathematically tractable functions. They are contrasted with *configurationally defined* objects, which can only be adequately described in terms of the actual configurations of the marks that instantiate them on a display surface. Character shapes in a PostScript page specification are computationally defined; the images on the printed page that result from the specification's interpretation are configurationally defined.

[15] *PostScript reference manual* (1985), p. 1. In the manual the word 'PostScript' is uniformly set in capitals and small capitals; I have transcribed it here in capitals and minuscules.

[16] In their 1982 paper Warnock and Wyatt had remarked that 'treating text characters like other graphic objects, and not as low level, device dependent primitives has been a big win'.

[17] Adobe's early history is summarized in Pamela Pfiffner's *Inside the publishing revolution* (2003).

Laser imagesetters and PostScript 167

industry;[18] Apple hoped to position it in the small-office market, which at the time was principally served by dot-matrix and daisy-wheel impact printers with little or no graphics capability.

113 Side view of the Apple LaserWriter (Apple Computer Inc). The machine was 41.5 cm (16.4 in) from front to back, excluding the paper trays, and 29.2 cm (11.5 in) high. It weighed 34.9 kg (77 lb).

The arrangement with Apple was financially very advantageous for Adobe, but it forced the company to tackle head-on the problems of rendering character shapes at low output resolutions.

In a sense, these problems are inherent in PostScript's view of the world. This is one in which page specifications are constructed in an ideal two-dimensional *user coordinate space*, and interpreted to instruct an output device to make marks in a particular non-ideal, resolution-limited *device coordinate space*. The principal advantage of this approach is device independence: a single specification can be presented to a number of different output devices, each of which (via its own PostScript interpreter) produces results which are as equivalent in terms of the size and disposition of the marks on the output material as the devices' differing performance characteristics allow them to be.

This state of affairs has become such a commonplace since the development of desktop publishing systems after 1985 that it is easy to lose

---

[18] The LaserWriter was originally priced at $6 995. The first Macintosh machine, with 128 kilobytes of main memory, cost $2 495. The Macintosh XL, with 512 kilobytes of memory and a 10-megabyte hard disk, cost $5 500 at its introduction. By contrast, the Breeze terminals in the Camex SuperSetter system, with four times as many pixels on their displays as the Macintosh and a graphics tablet for input, cost around $65 000 apiece. The 480-dpi BitPrinter was priced at $20 000 and the BitCaster RIP at $65 000. It is true that the SuperSetter system was not intended for the production of office documents.

sight of the conflict between the requirements of device independence and those of good character-image rendering. The appearance characteristics of easily readable character images remain the same, whatever the rendering technology: consistency of weight, size, alignment and spacing. In raster-scan devices, these characteristics translate directly into consistency of pixel dimensions between different images of the same character. However, the simple PostScript graphics model encounters two difficulties if it is used without modification to render character images in device coordinate spaces with output resolutions less than around 1000 dpi from character outlines specified in user coordinate space with no information added to them.

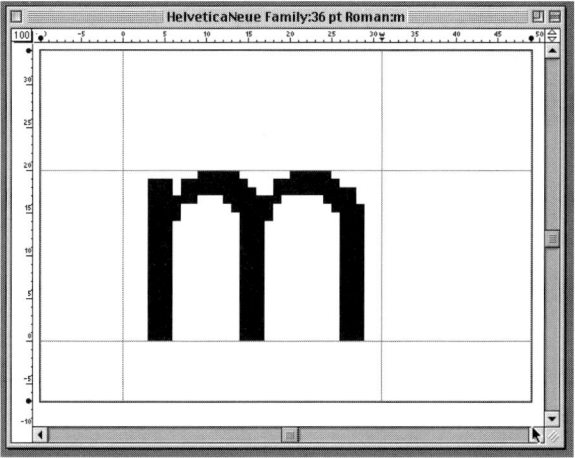

114 *The upright* m *of Adobe's Helvetica Neue family, rasterized with Letraset FontStudio to an x-height of 20 pixels. The first and second arches are respectively 8 and 9 pixels wide.*

One problem is that dimensions in the character outline itself may not map consistently into pixel dimensions in the character image. At 300 dpi, a 10-pt PostScript character has an em square of 42 pixels. If we take Jochen Schuchardt's typical value for the x-height of a present-day typeface as 46% of the em square, this yields x-heights for 10-pt characters of around 20 pixels.[19] The upright m of Adobe's Helvetica Neue family, rasterized to this size with no constraints applied, has arch widths that differ by one pixel (Figure 114).

The other, analogous problem is that character shapes that are consistently positioned in user coordinate space will not necessarily give rise to character images in device coordinate space that have the same consistency of positioning. For example, the nominal width of the i in Helvetica Neue is 222 PostScript units.[20] Three is side by side will have

---

[19] Schuchardt's results are discussed in Chapter 1. Adobe, following IBM, chose to define their version of the printer's point as exactly 1/72 inch.

[20] One unit of character width in PostScript is 1/1000 of the em square.

their left-hand reference points (the intersection of the left edge of the width and the baseline) with relative positions in user coordinate space of 0, 222 and 444 units. At 10 pt and 300 dpi, these positions round to 0, 9 and 19 pixels; so that the space between the second and third i in device coordinate space is one pixel more than that between the first and second. Errors of this size are easy to see, because of 'vernier acuity': the human visual system's remarkable ability to detect small differences in a repeating pattern.

What this means in practice is that a PostScript interpreter needs to handle character shape specifications somewhat differently from the specifications for other kinds of graphic object. There has to be some mechanism that controls the way in which character shape specifications are rendered at low resolution, so that dimensional consistencies within and between character shapes are maintained in the low-resolution images.[21]

In PostScript this mechanism has two parts. The first, known informally as 'the font machinery', is a component of every PostScript interpreter. It contains a procedure, Type 1 BuildChar, which acts on information from the second part of the mechanism: the 'hints' that are part of Adobe's Type 1 font format.

Type 1 is the format in which fonts manufactured by Adobe are distributed. At the time that PostScript was launched the details of the format were not made public, and significant parts of the information in Type 1 fonts were encrypted to protect them from copying or modification. However, Apple and the Microsoft Corporation announced in September 1989 that they would jointly develop fonts independently of Adobe, using a character shape specification language that had been under development at Apple since 1987.[22] Adobe responded in March 1990 by releasing descriptions of the Type 1 format and the encryptions it used, while keeping the details of the font machinery confidential.

Adobe's philosophy in the Type 1 font format has been to use *declarative hints* that express constraints on the size and positioning of character features.

> A declarative hint system depends on an intelligent rasterizing algorithm to render character outlines correctly ... the appearance of font characters created with declarative hints will continue to improve as hint handling algorithms improve, without modifying the Type 1 font programs.[23]

The hints in the Type 1 format are of two types. There are *font-level* hints that, for example, ensure that round and square characters such as

---

[21] 'In the PostScript language, characters have their own coordinate system distinct from the coordinate system used by a specific device.' *Adobe Type 1 font format* (1990), p. 25.
[22] This is the language that became known as TrueType. Its specifications were published in March 1991.
[23] *Adobe Type 1 font format*, p. 36.

O and H have the same calibre at low resolutions, and that the vertical and horizontal stems in different characters are rendered consistently. There are also *character-level* hints that deal with issues such as the consistency of stem and arch widths in small m. (In fact, since this particular requirement recurs in every roman font, it has its own hinting command.)

Adobe's approach to hinting – to do as well as one can, and allow rasterizing algorithms to improve – has the desirable consequence that fonts already in the marketplace do not have to be upgraded when a new version of the PostScript interpreter is released. It does mean, though, that new techniques for character-shape rendering that may be developed as a result of fontmaking experience cannot be applied retrospectively to existing fonts, and that their implementation in new fonts must be handleable by earlier versions of the interpreter. Examples of such techniques are 'hint replacement' for overlapping stemwidth hints, and the Flex mechanism for very shallow curves on vertical and horizontal edges.[24]

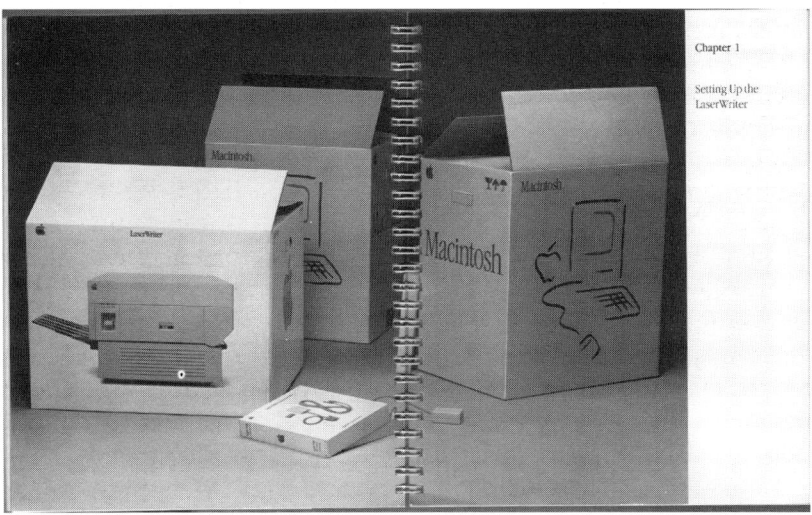

115 *Apple's vision for the LaserWriter, as a shared printer for local networks of Macintosh machines: from the 1985 owner's manual. An equivalent configuration would have been much more difficult and expensive to implement with other personal computers of the time.*

The LaserWriter was announced at Apple's stockholders' meeting on 23 January 1985, along with the low-cost AppleTalk network and the Macintosh XL computer.[25] With these, Apple and Adobe had produced

---

[24] *Adobe Type 1 font format*, ch. 8.

[25] The Macintosh XL was a rebadged Apple Lisa 2, which had been launched simultaneously with the Macintosh range in January 1984. The XL was discontinued in April 1985; Apple's 20 Mb external hard disk, which would work with the cheaper and more up-to-date Macintosh 512K, was introduced in the same year.

a combination of computer, page specification language and printer that was uniquely powerful in terms of its simple interface, its graphics capabilities and its ability to act as a front end to high-resolution imagesetters. However, there were few applications available at the time that could make full use of the potential the system offered. The idea of the Macintosh Office with which its marketing began stumbled over the unwillingness of office systems managers to abandon dot-matrix and daisywheel printers – which, after all, seemed at the time to be quite sufficiently fast and capable replacements for the typewriters and printing calculators around which the existing systems for office information management had evolved.

The situation was different, however, with Aldus Pagemaker, a program written specifically for the Macintosh that allowed the easy integration of text and graphics on a page. Pre-production versions of the program had been available at the time of the LaserWriter's announcement; it went on sale to the public in July 1985.[26] Pagemaker's output was text files in the PostScript language, that the LaserWriter could interpret and that could also be sent to a PostScript-equipped imagesetter for output at high resolution. With PostScript as their means of intercommunication, Macintosh, LaserWriter and Pagemaker together allowed fully made-up pages carrying both type and illustrations to be specified 'from the desktop' for the first time.

Although it was not the only page specification language that existed in 1984, PostScript was revolutionary because of the circumstances in which it appeared. The laser imagesetters of the period offered all the advantages of high-resolution full-page composition, but the front-end equipment needed to make full use of them was very expensive. There was no straightforward way of exchanging document specifications between one manufacturer's system and another's.[27] Although the mechanisms of PostScript's interpreter remained proprietary, the language itself was in the public domain from the moment of its introduction, and offered almost for the first time an effective solution to this problem. PostScript also provided much more comprehensive ways of dealing with continuous-tone images and colour than anything else available at the time.

---

[26] Jonathan Seybold's early assessment of the combination of Macintosh, LaserWriter and Pagemaker is in *The Seybold report on publishing systems* vol. 14 no. 9 (1985). The report is headlined 'An imagesetter for the rest of us'.

[27] TeX, written by D E Knuth at Stanford University and discussed in Chapter 18 below, had provided an interchange system for mathematical documents since 1978; but its typographical peculiarities made it unsuitable for general use in the graphic-arts market. Standard Generalized Markup Language (SGML), which was published as a draft international standard in October 1985, was a means of interchanging the content structure of documents rather than their graphic structure.

The accessibility of the language's interpreter on the LaserWriter's controller board was another revolutionary feature. It was not hard to establish two-way communication between a computer and the controller via the printer's serial port. A user could then send statements in the PostScript language to the interpreter, which would execute them if they were correct or return an error message if not. While this is not a feature that most graphic designers would find useful, it allowed programmers to establish a relationship with the language that was much closer than anything that could be achieved with other page specification languages of the time. This matched Apple's marketing strategy for the Macintosh, which sought to position it as the computer of choice for individual and individualistic users: 'If you can point, you can use a Macintosh'.[28]

---

[28] The celebrated television commercial of January 1984, in which a hammer-carrying woman runs between ranks of grey anonymous figures in a huge hall and smashes the screen from which their leader is praising the new Information Purification Directives, was another part of the same strategy. Informed viewers would have had no difficulty in recognizing the allusion to IBM and its efforts to make its own personal computer the industry standard.

17 The Stone typeface family

If the alliance with Apple obliged Adobe to confront the problems of character image rendering at low resolutions, it also brought into sharp focus the question of how the typefaces that PostScript-capable printers might use should be provided. This was the same question that had arisen, fifteen or so years earlier and in the context of a quite different technology, with the rush of small companies into photocomposing machine manufacture after 1965.[1] Adobe's approach was in marked contrast to the one that had prevailed at that time. Instead of copying existing designs without authorization, the company negotiated in good faith with established type manufacturers from the beginning.

A licensing agreement with Linotype was concluded in August 1984. This gave access to the large and well-respected range of designs in the Linotype library. Agreements with Bitstream and the International Typeface Corporation (ITC) followed, broadening the potential appeal of PostScript to the advertisement-typesetting market.[2] The company's founders, though, understood the boost to its standing in the graphic-arts world as a whole that a programme of original typeface design would provide.

Sumner Stone came to Adobe Systems as director of typography in the late summer of 1984. He had been working at Camex in Boston and before that at Autologic, where he was director of typographic development from 1979 to 1983. Part of his agreement with Adobe was that he should be able to produce original designs as well as overseeing the adaptation to PostScript of existing ones.

Soon after his arrival he began work on the design of a new typeface family in which he proposed to add an 'informal' to the more usual roman, italic and sanserif variants. His motivation for doing this was an understanding that

> ...as laser printing technology became more commonplace, there would be an increasing need for typefaces suited to personal communications generated by computer.[3]

Stone began the design of the family in a conventional way, by drawing variants of key letters in outline form on tracing paper or film.[4]

---

[1] See Chapter 13 above.

[2] Initially the agreement with Linotype covered only low and medium resolution output, while those with Bitsream and ITC were for all resolutions: *The Seybold report on publishing systems* vol. 14 no. 9 (1985), p. 10.

[3] 'The Stone family of typefaces: new voices for the electronic age', *Fine print* vol. 14 no. 3 (1988), pp. 123–126.

[4] Material from the design of the Stone typeface family is in the Houghton Library of Harvard College Library.

At the time the work was begun, the tools available at Adobe for the conversion of drawn outlines to numerical specifications were quite unlike the on-screen type-drawing packages such as FontStudio and Fontographer that made their appearance later in the decade. In a note to the author, Stone describes the method he used at the beginning of the project:

> I digitized many small increments on pencil outlines of about 6 in cap height and we started with vectors [*i.e.* straight-line segments joining the digitized points]. I got Bill Paxton [one of the computer scientists on Adobe's staff] to write a little routine that would turn the vectors into béziers and that's how I started.[5]

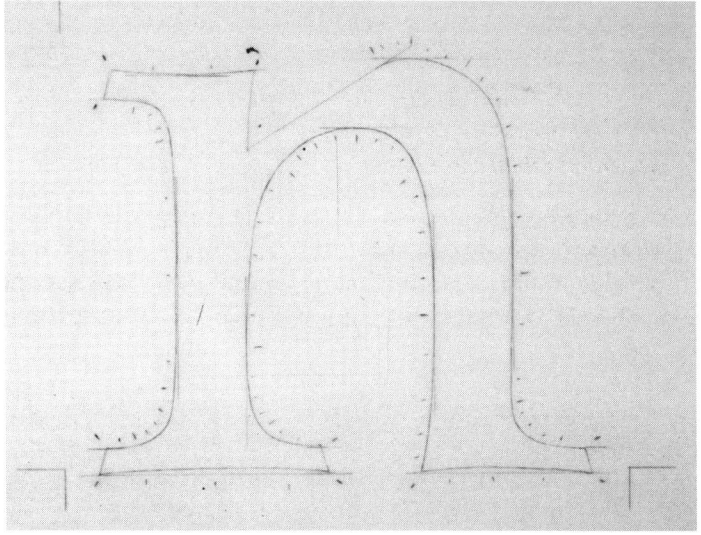

116 An early version of the informal minuscule n *[TypTS 970.88.462 (62) F, Department of Printing and Graphic Arts, Houghton Library, Harvard College Library]. Half actual size.*

Figure 116 shows one of these early drawings, marked up ready for data capture. The character shape is drawn in pencil on tracing paper, with guide points marked outside the outline. Using the cross-hairs on the digitizing cursor, it would not be hard to select points on the outline itself that corresponded to the position of each guide point. The heavier marks on either side of the verticals, denoting points where the contour runs vertically or horizontally, are red in the original, and the marks at the corners of the serifs are green.

Once converted to PostScript, character outlines could be filled and printed as solid shapes in a range of sizes, together with reference lines for widths and alignments. As Stone says,

> After digitizing, editing, and in some cases, redrawing on the computer,

---

[5] Personal communication, October 2003. Bézier cubic splines are the formalism that PostScript uses to specify curves.

some of the roman letters (along with guidelines) were printed on the laser printer. These proofs were then used as drawing paper for the italic, so that sketches of the the italic forms could be made next to the roman type.[6]

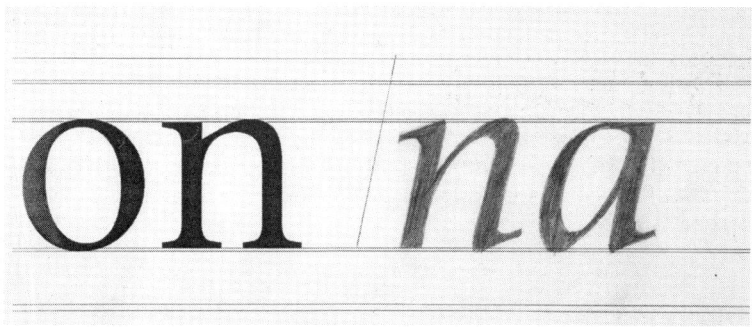

117 *Developing italic characters by drawing within the reference lines of the roman [TypTS 970.88.462 (68) F, Department of Printing and Graphic Arts, Houghton Library, Harvard College Library]. 20% actual size.*

The process is illustrated in Figure 117. A similar combination of printing and drawing was used to develop terminal shapes for roman f and r, with the modified shapes drawn on tracing paper laid over large laser-printer proofs with stem widths of 14 mm and an x-height of approximately 84 mm.

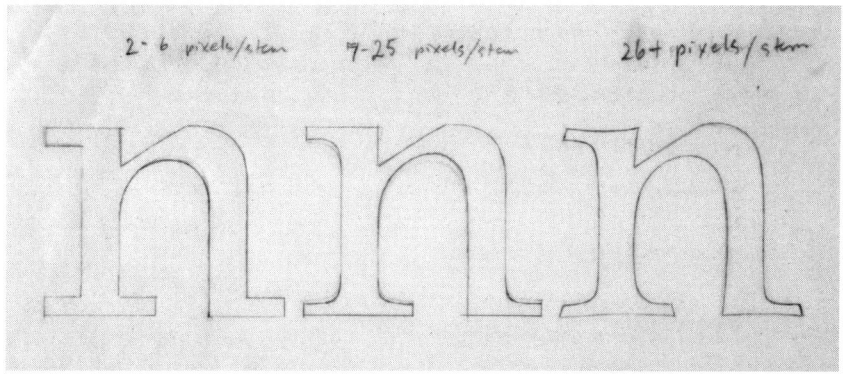

118 *'The very first drawings' for the Stone family [TypTS 970.88.462 (60) F, Department of Printing and Graphic Arts, Houghton Library, Harvard College Library]. 80% actual size.*

It is clear from the material in the Houghton Library that Stone was thinking about the problems of rasterization from a very early stage in the project. Indeed it was necessary for him to do so, since the Adobe font packages of the time contained a 'suitcase' of bitmapped screen-fonts, made for a resolution of 72 dots per inch, as well as PostScript specifications for the character shapes.

---

[6] 'The Stone family of typefaces', p. 125.

'The very first drawings were done on graph paper with the lc n at two pixels per vertical stem.'[7] This description corresponds to the drawing of three ns shown in Figure 118, where the widths of the stems are 0.25 in (6.35 mm) and the heights of the arches 1.25 in (31.75 mm). Thus the arches are five stem-widths high, in line with generally-accepted calligraphic practice. The notes above the characters read '2–6 pixels/stem 7–25 pixels/stem 26+ pixels/stem'. These ranges would be appropriate for normal text sizes on devices with resolutions of 72, 300 and around 1270 dots per inch (dpi).[8] 'The two numbers that were of paramount importance at that time were 72 dpi and 300 dpi.'[9]

Stone went on to make finished drawings of characters from the serif, sanserif and informal styles to the same small scale as his earliest drawings for the project. His policy with regard to stem widths was the same that Frutiger had adopted with the Univers family: to make the variant widths of a given weight have the same stem width, even though this meant that the visual weights of the variants differed from one another when they were seen *en masse*.[10] 'I thought that the consistent vertical stroke weight would provide a kind of visual anchor in the low res[olution] environment.'[11]

He followed up these small drawings with another series, which in effect are the first production drawings for the family. They are made to a stem width of 0.7 in (17 mm) and an x-height of approximately 3.35 in (85 mm). An italic variant (Figure 119) has been added to the upright roman, sanserif and informal of the earlier series. These drawings are on matt polyester film, with marks on an overlay of clear film that serve as guides to the locations of points on the outline for data capture. The serif and sanserif variants have drawings for A a B b E e G g H M N n o R r S v, the informal A B b E e G g H N n R S v and the italic a e g n o v. The serif has two and the sanserif three versions of g, with different bowl treatments and descender lengths; one of the sanserif gs, like both the seriffed ones, is two-storied. The data from this series of drawings served as the basis for the development of the computer-drawn designs that made up the complete family.

The drawings of the serif, sanserif and informal (the last described as 'Stone Relaxed' on the laser-printed proofs) were digitized between 7 and 20 March 1985.

---

[7] Personal communication, October 2003. The drawings in Figure 118 were probably made over, rather than on, graph paper with a 1/8-in square. A few sketches, but no finished drawings, in the Houghton collection are made on the graph paper itself.
[8] At 72 dpi the arch heights would be between 10 and 30 pt, at 300 dpi between 8.4 and 30 pt and at 1270 dpi 7.4 pt or more.
[9] Personal communication, October 2003.
[10] *cf.* Figure 77 in Chapter 10.
[11] Personal communication, October 2003.

The Stone typeface family

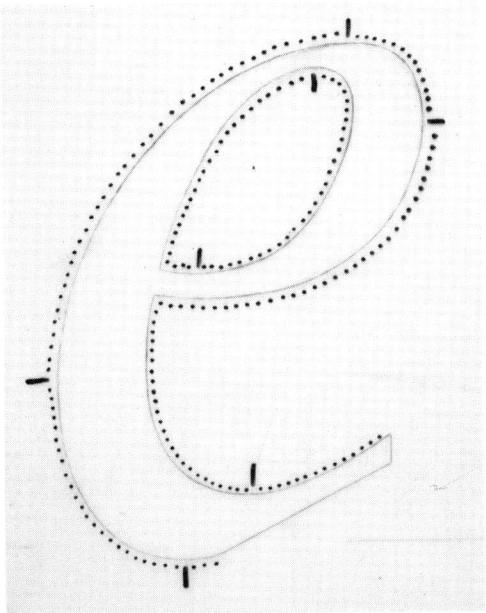

119 A finished drawing of the italic e, with guide marks for numerical data capture [TypTS 970.88.462 (248) F, Department of Printing and Graphic Arts, Houghton Library, Harvard College Library]. Approximately 80% actual size.

The first proof for each character was made from the raw data captured from the drawings, with the locations of the numerous points on the outline that had been indicated by guide marks on the drawing overlay shown on the proof by tick marks (Figure 120). The points marked g on the proof are corner points, where the direction of the outline changes abruptly; those marked r are points where it runs vertically or horizontally. At this stage the outline is constructed by joining the points with straight lines (Figure 121).

The next stage in making PostScript specifications for the character shapes was to reduce the mass of data represented by these points, with the objective of specifying Bézier cubic splines that would reproduce the outlines on which the points lay. This was the function for which Stone had had a routine written at the beginning of the project. Proofs made from the reduced data show the positions of the points or 'knots' on the outlines that denote the end-points of successive Bézier splines, as well as the locations, usually away from the outline, of the pairs of control points for each spline (Figures 122 and 123).

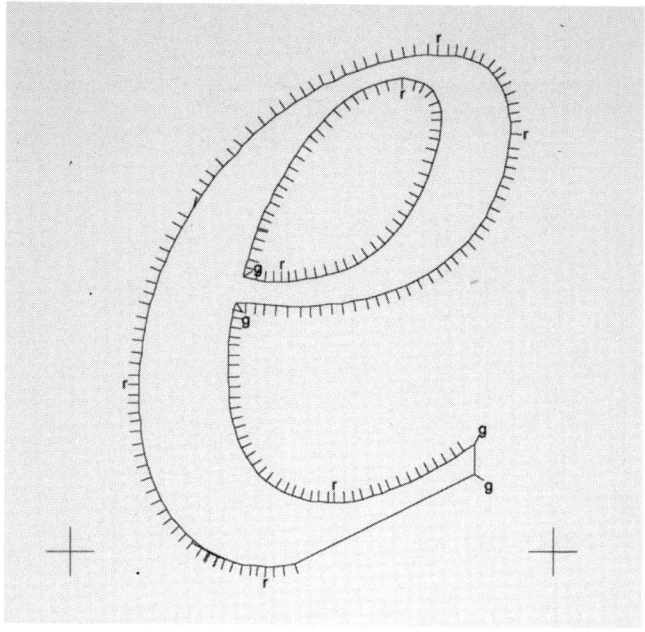

120 A proof of the italic e *in 'raw' format [TypTS 970.88.462 (256) F, Department of Printing and Graphic Arts, Houghton Library, Harvard College Library]. 76% actual size.*

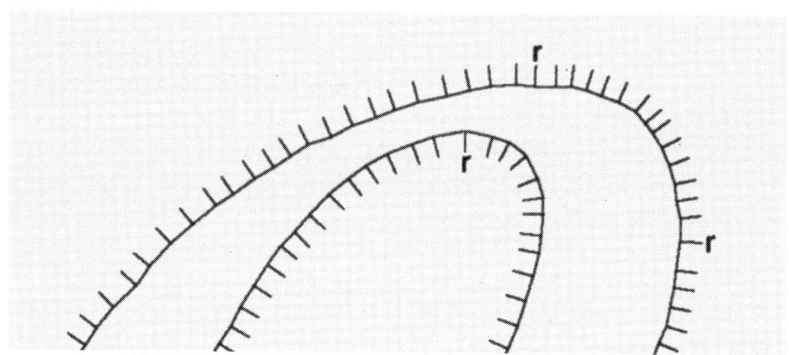

121 The upper part of Figure 120 in close-up. 150% actual size.

On the earliest of these proofs, produced on 10 March 1985, the data format is described as 'fitknots'. On the proof of roman b some of the points on the outline are ringed, with a pencilled note in the designer's hand:

> The circled "c's" are knots that the curve fitter threw in.
> Still have curves representing straight lines.
> Having fewer knot points doesn't really seem to make a difference.

On later proofs made from reduced data, such as that shown in Figures 122 and 123, the data format is described as 'bez' and there are no adverse comments.

The Stone typeface family

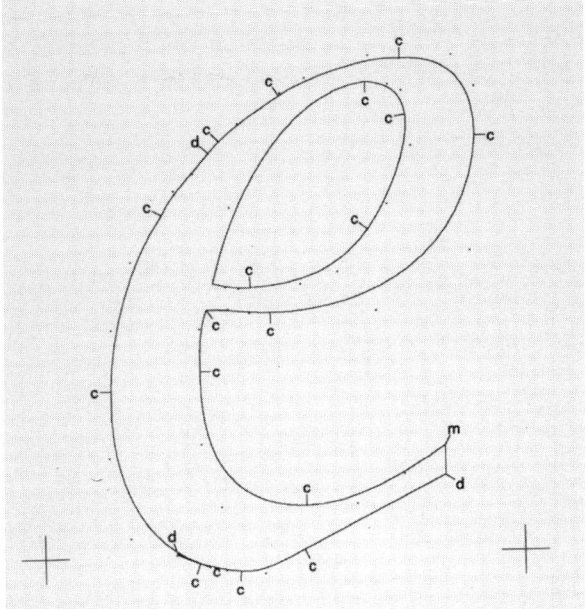

122 *A proof of the italic* e *in 'bez' format [TypTS 970.88.462 (255) F, Department of Printing and Graphic Arts, Houghton Library, Harvard College Library]. 76% actual size.*

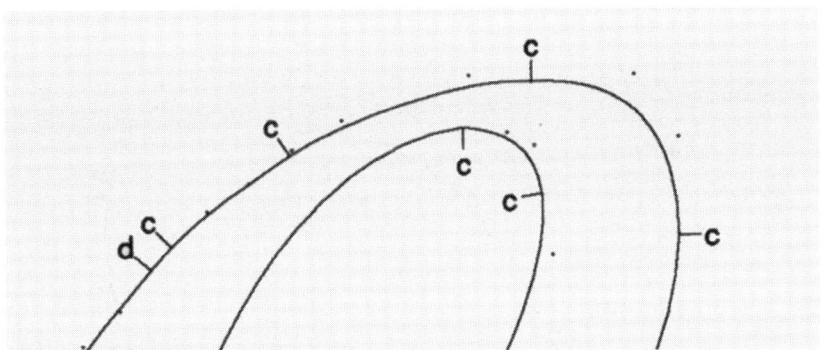

123 *The upper part of Figure 122 in close-up. 150% actual size.*

In Figures 122 and 123, the points marked c are the end-points of successive Bézier splines; the dots between them show the locations of the control points for each spline segment. The points marked d are the end-points of 'drawto' segments, which are straight lines appended to spline segments. The spline below the d mark in Figure 123 has a point of inflection: one of its control points is just inside the character outline, rather than on or outside it like the others in the illustration.

Of the proofs of type in the Houghton Library's collection, most are undated. The earliest dated proof is of the informal variant. It is one of a set of three showing incomplete alphabets of the serif, sanserif and informal variants, in a range of five sizes with capital-letter heights from 3.2 to 16.8 mm. The proof of the informal is dated 4-17-85 [17 April 1985], with a note 'Changes made 4/29/85'. A proof of the serif, with a slightly different text in the same range of sizes, is dated 5-8-85 [8 May 1985].

> VERBSGOHUMAN
> verbsgohuman
> *VERBSGOHUMAN*
> *verbsgohuman*
> VERBSGOHUMAN
> verbsgohuman
> *VERBSGOHUMAN*
> *verbsgohuman*
> VERBSGOHUMAN
> verbsgohuman
> *VERBSGOHUMAN*
> *verbsgohuman*

124 An early proof of six styles from the Stone family [TypTS 970.88.462 (302) F, Department of Printing and Graphic Arts, Houghton Library, Harvard College Library]. Half actual size.

The drawings of the italic were digitized on 30 and 31 July 1985. In his article in *Fine print*, Stone says that 'Most of the design work . . . was done by drawing with a computer'.[12] The next dated proofs in the Houghton collection, marked 'Oct '85', are evidence of this. Two show the serif and sanserif variants in a progression of weights; the other, upright and italic or oblique versions of serif, sanserif and informal (Figure 124). All of the oblique sanserif and informal characters in this illustration, as well as all the italic capitals and italic minuscule b h m r s, will have been generated by drawing on the computer.

---

[12] 'The Stone family of typefaces', p. 125.

Each style on the proof in Figure 124 carries one or more pencilled notes by the designer. In the roman, for example, capital B is marked 'narrower' and capital U M 'wider'. The corresponding characters in the upright sanserif are marked 'as serif'. Terminal serifs in capital E S in the upright informal are marked 'Smaller', and the note to the right reads 'Try again with one-sided serifs (for lower case)'. The oblique informal is marked 'as above'. The implication carried by these notes points up the fundamental difference between the interactive display-based technique that Stone used in developing his design and the drawing-based approach used in earlier techniques of numerical contour capture such as the Ikarus system.

In producing a numerical character shape specification, Ikarus demands a finished drawing as its starting-point. The system will indeed list the coordinates of points on an outline in a form that allows them to be changed interactively, but this facility is intended simply as a means of correcting errors in the description of the shape whose definition is embodied in the drawing. It cannot realistically be used to specify shapes that have not yet been realized in graphic form. In the display-based technique, on the other hand, the shape the designer sees is almost infinitely mutable. As Stone remarks,

> The points defining the spline outline can be pulled and pushed by the designer in a fashion that seems more like sculpture than drawing; this creates new shapes, or subtly modifies the existing shape. It is possible to use a letterform as raw material for creating another form.[13]

This mutability means that one style can grow out of another: 'all the bold characters were created from the medium characters'.[14] Equally, though, it allows the designer to postpone the moment of commitment to a particular version of a character shape to later and later stages in the development of a design.

In the strict technical sense, this was also true of earlier techniques. The multiple and complex procedures of matrix manufacture for hot-metal composition presented no absolute bar to the repeated revision of character shape specifications. The development of Times New Roman illustrates the point;[15] though designs for less illustrious clients, with sponsors less influential than Stanley Morison, might not have fared so well. The programs that generated the character images in Figure 124 will work with any technically valid configuration of Bézier splines;[16]

---

[13] 'The Stone family of typefaces', p. 125.

[14] *ibid*. The illustration on the same page shows how points on the outline of small b were moved in successive stages to go from one weight to the other.

[15] As Walter Tracy says, 'The number of recut punches [in the production of the typeface] was 1,075, a figure often mentioned, presumably as evidence of the earnestness that went into the work, though it is also evidence of an inability to make effective decisions at the drawing stage': *Letters of credit* (1986), p. 202.

[16] Invalid spline configurations are those in which the contour enclosing a shape crosses itself, so that the inside of the enclosed shape switches from one side of

and, unlike the hardware-based techniques of matrix manufacture, there are no cumulative costs associated with their repeated use. The only resource that gets used up is time. On the other hand, though, each iteration of the development cycle needs much less time than it did in the earlier technology:

> For the first time since the punchcutter used smoke proofs it is possible to get an almost immediate proof of your letterforms. In fact, these proofs are in some ways better than smoke proofs since they are the actual finished product created by the same machine(s) that will generate the type when the design is finished.[17]

Drawings of numerals 2 3 5 for the serif variant of the Stone family were digitized on 7 December 1985. A proof of complete alphabets of the serif and sanserif variants, in medium and bold weights, is dated 2/21/86 [21 February 1986]; a weight progression of the serif variant, marked 'Book. Bold. Black. Heavy' at a capital-letter height of 8.8 mm, is dated 3/3/86 [3 March 1986]. The last dated proof in the Houghton collection is of the italic at the same capital-letter height, marked 'Critique 4/24/86 [24 April 1986]'.

Copies of Adobe's original font packages in the designer's collection are dated October 1987.[18] The family's first public appearance seems to have been in March 1988, in Adobe's *Colophon* newsletter. The ITC version was announced in November of the same year.

---

the contour to the other: see *The Metafontbook* (1986), p. 228.
[17] 'The Stone family of typefaces', p. 126.
[18] Personal communication from Sumner Stone, March 2004.

Part 4: Making type with programs

18 Computer science and typography

Donald Ervin Knuth was born in Milwaukee, Wisconsin in 1938. After postgraduate work at the California Institute of Technology he came to Stanford University in 1968 as Professor of Computer Science. *Fundamental algorithms*, the first volume of his planned seven-volume series *The art of computer programming*, was published by Addison-Wesley in the same year. The second and third titles in the series, *Seminumerical algorithms* and *Sorting and searching*, followed in 1969 and 1973.

These volumes had been printed by offset lithography from reproduction proofs composed on Monotype equipment. Knuth had prepared a second, extensively revised edition of *Seminumerical algorithms* which was to be published in 1976. By this time Addison-Wesley had abandoned Monotype composition because of its cost, and trial settings for the new edition were made with direct-photography photocomposition. Knuth was very disappointed with their appearance.

On 7 February 1977, however, while examining proofs of a new book that had been proposed for his department's courses, he became aware of the technology of high-resolution digital photocomposition.[1] In his own words (written in 1996),

> Metallurgy and hot lead have always been complete mysteries to me; neither have I understood lenses or mechanical alignment devices. But letters made of little dots – that's computer science! That's just bits, binary digits, 0s and 1s! Put a 1 where you want ink, put a 0 where you don't want ink, and you can print a page of a book!
>
> ... the problem of printing books had changed from a problem of metallurgy to a problem of optics and then to a problem of computer science. The fact that Gutenberg had made books from movable metal type was suddenly only a 500-year-long footnote to history. The new machines have made the old mechanical approaches essentially irrelevant: The future of typography depends on the people who know the most about creating patterns of 0s and 1s; it depends on mathematicians and computer scientists.[2]

Knuth's diary entry for 30 March 1977 reads, in part,

> Galley proofs for vol. 2 [*i.e.* the new edition of *Seminumerical algorithms*] finally arrive, they look typographically awful ... I decide I have to solve the problem myself.[3]

The month of April was taken up with other work, but on 4 May Knuth

---
[1] The book was P H Winston's *Artificial intelligence* (1977). Knuth's account of the incident is in Chapter 24 of *Digital typography* (1999), a collection of his lectures and publications on computer-aided page formatting and type design published by the Center for the Study of Language and Information at Stanford.

[2] *Digital typography*, pp. 6–7.

[3] *Ibid.*, p. 482. Knuth reproduces many passages from his diary in Chapters 24 and 25.

'Went through first 30 galleys until Belfast typesetting system [the system that had produced the new proofs] understood', and the next day 'Read about Bell Labs typesetting system / Major design of TeX started.' TeX was Knuth's name for his proposed page-formatting language.[4]

The draft report that Knuth wrote on 12–13 May 1977, as he says 'mostly as a memo to myself' to clarify his ideas about the language whose structure he was forming in his mind, already mentions its fundamental concepts of 'boxes' and 'glue'.

> The main idea is to consider the process as an operation on two-dimensional "boxes"; roughly speaking, the input is a long string of characters culled from a variety of fonts, where each character may be thought of as occupying a small rectangular box, and the output is obtained by gluing these boxes together either horizontally or vertically... Furthermore, TEX has another important basic concept of elastic glue between boxes, a type of mortar that stretches and shrinks at different specified rates so that box patterns will fit together in flexible ways.[5]

During the weekend of 14–15 May Knuth went with his wife on a tour organized by the Associates of the Stanford University Libraries. They saw work from Aldus's press and a page from a Gutenberg bible at the offices of the Sacramento *Bee*, and also visited a large private library specializing in Californian history. Here Knuth found Goudy's *Typologia* (1940), which he borrowed from the Stanford library on his return. This in turn led him to discover the library's Gunst collection of books on the history of typography and printing.[6]

Knuth's diary entry for 18 May records that he 'took slides of 20 pp from vols 1 & 2': Addison-Wesley had sent him copies of the reproduction proofs from which the first editions of *Fundamental algorithms* and *Seminumerical algorithms* had been printed. In his paper 'Lessons learned from Metafont'[7] Knuth describes how he hit on the fundamental concepts of the character shape specification language that he called Metafont while he was projecting the images from these slides

> ...about 8 meters onto a wall in my house where I could make pencil sketches of somewhat blurry images about 5 cm high.

> The three p's of Metafont – drawing with *pens* and *parameters*, via *programs* – popped into my mind within an hour or so after I started to make those sketches. It suddenly dawned on me that I should not simply try to copy the shapes. A human being had originally drawn them, so I really wanted to learn as much as possible about what was in that person's mind at the time, and I wanted to incorporate that knowledge into a computer program.

---

[4] Knuth normally sets the word as T_EX, or TEX in reproductions of computer files. I use TeX and TEX instead of T_EX and TEX.
[5] *Digital typography*, p. 483.
[6] Personal communication from Prof Knuth, August 2003.
[7] *Visible language* vol. 19 (1985), pp. 35–53; reprinted as Chapter 16 of *Digital typography*.

The first part of the diary entry for 19 May reads 'Using slides, found out how the lower case works', and on the following day '... at 5 a.m. had rough drafts of l.c. and u.c. Roman and italics and digits 0-9'.[8]

Thus in just over two weeks, between 4 and 20 May 1977, Knuth had formulated the underlying concepts not only of a page-formatting language that would subsequently be used to produce many thousands of scientific and mathematical papers (and this book) but also of a character shape specification language that worked on principles that were quite different to any others in use at the time; and he had used the latter to produce at least a first version of the latin alphabet in two styles of type.

Knuth's account makes it clear that he approached his new project with a definite objective in mind. He needed a technique that, in the short term, would allow him to replace the unsatisfactory typesetting in the new edition of *Seminumerical algorithms*, and in the longer term would allow him to complete the remaining volumes of his projected series in the same style. His typographical reading, drawing as it did on collections dealing with the history of the book, biased him towards metal-type composition – hand composition, indeed, rather than the Monotype system by which the first editions of his first two volumes had been composed – as the model he proposed to emulate. This is clear from a passage in *The TeXbook*, the user manual for the published version of his page-formatting software:

> Let's take a look at what TeX does behind the scenes, by comparing the computer's methods with what you would do if you were setting metal type by hand. In the time-tested traditional method, you choose the letters that you need out of a type case – the uppercase letters are in the upper case – and you put them into a "composing stick"... This isn't much different to what TeX does, except that different words are used; when TeX locks up a line, it creates what is called an "hbox" (horizontal box) because the components of the line are pieced together horizontally.[9]

The character-sized rectangular boxes that Knuth already describes in his report of 12-13 May 1977 are exact two-dimensional analogues for the face of three-dimensional metal types. Equally, justifying a line by expanding or contracting the notional elastic glue between words is a close analogy to the process by which the same operation is performed in the Monotype system, which itself is a mechanical reimplementation of the compositor's actions in straightforward justification.

The method that Knuth chose to define character shapes and produce image specifications from them, on the other hand, was quite unlike anything that had previously been used in type manufacture. It is perhaps surprising, given that Goudy in *Typologia* describes in some detail the procedures he used for pattern-cutting and matrix engraving,

---

[8] *Digital typography*, p. 503.
[9] *The TeXbook* (1984), p. 64.

that Knuth's first approach to the problem of character shape specification was not based on the mathematical description of outlines.[10] His diary entry for 17 May 1977, the day before he photographed the reproduction proofs of pages from his first two volumes, mentions an unsuccessful attempt to replace cubic splines by piecewise quadratics; but it is not clear whether at that stage of his explorations he was seeking to specify outlines or pen tracks. However, by the time he delivered the Josiah Willard Gibbs Lecture in January 1978 he was fully committed to the use of parameterized virtual pens for drawing character shapes.[11]

In the lecture Knuth makes it clear that he was concerned to find a technique for character shape specification that would not be overtaken by changes in composing technology.

> One of the most important factors in my motivation was that the problem would be solved once and for all, if I could find a purely mathematical way to define the letter shapes and to construct the corresponding raster patterns... any new [composing] machines are almost certain to be based on a high precision raster; and although the precision of the raster may change, the letter shapes can stay the same forever, once they are defined in a machine-independent form.

From this point of view, correct raster patterns are the primary objective. Knuth's experiments with the direct rasterization of character images using television cameras had been unsuccessful,[12] and in any event the technique would not have met his requirements for resolution independence. Given the quality of the enlarged photographic images that he was able to produce from the proofs supplied by Addison-Wesley, it is understandable that his mind turned towards a method of character shape specification based on the notion of an underlying form that was common to different character styles.

This notion seems to have come from his brief but intensive reading of typographic history. (Only eight months had elapsed between Knuth's decision to tackle the problem of improving the appearance of his books himself and his delivery of the Gibbs lecture, and for much of that time he had been working on his TeX page-formatting language.) In the lecture, after a mathematical discussion of what he describes as pleasing curves, Knuth describes his approach to constructing specifications for the digits 0–9.

> Most of these digits are drawn by using another idea taken from the history of typography, namely to imitate the calligrapher who uses pen and ink...
>
> Notice that instead of describing the boundary of the character as the Renaissance geometers did, my Metafont system describes the curve

---

[10] His second approach, in the version of Metafont released in 1986 and discussed below, did make use of outlines.

[11] *Bulletin (new series) of the American Mathematical Society* vol.1 no.2 (1979), pp.337–372. The lecture is reprinted in *TeX and METAFONT: new directions in typesetting* (1979) and as Chapter 2 of *Digital typography*.

[12] *Digital typography*, pp. 8, 319.

traveled by the *center* of the *pen*[13] and the pen's shape is allowed to vary as the pen moves. The main advantage of this approach is that the same definition readily yields a family of infinitely many fonts of type, each font being internally consistent.[14]

This ability to generate several styles of type from a single parameterized specification constitutes the 'meta'-ness of Knuth's approach to specifying character shapes. As he says, in a paper written in 1981,

> ... a "meta-font" is *a schematic description of how to draw a family of fonts*, not simply the drawings themselves. Such descriptions give more or less precise rules about how to produce drawings of letters, and the rules will ideally be expressed in terms of variable *parameters* so that a single description will actually specify many different drawings. The rules of a meta-font will thereby define many different individual fonts, depending on the settings of the parameters.[15]

The experimental programs for character shape specification whose results Knuth presented in the Gibbs lecture had been written in SAIL, an Algol-like compiled programming language developed at the Stanford Artificial Intelligence Laboratory. In 1979 Knuth developed a new interpreted language which took over the name Metafont.[16] He used the new language to program a family of 35 fonts, intended for the composition of the second edition of *Seminumerical algorithms* and subsequent volumes in the series. The family was first published, under the name 'Computer Modern', in January 1980.[17]

The American Mathematical Society, the sponsors of the Gibbs lecture, had formed a committee in the autumn of 1979 to consider the relationships between digital photocomposing technology and mathematical typesetting. Unsurprisingly, Knuth was a member of the committee. The Society, however, made the imaginative gesture of inviting Hermann Zapf to join it as well. Zapf wrote to Knuth in October 1979:

> ... We should work out carefully with Metafont the basic structure for a scientific alphabet, neutral in its forms, and the best solution for all sorts of typesetting devices ...[18]

---

[13] The emphases in this and the following quotation are in the original text.

[14] *Digital typography*, p. 46.

[15] 'The concept of a meta-font', *Visible language* vol. 16 no. 1 (1982), pp. 3–27; reprinted as Chapter 15 of *Digital typography*.

[16] In *Mathematical typography* Knuth calls his system METAFONT; in subsequent material METAFONT. I have transcribed the name uniformly as Metafont.

[17] D E Knuth, *The Computer Modern family of typefaces*, Stanford Computer Science Department report STAN-CS-80-780 (1980).

[18] Extracts from the correspondence between Knuth and Zapf are published in 'AMS Euler – a new typeface for mathematics', *Scholarly publishing* vol. 20 (1989), pp. 131–157; reprinted as Chapter 17 of *Digital typography*. The name Euler had been suggested for the new family at a meeting of the font committee at the end of February; it was christened AMS Euler in recognition of the Society's sponsorship.

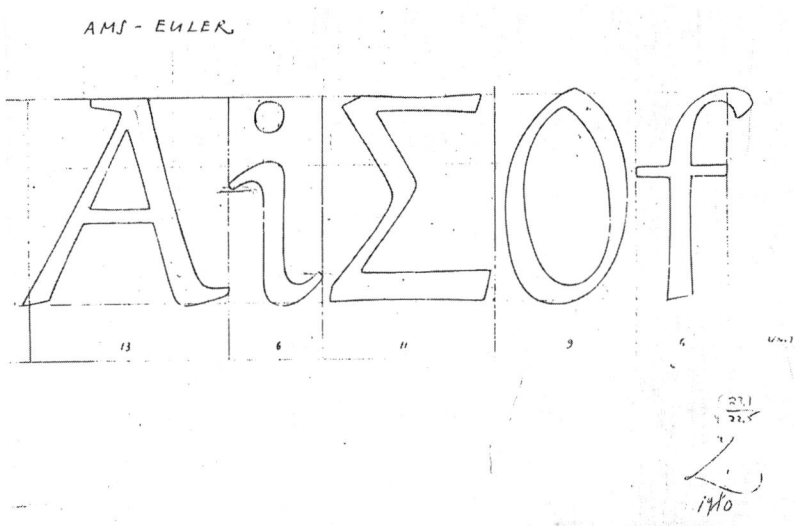

125 Zapf's handwritten designs for the roman and greek of AMS Euler. 40% actual size.

126 Zapf's first outline drawings for the medium weight of AMS Euler. 40% actual size.

Computer science and typography

127 Zapf's handwritten designs for the fraktur and script capitals of AMS Euler. 40% actual size.

Knuth invited Zapf to Stanford in February 1980 to introduce him to the practical aspects of Metafont. In March Zapf sent Knuth a number of sketches for a new typeface family intended for the composition of displayed mathematics. On 3 May 1980 the trustees of the Society agreed to commission from Zapf a set of seven new alphabets in four styles: capitals and minuscules in roman, greek and fraktur, and script capitals.

By the beginning of September 1980 Zapf had produced a first set of 119 handwritten sketches of roman and greek characters, along with some outline drawings at a larger size in medium and bold weights (Figures 125 and 126).[19] The sheet with Zapf's sketches was photocopied with typewritten numbers added to it, and circulated to members of the font committee with a request for comments. A second sheet of handwritten sketches, with fraktur capitals and minuscules, script capitals and alternative versions of some characters followed in November (Figure 127).[20]

---

[19] Figures 125–127 are reproduced from photocopies in the author's collection, several generations removed from the originals. In Figure 126 the characters have been marked with their widths on an 18-unit system. The illustration on p. 351 of *Digital typography* has a fraktur **R** in addition to the five characters shown here, with no widths or reference lines.

[20] The same drawing is reproduced without annotations on p. 355 of *Digital typography*.

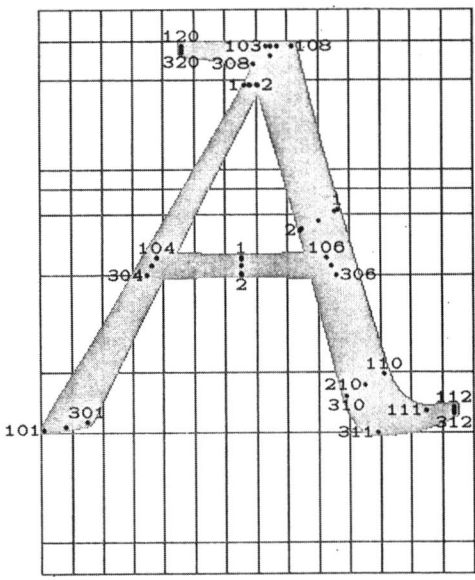

128 A Metafont proof of Scott Kim's rendering of Zapf's medium-weight A, *produced in April 1981. The proof was made on a Xerox Dover xerographic laser printer, which was incapable of reproducing large areas of solid black.*

129 Three stages in the construction of the A *shown in Figure 128; photographed from a DataDisk terminal display in the Computer Science Department at Stanford in April 1981. A reflection in the display screen affects the appearance of the upper right-hand stroke.*

Scott Kim, a graduate student of Knuth's, volunteered to encode Zapf's designs with Metafont. He began work with the five characters shown in Figure 126, and by mid-February of 1981 had produced preliminary versions of them. Figure 128 shows a proof produced by Metafont from his program for the A, and Figure 129 the way in which the character image is built up with successive strokes from different virtual pens. Kim's programs allowed a range of weights to be interpolated or extrapolated from the two weights defined by Zapf's drawings.[21]

---

[21] *cf.* the first illustration on p. 357 of *Digital typography*.

Computer science and typography

While Zapf had been working on his designs for the Euler family and Kim was beginning his programming work, Knuth had been preparing the second edition of *Seminumerical algorithms* for production with his new system. The pages were formatted with his TeX language, and the fonts produced with the programs described in the 1980 report. Typesetting was done on the Alphatype CRS photocomposing machine in the computer science department at Stanford. The book was published in January 1981.

The typeface that had been used to set the first two volumes of *The art of computer programming* in their first editions was Modern Series 8A from the Lanston Monotype Company (the American associates of the Lanston Monotype Corporation). Figure 130 shows the 10 pt size from the manufacturers' specimen.[22]

> the learned sciences, and the professions surround themselves with the history, literature, and concrete examples of the work with which they are particularly
> 12345   abcdefghijklmnopqrstuvwxyz   67890$
> ABCDEFGHIJKLMNOPQRSTUVWXYZ
> ABCDEFGHIJKLMNOPQRSTUVWXYZ
> *12345   abcdefghijklmnopqrstuvwxyz   67890$*
> *ABCDEFGHIJKLMNOPQRSTUVWXYZ*

130 10 pt Modern Series 8A; actual size.

Mathematics books and journals do not look as beautiful as they used to.

131 10 pt Computer Modern Roman; actual size.

Mathematics

132 The first word from Figure 131; four times actual size.

Figure 131 shows the 10 pt size of the roman type made with Knuth's 1980 programs, and Figure 132 an enlargement of the first word in the line.[23]

---

[22] The specimen was kindly made available for photography by the St Bride Printing Library.

[23] Figures 131, 132, 134 and 135 are reproduced from proofs made on the Alphatype CRS machine at Stanford in October 1981. By normal graphic-arts standards the type is somewhat over-exposed.

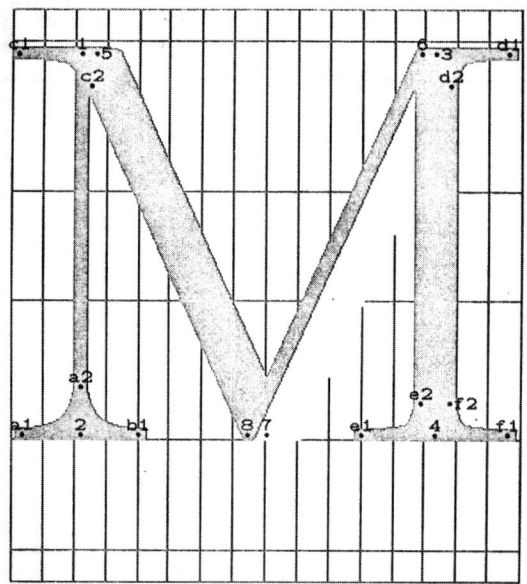

133 A Metafont proof of the M *from Figures 131 and 132. The originals of this and Figure 136, like that of Figure 128, were made on a Xerox Dover printer.*

Metafont's construction of the M in Figures 131 and 132 is shown in Figure 133.[24] The main part of the character is drawn with virtual pens and erasers of different types. Two of the pens are horizontal ellipses, with widths corresponding to the weights of the left-hand and right-hand verticals. The first of these draws a stroke with its centre aligned on the marked points 1 and 2; the second a stroke between 5 and 7. The elliptical shape of the pen accounts for the fact that the upper right and lower left corners of the descending diagonal are slightly rounded. The excess at the lower right of the diagonal is removed by a rectangular eraser with the same width as the pen that drew the diagonal; in Metafont's proofing mode this eraser also removes lines in the background grid that lie in its path. The ascending diagonal is drawn between points 8 and 6 by the same pen that drew the left-hand vertical; because the pen is a different width from the one that drew the descending diagonal, the upper left corner is differently rounded. The right-hand vertical between points 3 and 4 is drawn by the same pen that drew the descending diagonal. Serifs are drawn at the ends of the verticals by separate routines.

Figures 134–136 illustrate the approach that Knuth adopted in his original Metafont programs to the parameterization of character shape specifications. The bold sanserif shown in the illustrations is generated

---

[24] Figures 133 and 136 are reproduced from Metafont proofs produced at Stanford on 17 November 1981.

by the same programs that produced the characters in Figures 131–133. The widths of the two elliptical pens are set to be the same, and the serif-drawing routines used for the roman character are switched off by conditional statements in the programs.

Mathematics books and journals do not look as beautiful as they

134 10 pt Computer Modern Sanserif Bold; actual size.

Mathematics

135 The first word from Figure 134; four times actual size.

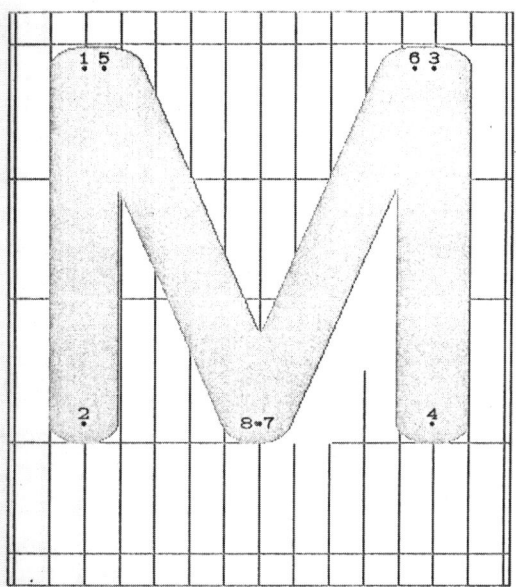

136 A Metafont proof of the M *from Figures 134 and 135. 80% actual size.*

This first approach of Knuth's to character shape specification, with elliptical virtual pens of different widths, relatively simple notions of character construction and an unsophisticated view of the relationships between different styles of typeface, was not really robust enough to bear the load that its author had placed on it with the production of *Seminumerical algorithms*. The appearance of the type on the pages of the 1981 edition was a great disappointment to its author.

> ... the new text was readable, and I could console myself a little with the thought that it was not as bad as some other books that were being printed at the time; but it was not at all what I was hoping to achieve. The sans-serif was totally wrong; the weights of roman versus italic versus numerals were

not quite right; and the high resolution [of the photocomposing machine] revealed unsuspected deficiencies in many individual characters.[25]

Knuth's article 'The concept of a meta-font' was published in January 1982.[26] He had spent much of the summer of 1981 in preparing it, first rewriting the software that drove the Alphatype machine on which the camera-ready copy was produced and then generating the many new high-resolution fonts the paper made use of.

The LORD is my shepherd;
    I shall not want.
He maketh me to lie down
        in green pastures:
    he leadeth me
        beside the still waters.
He restoreth my soul:
    he leadeth me
        in the paths of righteousness
        for his name's sake.
Yea, though I walk through the valley
        of the shadow of death,
    I will fear no evil:
    for thou art with me;
        thy rod and thy staff
        they comfort me.
Thou preparest a table before me
        in the presence of mine enemies:
    thou anointest my head with oil,
        my cup runneth over.
Surely goodness and mercy
        shall follow me
        all the days of my life:
    and I will dwell
        in the house of the LORD
        for ever.

137 Knuth's Metafont rendering of the 23rd Psalm.

Figure 137 reproduces the rendering of Psalm 23 shown in the paper: a *tour de force* of Knuth's original approach to fontmaking.

---

[25] *Visible language* vol. 19 no. 1, pp. 41–42; *Digital typography*, p. 322. The problem with the sanserif's appearance that Knuth mentions is exacerbated in Figures 134 and 135 by the over-exposure of the Alphatype output. The proof from which those illustrations were made was produced in October 1981, however, and the adjustment of the machine may have changed since the camera-ready copy for *Seminumerical algorithms* was typeset around a year earlier.

[26] *Visible language* vol. 16 no. 1, pp. 3–27; *Digital typography*, Chapter 15.

Responses to Knuth's article from a number of type designers and other graphic-design professionals, along with a critique of his ideas by D R Hofstadter, were published in *Visible language* in October 1982.[27] Meanwhile Knuth had solicited more detailed criticisms of four of the Computer Modern family of fonts from several type designers,[28] and Scott Kim was continuing his work of rendering Zapf's drawings for AMS Euler.

It gradually became clear that Metafont's virtual pens were unsatisfactory tools for specifying the configurations of real characters.

> [Kim] wanted to take advantage of Metafont's ability to follow the path of an imaginary pen as it travelled along the center of each stroke. Variations could then be made by changing the angle and width of the pen. The problem was that the strokes did not have well-defined center lines.[29]

In 1981 the AMS had commissioned a report from the designer Charles Bigelow on the feasibility of using Metafont for the production of mathematical characters. Part of his conclusion was that

> ... Metafont is unique as a tool for research and experiment in type design, and has an extremely promising future in this area. As a production tool, Metafont has the potential for practical use, but this potential is not realized in the present implementation.[30]

Bigelow pointed out that practising type designers often made finished drawings by constructing contours with a fine pen and filling in the resulting shape with a brush. Metafont's ddraw routine, extensively used by Kim in his trial versions of Zapf's characters, produced a solid shape by outlining it with two curves and then filling in the space between them with a series of curves interpolated between the outlines.[31] This seems at first sight like an analogous operation to the designer's work; but the interpolated curves that filled the shape were drawn with a virtual pen of the same size as the one that drew the outlines. This meant that the routine would be very slow if it were used for filling large shapes that had been outlined with a small pen for accuracy's sake.

At the end of 1982 Bigelow came to Stanford from the Rhode Island School of Design at Knuth's invitation, to run a new joint programme in digital typography between the Departments of Computer Science and Art. Two of his students, Dan Mills and Carol Twombly, began to build Metafont programs that rendered Zapf's characters by the ddraw method in spite of its disadvantages. They overlaid the drawings with

---

[27] *Visible language* vol. 16 no. 4 (1982), pp. 309–359.

[28] Charles Bigelow, Matthew Carter, Sumner Stone, Hermann Zapf and the present author. The fonts in question were the roman, text italic, sanserif slanted and sanserif bold.

[29] David R Siegel, *The Euler project at Stanford* (1985), p. 5.

[30] Quoted by Siegel: *op. cit.*, p. 7.

[31] See pp. 46–49 of 'Metafont, a system for alphabet design', in *TeX and Metafont* (1979).

graph paper, marked significant points on the outlines and measured their coordinates. Metafont ddraw statements were constructed by hand from the measurements, and the shape drawn by the program checked on the terminal display for errors resulting from mistyped coordinates. Printed output from the program was compared with Zapf's drawings on a light-table.³²

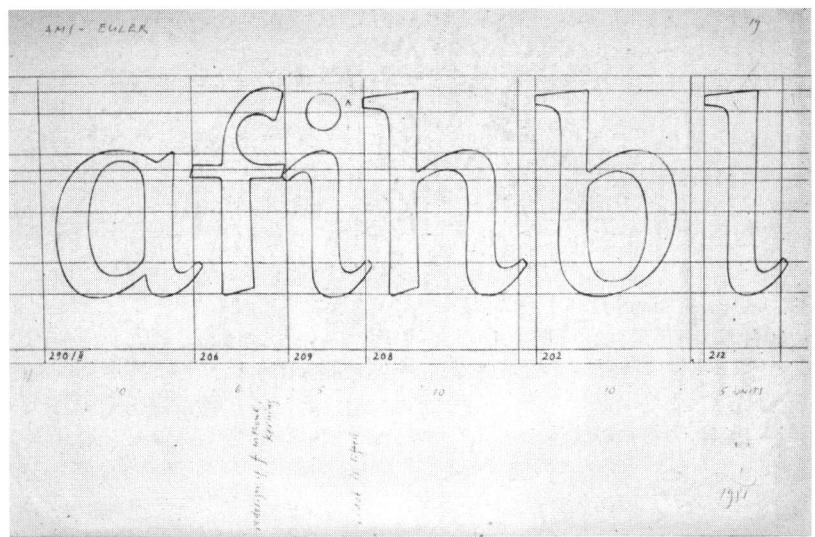

138 *Sheet 19 of Zapf's production drawings for AMS Euler, with characters from the bold variant. From a photograph taken at Stanford in 1984; approximately 40% actual size. Zapf has given the characters serial numbers and pencilled their unit widths below them. The notes at the bottom of the sheet read 'redesign of f without kerning' and 'i: dot is lifted'.*

David Siegel, another of Bigelow's students, wrote a program in the spring of 1983 that simplified the tedious process of coordinate measurement by the use of a digitizing tablet and cursor. Using this, the character shape data from all Zapf's drawings was captured by the end of July 1983.

The Association Typographique Internationale held its fifth working seminar at Stanford in the summer of 1983, under the title *The computer and the hand in type design*.³³ At the seminar Knuth presented the paper 'Lessons learned from Metafont' from which the description of his reaction to the appearance of the new edition of *Seminumerical algorithms* has already been quoted. After describing some aspects of the revision of the Computer Modern sanserif that was undertaken in 1982, Knuth goes on to say that

---

³² The process is illustrated on pp. 8 and 9 of *The Euler project at Stanford*.

³³ The proceedings of the seminar are published in *Visible language* vol. 19 no. 1 (1985).

> I can summarize this recent work by saying that we are now paying a great deal of attention to the edges... I realize now that I was extremely naïve in 1977 when I believed that the edges would take care of themselves if I simply drew with a pen that had the right shape.

In the next sentence, however, he returns once again to his original insight:

> On the other hand, we are not abandoning the pen metaphor, because it gives the correct "first-order" insights about how letters are drawn; the edge details are important second-order corrections that refine the designs, but they should not distract us from the chief characteristics of the forms.[34]

The latter part of 1983 was a period of intense discussion within the digital typography group at Stanford about the form of the new version of Metafont that Knuth had foreshadowed in his lecture.[35] A principal thread of the discussion centred around the notion of 'meta-design': the specification of a number of stylistically distinct typeface variants by means of a single set of parameterized functions. This was the truly novel feature of Knuth's Computer Modern family, exemplified in the programs in his 1980 report. It is clear from documents circulated within the group that Knuth's own reservations about the typographic quality of the results were widely shared, but the problem lay deeper than that. Members of the group who were familiar with the design methods used in current and traditional type manufacture found it hard to reconcile their own experience with Knuth's unspoken assumption that what might be called *a priori* meta-design – the specification of new variants by new parameterizations of a single underlying structure – was capable of producing results that would be acceptable in terms of the traditional criteria of typeface quality.

The alternative to Knuth's approach seemed to be an extension of the one adopted for the Euler project: programs would be written to generate, and interpolate between, character shapes that had already been defined as drawings. While this *a posteriori* approach to meta-design appeared more likely than the *a priori* one to yield technically satisfactory results, it did not offer anything in practical terms that was not already available from systems like URW's Ikarus. It also demanded the step that Mills, Twombly and Siegel had found so laborious: the conversion of shape specification data from the graphic language of the designer's drawings to the symbolic language of the Metafont programs.

Because the discussion of meta-design took place among a group of people all of whom had some acquaintance with conventional techniques of type design by drawing, it was carried on under the implicit assumption that character shape specifications would be presented to an eventual rendering system in the form of outlines. Knuth, meanwhile, was working with his graduate student John Hobby on algorithms for

---

[34] *Visible language* vol. 19 no. 1 (1985), pp. 46–47; *Digital typography*, pp. 329–330.
[35] The present author joined the group in September 1983.

virtual pens to be incorporated in the new Metafont. The difference in emphasis is understandable, given Knuth's views on the role of pens in character-shape construction and the amount of work he had already invested in pen-based specifications for the Computer Modern family.

While the form of the new Metafont was being decided, Siegel was continuing his work on rendering Zapf's drawings for AMS Euler with the old version of the system. 1446-dpi bitmap fonts of Euler's roman variant were produced in January 1984, and proofed on the Autologic APS-5 CRT photocomposing machine which was by then installed in the Department of Computer Science. The proofs showed a number of 'off-by-one' strokeweight errors: errors, that is, in which the widths of strokes differed by one pixel from their intended values. These were a consequence of the fact that the smallest virtual pen available to old Metafont's ddraw routine still had a finite width, even though Siegel's program was using it to draw the boundaries of character shapes. Hobby wrote algorithms to relocate the pen in such a way that its edge, rather than its centre, traced out the contour whose shape had been captured on the digitizing tablet.

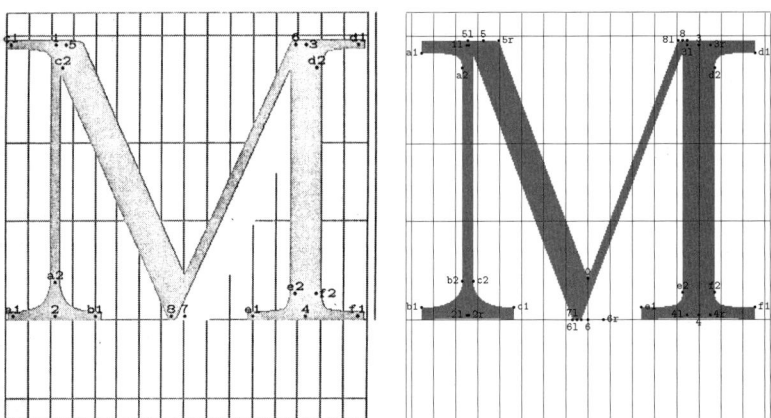

139 *Metafont proofs of 10-pt roman* M *from Knuth's original Computer Modern roman (left) and the new version. The left-hand image is reduced from Figure 133. The right-hand image was made by running the* cmr10 *program in the new Metafont, and is scaled so that the calibres of the two characters are the same.*

A preliminary version of the new Metafont appeared in the spring of 1984, and was introduced with a programming course at Stanford that stretched the resources of the digital typography group to their limits.[36] After the course, Siegel used Hobby's pen-relocation algorithms and the old version of Metafont to produce a first series of the Euler fonts which were sent to the AMS in September 1984 for approval.

---

[36] D E Knuth, 'A course on Metafont programming', *TUGboat* vol. 5, pp. 105–118; reprinted as Chapter 19 of *Digital typography*.

Also in 1984, Knuth learned that the Lanston Monotype Company's patterns for Modern Series 8A had survived in San Francisco. For the first time he was able to acquire reliable information about the actual shapes of the characters with which he had been working for so long. Figure 139 shows how the structure of capital M changed between the old and new versions of Computer Modern.

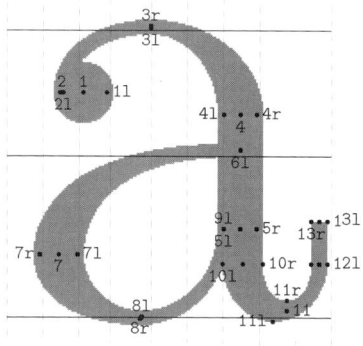

140 *The pattern for the 10-pt roman* a *of Modern 8A (left) and the same character from the new Computer Modern. The pattern is actual size; the Metafont proof is scaled to it so that the calibres of the two characters are the same.*

As Figure 140 suggests, however, Knuth often reinterpreted the shapes on the patterns into the idiom of his existing design, rather than modifying the design itself in order to copy them exactly. As he says, in the introduction to the book that lists and illustrates the programs for the whole of the new Computer Modern family,

> It never was my intention to make a slavish copy of any particular typeface, but the chance to work with these real artefacts made it possible to understand many of the intentions of the original designer.[37]

The new Metafont continued to evolve during 1984 and the spring and summer of 1985.[38] During this period Hobby wrote programs to convert the original shape data for the Euler characters into a form that the new Metafont would accept. Proofs of type were sent to Zapf in August 1985, and the completed family was delivered to the AMS in September.[39]

Early in 1984 the present author began work on the implementation of a new typeface design, making use as they became available of the facilities that the new version of Metafont offered. The objectives of

---

[37] *Computer Modern typefaces* (1986), p. vii.

[38] A summary of the language's syntax, dated 4 April 1985, carries the warning 'Beware: These specifications change daily!'.

[39] Knuth himself subsequently altered the fitting and alignment of certain of the Euler characters: see his article 'Typesetting concrete mathematics' in *TUGboat* vol. 10 (1989), reprinted as Chapter 18 of *Digital typography*.

the project are summarized in a paper written in 1986.[40] Briefly, they were to explore the feasibility of making a set of Metafont programs that would produce technically satisfactory fonts with parameterized weights and widths over a range of sizes that were much smaller in terms of pixel dimensions than those for which the Computer Modern family was primarily intended.

The motivation for this was the increasingly important role that the composition and display of text on CRT-based computer terminals was coming to play in academic as well as in commercial life. In the event, although not every character of the new design's minuscule roman alphabet had a completed program and there were none at all for the capitals, those programs that did exist performed reasonably well at x-heights down to seven pixels. This is a reasonable size for text display on electronic devices, although it is impractically small (corresponding to a nominal size of 2.88 pica points) at the 300-dpi resolutions which were the norm for the xerographic laser printers of the time.

In contrast to the pen-based approach that Knuth used with the Computer Modern family, the character shapes in the new design were built up from outlines defined by the Bézier cubic splines that Metafont used in common with PostScript as its curve-drawing formalism.[41] While this approach undoubtedly made it more difficult to arrive at satisfactory rasterizations of the character shapes at small sizes, it also made it possible to specify features that were important to their performance in the same circumstances: in particular, flat-bottomed notches at stroke junctions in small v and w, which prevented the junctions from filling in on write-black laser printers.

At the same time that the author was working on this design and Knuth was completing the coding of the new Metafont, N N Billawala was beginning the development of the parameterized pen-based routines that she used in her Pandora typeface family.[42] Thus in 1986, at the time that the manual for the new Metafont was published, two completed Metafont typeface families existed and there were two development projects in hand. The completed families were Knuth's own Computer Modern, extensively revised in its new version, and the Euler family; the development projects were Billawala's Pandora and the present author's design. The first family of each pair used Knuth's

---

[40] 'Designing a new typeface with Metafont', in J Désarmenien (ed.), *TeX for scientific documentation* (1986). Much of the work on the project was done in the Département de Mathematique at the Université Louis-Pasteur in Strasbourg, under the auspices of Prof Dominique Foata.

[41] PostScript's splines are defined with explicitly specified off-curve control points. While these can also be used in Metafont, the language has a **tension** primitive that allows control points to be defined implicitly: see *The Metafontbook* (1986), ch. 3.

[42] *Metamarks: preliminary studies for a Pandora's Box of shapes*, Stanford Computer Science Department report STAN-CS-89-1256 (1989).

virtual pens to specify character shapes; the second adopted what in terms of conventional type manufacture was a more normal approach, by using outlines.

Since 1986 the combination of TeX and Metafont has been very extensively used in mathematical publication. Knuth himself produced the Concrete family, a reparameterized version of Computer Modern first used in the book *Concrete mathematics* which he coauthored.[43] The roman of Concrete is much more even in colour, and consequently easier to read, than that of Computer Modern, although the shapes of certain characters (particularly minuscule t) are still some way away from accepted norms.

The same combination has also proved useful for authors, academic or otherwise, who need scripts that cannot be realized economically in normal type manufacture. A quick look in the fonts directory which is part of CTAN, the comprehensive TeX archive network on the Internet, reveals Metafont sources for elvish and klingon as well as for cyrillic, devanagari, etruscan, phoenician, runic and many other scripts. The virtual pens which are fundamental to Knuth's original conception of the Computer Modern family have turned out to be powerful and versatile tools for rendering scripts less distanced from their pen-written roots than are the forms of the latin alphabet. 'The metaphor of penmanship used in Metafont requires some modification and adjustment when applied to a Latin-letter font, but it is ideal for scripts based on handwriting.'[44]

---

[43] R L Graham, D E Knuth & O Patashnik, *Concrete mathematics* (1989).
[44] Pierre Mackay, 'Typesetting problem scripts', *Byte* vol. 11 no. 2 (1986).

19 The Colorado typemaking project

[Some of the material in this chapter originally appeared in a paper presented at the fourth international conference on raster imaging and digital typography, held at St Malo in March 1998. The proceedings of the conference are published by Springer as *Lecture notes in computer science*, no. 1375.]

The Galfra family of telephone-directory typefaces, already mentioned in Chapter 14 above, was commissioned by the Società Elenchi Ufficiali Abbonati al Telefono (SEAT) from Ladislas Mandel as a consequence of his work on small-advertisement typefaces for International Photon Inc in the 1970s (Figure 141).[1]

141 *Trial pasteups of Ladislas Mandel's Univad and Edgware designs for International Photon. Actual size. The baseline separation is 4.75 pica points. The objective of the project was to produce designs that were more legible than Linotype's Doric and Maximus at comparable image sizes.*

Following on the success of Galfra after its appearance in 1978 Mandel produced two more new designs, Lusitania and Nordica, for use by the directory-publishing interests of ITT. Meanwhile Galfra was licenced by the SEAT to a number of publishers including US West Dex (USWD), the directory-publishing arm of US West Inc, in Denver, Colorado. In 1993 Mandel was approached by USWD to produce a new family of typefaces for use in their directories.

Taken in the broadest terms, entries in a residential telephone-directory listing all have identical structures. Each entry contains a subscriber's name, an address and a telephone number. Within this overall structure,

---

[1] Figures 141–147 are taken from material in the designer's collection.

however, there are surprising variations, both between one country and another and even between regions in a single country.

In western societies, for example, most peoples' names have two parts: a *family name*, which itself may contain more than one word, and a group of one or more *given names*. How much of the name gets written down in a residential directory entry, and in what form, depends entirely on the policy adopted by the directory's publisher. Where, as is very often the case, the entry is one of a succession with the same family name, this may be repeated in each entry (some American directories) or replaced by a ditto mark of some sort (French or Italian directories) or simply by an indent (British and some American directories). The given names in an entry may be written out in full (French or Italian directories) or replaced by their initials (British directories). In the same way street addresses may be extremely short, as in Manhattan's 105 W 11, or more extensive as in 10340 Hummingbird St NW from the suburbs of Minneapolis-St Paul, or both extensive and cryptic as in 365 qd1lt1/4ap1004 av M João from Anàpolis in Brazil.

In his designs for telephone-directory typefaces, Mandel's objective has always been to render the differing structural conventions that directory entries follow in different countries by means of appropriate visual structures in the printed entry. His view is that the user's first response to a text is always cultural in nature, and that the appearance of a directory (or, indeed, of any other text) has to be in tune with its users' cultural expectations for their use of it to be effective. In this respect his approach to USWD's commission was conditioned in part by the very wide area of the western United States that their territory covered, from the Dakotas in the north to New Mexico in the south, and in part by the interests that the company had at that time in the Brazilian directory publishers Listel.

Mandel also works to a particular schematic model of residential directory use, illustrated in Figure 142. The user, knowing a subscriber's family name and given names and perhaps their address, goes to the directory to search for their telephone number. The search is top-down and hierarchically organized. It begins with the family names or name-initial pairs in the headlines of the directory pages (which are not shown in Mandel's illustration). These identify the page on which the target family name and given names appear. The user then scans vertically down the left-hand edge of successive columns on the page, looking for the first occurrence of the target family name. If the name is unique in the directory the search is over when it is found. If it is not, a visual cue of some kind shows the range of entries over which it is repeated, and the user scans given names within this range. Once again, if the target combination of given names is unique within the range of repeated family names the search is finished when they are located. If not, the user continues a vertical scan of the addresses in successive entries until the correct one is found. Although Mandel's model does not deal with every aspect of the use of residential listings, it provides a firm conceptual basis for their typographic design.

142 Mandel's illustration of the 'visual itinerary' in his model of the directory search task.

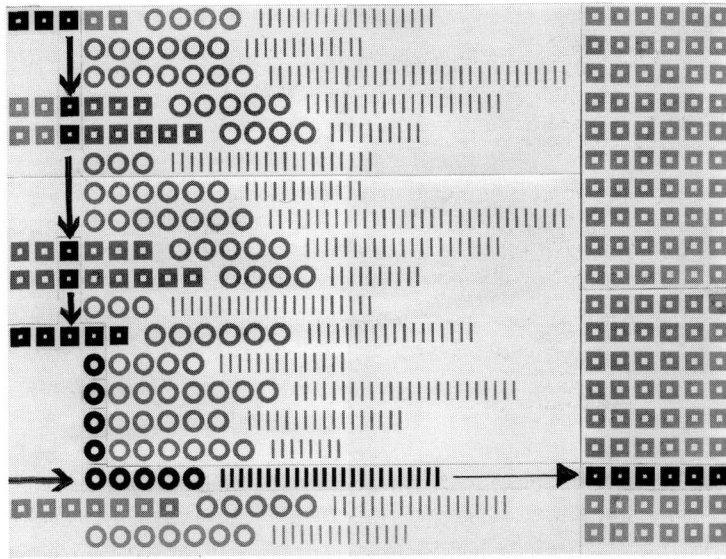

143 A practical realization of Figure 142: part of a residential listing for Milan, in an early version of Galfra. 150% actual size. The indent that signifies a repeated family name in Figure 142 is supplemented here by a chevron-shaped ditto mark.

Mandel began work on the USWD project by making photographically reduced pasteups, in four different combinations of variants, of a few typical entries (Figure 144). He drew the characters for these at the 18-cm em size which he had used in the Lumitype drawing office for many years. The type has an unusually large x-height – 70% of the em size – and the lower part of the bowl of g is raised well above the baseline to separate it visually from the very short descender (Figure 145). Although the type is not a conventionally seriffed design, the terminals of strokes are shaped to emphasize the initial and final attack of the characters (*cf.* l and u in Figure 146).

The Colorado project

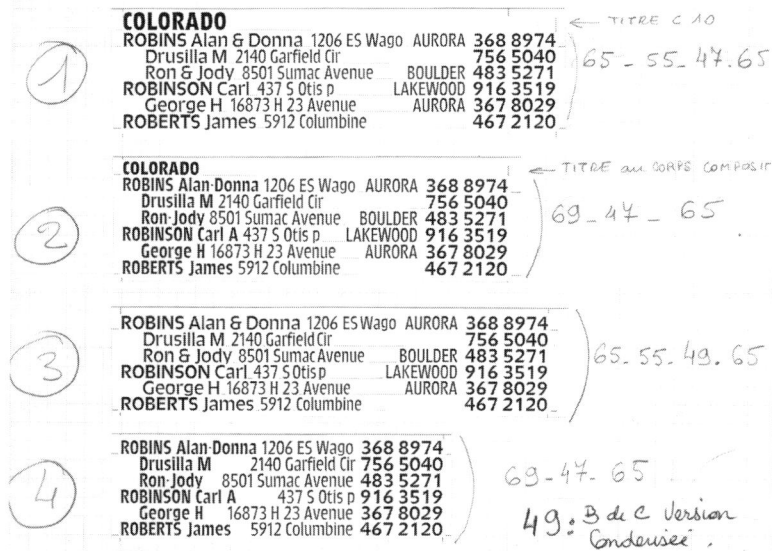

144 Photographic reductions of Mandel's first trial pasteups for the Colorado family. The handwritten numerals on the right of each pasteup denote the weights and widths of the variants used in it, on the Lumitype system (see Chapter 9). The illustration is half the actual size of the reductions, giving it a realistic baseline separation of 6 pica points.

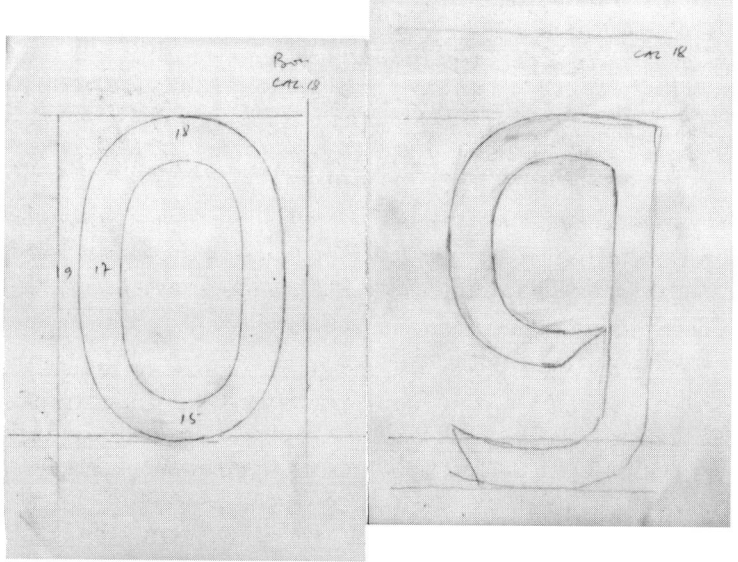

145 Early sketches for o and g in the light condensed variant of the new design. One-third actual size. The numerals in the drawing of o are strokeweight and sidebearing dimensions, in millimetres.

The crotches of diagonal characters are opened out to avoid filling-in on the press, and joining strokes like those in u and the lower bowl of a barely touch for the same reason. The lower horizontal curves of round characters are lighter than the upper ones: this helps to increase the counter height without decreasing the weight of the character too much.

146 Part of the first-stage reduction from Mandel's 18-cm drawings to make the first of the pasteups in Figure 144. Actual size.

147 Trial pasteups superimposed on a printed directory page. Actual size. The illustration shows two of the four columns on the original page, and has been modified from the original to decrease its vertical size.

Figure 147 shows copies of two of the trial pasteups from Figure 144 superimposed on an actual directory page set in the Galfra typefaces that USWD were using under licence at the time the Colorado project began. The difference in appearing size between the type on the printed page and that in the pasteups is striking. The illustration also shows the variability of entry content in USWD's directories. In this rural part of New Mexico the content of the address component ranges from the conventional 1725 S Avenue D Portales of The Video Vault to the simple Floyd of Albert Vidlar's entry (Portales and Floyd are both

The Colorado project

locality names). Name components are similarly variable, even in this short extract: from VICUNA Jesus & Veronica to [VIERA] JJ, both in the left-hand column of the illustration.[2]

148 Ladislas Mandel (left) and the author, September 2002; from a photograph by Lionel Roux.

Mandel first contacted me about the Colorado project early in 1994. At that time USWD had interests in Eastern Europe, and were envisaging the use of xerographic laser imagesetters with comparatively low output resolutions for directory work because the unreliability of electricity supplies there made the consistent processing of photographic output from higher-resolution devices problematic. Mandel knew that I had made a number of designs for low-resolution electronic displays, and felt that my experience in this area would be useful in developing the small character images needed for the directory-composition task. The xerographic imagesetter that was being considered for the project at the time had asymmetric vertical and horizontal resolutions of 900 and 1800 dots per inch (35 and 70 dots per mm) respectively. At this vertical resolution a capital letter of the design that Mandel was envisaging would be around 50 pixels high at a nominal size of 5 pica points.

A photographic imagesetter that was also under consideration had a resolution of 1016 dots per inch (40 dots per mm) in both directions: a 5-pt capital letter from this device would be around 60 pixels high.

In our early discussions, Mandel was emphatic about the degree of control over typographic parameters such as strokeweight and character

---

[2] The brackets denote a repeated family name omitted from the typeset listing.

spacing that he wanted in the finished fonts. As described in Chapter 14, much of his early directory work had been for CRT photocomposing machines, in which a single bitmap font is made to provide character images over a size range of around 4:1 by varying the deflection sensitivity of the electron beam and consequently the writing resolution of the device. In a system of this kind the designer has complete control over the configurations of the character images. The machine imposes no interpretations of its own on the information contained in the font.

With laser imagesetters, on the other hand, the fixed-resolution bitmaps the imagesetter writes for each character image size are normally produced by separate rasterizations of a single set of outline character shape specifications, with all the possibilities for inconsistency of strokeweights and character spacing that present-day font formats are designed to minimize. It appeared from our initial conversations about the Colorado project that Mandel's experience with outline renderings of his designs had been uniformly bad. He would not acknowledge that PostScript fonts could ever perform as he wished them to, and looked to me to provide an alternative.

Mandel's insistence on the accurate control of the relationships of typographic colour between the different variants in his directory typeface families meant that there had to be enough pixels in the em square of the output character image size to accommodate the necessary differences in strokeweight. In medium-resolution environments such as those under consideration for the Colorado project, this requirement imposes a lower limit on the image sizes that can be composed. Mandel wanted an em at least 89 pixels square for his new designs. At 1016 dpi this equates to a nominal size of 6.33 pica points, larger than is desirable or necessary for directory setting. In his original proposal to USWD Mandel therefore envisaged photographic reduction of composed pages to a nominal type size of 4.5 pt from camera-ready copy produced at 6.33 pt on 1016-dpi machines.

With this in mind, Mandel began preparing character designs on an 89-square grid. At the same time I began to review the options for font production, using as test material some drawings provided by Mandel of his Clottes typeface (named for the then director of France Télécom's directory operations), which he had designed for use at 3.3 pt Didot in their A5-format 'mini-directories' (Figure 149).[3]

One possible alternative was to follow Mandel's thinking and produce a single set of bitmaps for each variant at the 89-pixel size. These could be realized as PostScript Type 3 fonts to satisfy USWD's imagesetters, whose raster image processors only accepted PostScript input at that time.

---

[3] 3.3 pt Didot is approximately 3.5 pica points. Figures 149–153 are taken from material in the author's collection.

149 Three drawings by Mandel of characters from his Clottes design. One-quarter actual size. The lowered arch of h *and the raised bowl of* p *also occur in the Colorado design.*

However, at a meeting in July 1995 the possibility was raised by USWD that direct-to-plate composition might be introduced in the fairly near future for directories with relatively short print runs. Such directories very often contain combined residential and business listings, in which different type sizes are mixed on the same page. It thus became clear very early in the project that no fontmaking solution that restricted output character images to a single size would fulfil USWD's actual requirements except in the immediate future, and probably not even then.

At this point the obvious course might have appeared to be to render Mandel's drawings with conventional techniques of numerical contour capture and on-screen hinting, to produce a set of PostScript Type 1 fonts. However, there were a number of reasons that dissuaded me. For one thing, as already mentioned, Mandel wanted control of the *differences* between strokeweights and counter widths of the different variants in the finished fonts. These differences were expressed on his drawings in terms of pixel counts, and I knew he would want to check them in the same terms on any proofs that might be produced. I was not certain that the resources provided by Type 1 hinting would be adequate to meet this challenge reliably at the small pixel sizes with which we were concerned.

Related to this was the question of rasterization effects. On the comparatively coarse pixel grids we were dealing with, rasterization necessarily distorts the proportions of characters to some extent. Taking small h from the light condensed variant of the new design as an example, vertical strokeweights of 8 pixels on the 89-pixel grid scale arithmetically to 7.55 at 84 pixels (which is 6.0 pt at 1016 dpi), while the counter width of 20 pixels scales to 18.88. Normal rasterization rounds the strokeweights back to 8 and the counter width to 19 pixels, so that the proportion of counter width to strokeweight decreases by 5%. I wanted the option of maintaining the counter width at 20 pixels in the smaller size, and doing the same with the other variants, to preserve the visual differentiation between them.

This requirement is in fact an aspect of the more general issue of non-linear scaling. Following Harry Carter and Walter Tracy[4] as well as Mandel's views and my own, I anticipated that we would need to widen the counters of the USWD characters relative to the weights of vertical strokes, as well as rounding the strokeweights upwards, as character image size decreased. The same mechanism, hypothetical as yet, that compensated for rasterization effects could also be used for this task.

Quite apart from these issues of strokeweight differences and character proportions, however, was another consideration that appeared to rule out any contour-based approach completely. We wanted some parts of the character shape specifications to be scaleable, and others not.

This requirement comes from the nature of telephone directory publishing, whose demands in many ways resemble those of classified-advertisement publishing in newspapers. Newspaper classifieds are made small to maximize revenue, and directory entries to minimize cost; but the technical challenges are very similar in the two cases. The size of the type means that great craft and skill are needed to maintain its legibility; long print runs, high web speeds, inexpensive paper and thin ink mean that the character images on the printing plates must be physically robust.

In his work for CRT photocomposing machines, Mandel had taken advantage of the control over character image configuration the technology gave him to add pixel-scale details to his designs that increased their robustness. Examples of such details are finials at the squared ends of strokes, and cutouts or rebates at right-angled interior junctions.[5] These are put there to be sacrificed during typesetting and printing, leaving behind them the 'real' intended shape of the character. Without finials or cutouts, square corners would become rounded and interior junctions fill in.

Because they are not part of the character shape, details of this kind should not scale with the rest of the shape specification. Their dimensions depend on the magnitude of the effects for which they are intended to compensate. These are absolute, in terms of radii on the photographic material or distances on the printing plate, rather than relative to the dimensions of character images. A cutout or a finial should retain its specified size, whatever the size of the image of which it forms a part. I could not see how to achieve this behaviour with PostScript outline specifications.

---

[4] 'Optical scale in typefounding', *Typography* vol. 4 (1937), pp. 2–6; *Letters of credit* (1986), ch. 6.

[5] Visible on the dot of **i** and the upper left corner of the bowl of **D** in Figure 146.

Taking all these factors into account, I concluded that the character image specifications in the USWD fonts would need to be explicitly programmed. A choice of programming language therefore had to be made.

Although in principle the field was open between PostScript and Metafont, with TrueType on the outside, in practice there was no contest. From my previous experience with Metafont (referred to in Chapter 18) I knew that the language would respond to all of Mandel's requirements. Since it allowed the use of both image-related and absolute dimensions it was well suited to his methods of working. Although my earlier work had not resulted in a completed typeface, it had produced a number of useful tools for font development: in particular, procedures for printing out enlarged views of the pixel configurations of characters in the fonts and the outlines from which they were derived. I had also made use of the elegant technique for non-linear scaling of character dimensions devised by John Hobby.[6]

I wrote Metafont programs for the Clottes characters which performed reasonably well both at the 89-pixel size and at sizes down to 38 pixels (9 pt at 300 dpi; 2.7 pt at 1016 dpi). These tests showed that consistencies of character proportion could be properly maintained across a range of pixel sizes. They told us nothing, however, about the problems of mixing different weights.

Mandel made the first production drawings for the USWD typefaces in September 1995 on tracing paper over an 89-pixel grid, with stroke-weights specified in pixels and curves drawn in the normal way as continuous lines (Figure 150). It soon became clear that drawings of this kind, showing character *shapes*, were not sufficiently informative to serve as originals for a system that could output as proofs the *configurations* of the character images the fonts it produced would give rise to. Mandel, in drawing character details such as cutouts at junctions and the pointed ends of terminals, was evidently visualizing particular arrangements of pixels; but it was impossible for me to tell by looking at the resulting outlines exactly what those arrangements were. It was also difficult to reproduce Mandel's corrections, which as Figures 107 and 152 show were normally made by adding and deleting pixels on enlarged proofs of font characters, by modifying curves that were specified as Bézier cubic splines in the ordinary way.

I therefore suggested to Mandel that he return to a design technique with which he was familiar, and make pixel diagrams (which he called pre-digitized drawings) that showed the exact character configurations he wanted (Figure 151).

---

[6] See *The Metafontbook* (1986), Appendix D.

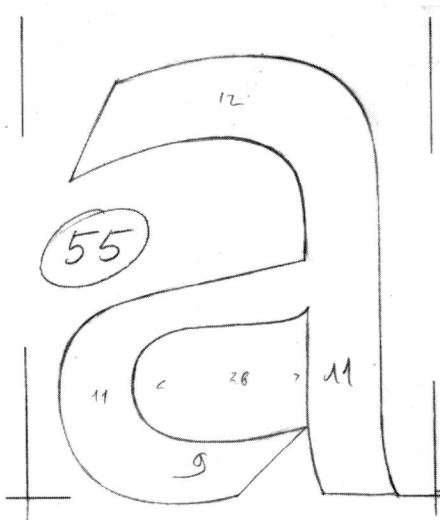

150 Continuous-curve character drawing for a *in the medium-weight normal-width variant. Half actual size.*

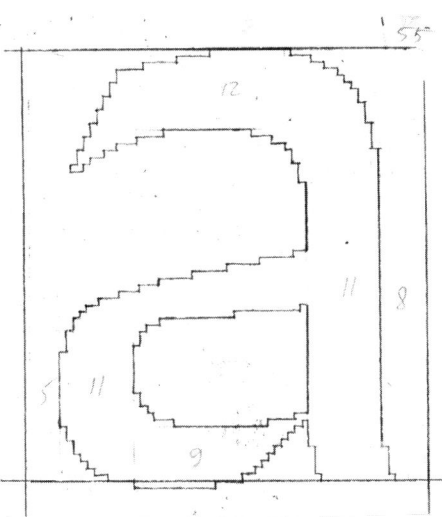

151 Pre-digitized drawing for the same character. Half actual size. The small numbers in both drawings are pixel counts on the 89-pixel grid.

We made the change from continuous-curve drawings to pixel diagrams because the former did not allow Mandel to define his requirements precisely enough for me to understand them. By their nature, though, the definitions in the diagrams were only fully precise for the nominal character image size that corresponded to the pixel grid on which they were made. Given that USWD needed fonts in a range of sizes,

The Colorado project

my problem now was to find a way of turning descriptions of pixel configurations into character shape specifications that could be satisfactorily scaled, while retaining the control over image parameters that Mandel demanded.

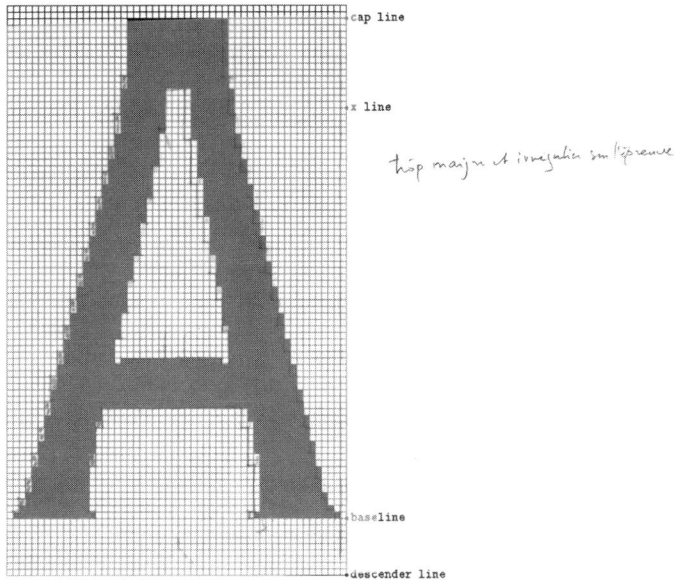

152 *Mandel's corrections to a proof of the first Metafont version of A in the light condensed variant. Half actual size. The designer has marked pixels to be added or deleted on a tracing-paper overlay. His pencilled note reads 'Too light and uneven on the proof'.*

In my first attempt at doing this I followed a conventional approach, specifying the shapes of curves to be rasterized by locating tangent points on the pixel grid and controlling curvature with the tension mechanism that is part of the Metafont language. This did not work at all well, mainly because it demanded too many arbitrary choices. Where, for example, is the tangent point of a curve described as a sequence of decreasing steps? In effect, as far as curves were concerned, I was trying to turn pixel diagrams back into continuous outlines, introducing inaccuracies as I went. It was clear from the extent of Mandel's corrections to the proofs of the two variants I had produced by the end of May 1996 with this technique (*cf.* Figure 152) that I needed to pay more attention to the pixels as he had drawn them. I therefore devised a set of Metafont procedures that reproduced the 89-square pixel diagrams exactly, and also generated character shape specifications that would scale satisfactorily.

The key to this new approach was a view of the character shapes that saw them made up of straight and curved strokes and what might be called 'features'. Examples of such features include the cut-off terminals at the upper left and in the lower bowl of the a in Figure 150, the cutout at the upper right corner of the lower bowl, and the curved terminal at the lower right of the descending stroke.

Mandel's pre-digitized drawings told me what the pixel configurations were that represented these features at the 89-pixel size. My task was to find procedures that not only regenerated the configurations on the drawings, but also yielded configurations at other sizes that were equally effective at rendering the appearance characteristics that Mandel called for. For example, the sloping line of a cut-off terminal (which, as Figure 151 shows, had been drawn by Mandel as a regular succession of steps) should always rendered by the closest possible pixel approximation to a straight line, rather than by an arrangement that gave rise to bumps or concavities in the character image.

The new approach had the immense benefit of making correction a solvable problem. If I could reproduce exactly, in a single pass, every detail of Mandel's changes to the configurations in the 89-pixel fonts, we would not become trapped in the endless loop of modification and correction that the earlier approach had threatened.

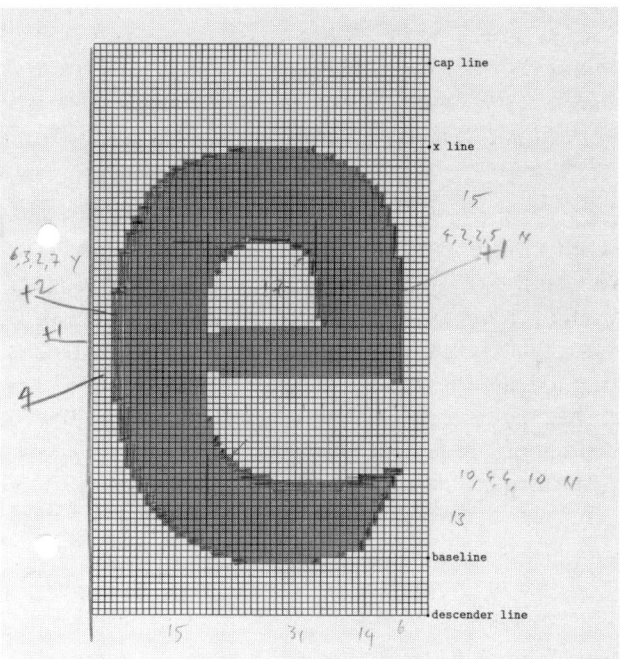

153 *Mandel's design for* e *of the extrabold extracondensed variant of Colorado. Half actual size. The designer has marked additional pixels and sidebearing modifications on a proof of the extrabold condensed. The pencilled groups of four numbers and a letter are parameters that describe the curves of the new variant in the dialect of Metafont developed for the project.*

It also allowed new variants to be built up by modifying the pixel diagrams of earlier ones, with complete confidence that the relationships so created would be preserved in the fonts. Indeed Mandel designed the minuscules of the extrabold extracondensed variant in just this way, by drawing with a felt-tipped pen on the enlarged font-character proofs of the extrabold condensed (Figure 153).

Using this approach, the Metafont programs for the seven variants of the Colorado family were completed by September 1997. Figure 154 shows the capital and minuscule (or small-capital) alphabets of all the variants.

Medium regular	ABCDEFGHIJKLMNOPQRSTUVWXYZabcdefghijklmnopqrstuvwxyz
Semibold regular	ABCDEFGHIJKLMNOPQRSTUVWXYZabcdefghijklmnopqrstuvwxyz
Light condensed	ABCDEFGHIJKLMNOPQRSTUVWXYZabcdefghijklmnopqrstuvwxyz
Semibold condensed	ABCDEFGHIJKLMNOPQRSTUVWXYZabcdefghijklmnopqrstuvwxyz
Extrabold condensed	**ABCDEFGHIJKLMNOPQRSTUVWXYZ**
	abcdefghijklmnopqrstuvwxyz
BOOK EXTRACONDENSED	**ABCDEFGHIJKLMNOPQRSTUVWXYZ**
	ABCDEFGHIJKLMNOPQRSTUVWXYZ
Extrabold extracondensed	**ABCDEFGHIJKLMNOPQRSTUVWXYZ**
	abcdefghijklmnopqrstuvwxyz

154 The seven variants of the Colorado family. The first four are set at a nominal size of six pica points with a baseline separation of 6.5 pt. This was the largest of the sizes used by USWD for residential entries. The extrabold condensed is in 8 pt with 9 pt baseline separation; it was not intended for use in sizes smaller than 7 pt. The two extracondensed variants are in 10 pt with 11 pt baseline separation, the smallest size in which they were intended to be used.

In the later stages of the design work we began to feel the need for realistic testing with more extensive material than a few hand-keyboarded entries. USWD sent me 5000-entry extracts from representative examples of their data files; I wrote TeX programs that interpreted the markup in the files. We were thus able to experiment freely with different entry styles; particularly with the position and capitalization of locality names, and the positioning of the postal code before or after the locality.

The final stage of the project was to produce a set of guidelines for the use of the Colorado family in all the types of directory produced by USWD. This was necessary because directory production, rather than being centrally controlled, was distributed among a number of regional centres, and it was felt to be important that the new family should be consistently used across the whole of USWD's territory. Figures 155 and 156 are taken from the guidelines.[7]

---

[7] In order to avoid inadvertently using real names and addresses in the examples, I borrowed the names and professions of characters from Edgar Lee Masters' *Spoon River anthology* (1915) and made up addresses for them.

```
BONE Richard headstone cutter
    23605 W Petersburg Hwy............... SPOON RVR 61554 309 790-7063
    Fax.................................................................. 309 586-9854
    ⊕ www.stonecutter.com
HILL J Dr Spoon River Family Practice
    200 Main......................................... SPOON RVR 61549 309 547-2010
    Res 3955 Birch............................... SPOON RVR 61550 309 587-4795
JONES Franklin 3850 Beech........... SPOON RVR 61550 309 587-7895
    Hywel & Margaret
        25652 N Railroad Av .............. SPOON RVR 61558 309 672-8582
    William 6790 W Elm ..................... SPOON RVR 61551 309 560-6542
MCNEELY Harry 3925 Hamilton..... SPOON RVR 61550 309 589-6927
    Paul 6650 Beech ............................ SPOON RVR 61550 309 587-5986
    Modem............................................................ 309 588-3956
        ⊕ mcneelypaul@hotmail.com
    W H 1001 Cedar............................. SPOON RVR 61551 309 560-2020
MEYERS Herbert MD—
    General Medicine
    Telephone Answered 24 Hours
        Main Street Medical Building .......... SPOON RVR 61549 309 547-2011
        Res 5775 Willow............................ SPOON RVR 61550 309 587-8976
PANTIER Benjamin atty
    290 S Main..................................... SPOON RVR 61549 309 547-7192
PEET Abner H Rev DD 501 Main....... SPOON RVR 61549 309 547-7122
SIEVER C 11615 Old Lewistown Rd..... SPOON RVR 61553 309 876-5983
SLACK John H & Margaret F
    10329 Old Lewiston Hwy................ SPOON RVR 61553 309 876-6221
SMITH L 3600 Cherry........................ SPOON RVR 61550 ♦309 587-7325
SOMERS Augustus 1301 Laurel........ SPOON RVR 61550 309 587-6980
    Jonathan S 21580 W Chestnut Cir ...... SPOON RVR 61552 309 560-6839
SPARKS Emily................................................ 309 587-7902
SPEARS Cyrus & Lois 5625 Cherry.... SPOON RVR 61550 309 587-1995
    Childrens' Line............................................ 309 587-2963
```

155 Example residential entries, in 5.5 pt on 6 pt baseline separation.

```
MEYERS Herbert MD—
    General Medicine
    Telephone Answered 24 Hours
        Main Street Medical Building ........... SPOON RVR 61549 309 547-2011
        Res 5775 Willow............................ SPOON RVR 61550 309 587-8976
PANTIER Benjamin atty 290 S Main .... SPOON RVR 61549 309 547-7192
PEACE OF MIND PET SITTING ............................ 309 587-6300
PEET Abner H Rev DD 501 Main ........ SPOON RVR 61549 309 547-7122
PENNINGTON'S ANTIQUES
    1650 Cherry.................................... SPOON RVR 61550 309 588-8192
```

PENNIWIT PHOTO
```
    190 Broadway................................. SPOON RVR 61549 309 548-7010
PETIT BOOKS & GIFTS 1800 Laurel...... SPOON RVR 61550 309 588-9156
PHIPPS Henry CPA 300 Main ........... SPOON RVR 61549 309 547-9000
```

PIERSOL MARKETS—
```
    Head Office—
        255 Broadway............................ SPOON RIVER 61549 309 548-6000
        Employment Enquiries................................ 309 548-6100
        Information.................................................. 309 548-6000
    Stores—
        Lewistown—
            200 E Main ........................... LEWISTOWN 61642 309 276-1470
            Deli-Bakery............................................. 309 276-1475
            Pharmacy................................................ 309 276-1480
        Spoon River—
            2020 Alexandra........................ SPOON RIVER 61557 309 670-2976
            865 Broadway.......................... SPOON RIVER 61549 309 548-2880
            Catering.................................................... 309 548-2885
            16000 Commerce Wy.................. SPOON RIVER 61558 309 672-4768
POTTER FARMS Hwy 103............. SPOON RVR 61580 309 656-9873
SIEVER C 11615 Old Lewistown Rd.......... SPOON RVR 61553 309 876-5983
SLACK John H & Margaret F
    10329 Old Lewistown Rd................. SPOON RVR 61553 309 876-6221
```

156 Example entries from a combined listing.

The Colorado project

The Colorado project raises in a particularly direct form the issue of the translation between shape and appearance that takes place in all industrial methods of type manufacture. I suggested in Chapter 1 that in a type manufacturing system there are three personalities: the client, the typeface designer and the font producer. The client's task is to define the requirements the new typefaces are to fulfil. The designer's task is to make appearance specifications for characters that satisfy the client's requirements. The producer's task is to make fonts that give rise to character images whose appearance matches the specifications provided by the designer. Putting the same idea another way, the character images that result from the producer's work should make statements about the appearance of a script that are equivalent to the statements made by the objects the designer produces.

In the traditional technique of matrix manufacture for hot-metal composition (see Chapter 5) the font producer begins by making intermediates that specify character shapes in the form of contours. These intermediates are the outline drawings from which the punchcutting patterns are produced, and also the patterns themselves.

Contour-defined objects such as these cannot speak of appearance in the same way that character images do. For one thing they are normally much larger, and the appearance of an object changes with its size. For another, they are defined by boundaries of a different kind. The drawings and patterns have *shapes*, bounded by smooth curves. Character images, whether produced by ink transfer, photography or xerography, have *configurations*, but they do not have shapes in the same sense that outline drawings do. It is only in very exceptional circumstances that the boundary of a text-sized character image is smooth enough to allow a contour-defined shape to be derived from it without a great deal of abstraction.

Part of the font producer's skill in the manufacture of type for hot-metal composition and direct-photography photocomposition, as well as that of designers who were at ease with the production process, was a mental ability to translate the shapes of large contour-defined objects into the appearance of the smaller configurationally defined objects they would give rise to. As Walter Tracy says,

> Personal experience has shown that given the opportunity to compare the large letter drawings with proofs of the characters at actual type size it is possible, after a time, to develop fairly reliable judgement as to what will be the final effect of a letter that is drawn many times larger than life.[8]

But in those techniques the marking processes that produced the character images had little influence on the images' metric characteristics. Inking and impression do not alter the underlying proportions of the letter on the face of a type.

---

[8] *Letters of credit* (1986), ch. 16.

In what we may call the classical technique of numerical fontmaking described in Chapter 17, the font producer still translates from the designer's appearance specifications to the shape specifications of a contour-defined intermediate; using, if designer and producer are the same person and the contours are specified directly, the same skill that Tracy describes. However, in this technique it is the rasterizer that translates from the intermediate's shape to the image's configuration; and, as was suggested above, at small pixel sizes a rasterizer working in unmodified character coordinate space necessarily mistranslates some of the metric characteristics of the design in certain circumstances. Because he sets such store by the relationships between the weights and proportions of the variants in his typeface families, it was these mistranslations that Mandel complained of in his strictures on the performance of PostScript fonts. Type 1 strokeweight hinting is no help here; all it can do is to make sure that the rasterizer mistranslates consistently.

I originally asked Mandel for pre-digitized drawings of the Colorado designs because, in my role as font producer, I could not translate faithfully enough from the shape language of the outlines he had provided into the appearance language of the character configurations he had in mind. In making the new drawings, though, Mandel hoped for an opportunity to short-circuit the translation process altogether, describing image appearance directly in terms of image configuration as he had with his designs for CRT photocomposing machines. Making Type 3 bitmap fonts directly from the drawings would have allowed him to do this, but did not meet USWD's requirements for variable character-image size on fixed-resolution laser imagesetters.

The 'strokes-and-features' approach that I developed as my second attempt to render Mandel's pre-digitized drawings was essentially conceived in terms of character configurations, although its procedures necessarily made use of Metafont's outline-drawing capabilities. The correctness criterion for the procedure that rendered a given feature was whether or not it would generate satisfactory pixel configurations over the target range of character image sizes: em squares from 70 to around 200 pixels, or 4 to 12 pt at 1270 dpi.[9] Metafont's strength, and the reason why I used it in preference to PostScript, was that it made it possible to control the rendering of character features at the pixel level as well as providing PostScript-like facilities for rasterizing straight and curved strokes.

In this respect PostScript and Metafont are fundamentally different. The path specifications in a PostScript font are descriptions of character shapes which have already been completely defined prior to the font's

---

[9] The 1016-dpi imagesetters with which we began soon dropped out of the picture. All the development work in the main phase of the project was for 1270-dpi machines.

production. 'The character paths must accurately express the true analog shapes of the original design.'[10] The horizontal and vertical hinting mechanisms in the Type 1 font format are ways of preserving, across the hazards of scaling and rasterization, consistencies that are assumed to be present in the original shapes. They modify, rather than define, the character paths. Metafont, on the other hand, takes consistency as its starting point, and derives the shapes it rasterizes from the resulting system of constraints. The ability that it provides in common with other programming languages, to define named variables with values specified by functions of arbitrary complexity, also offers a tractable alternative to PostScript's hinting. If, for example, a Metafont program contains a dimensional variable called stemwidth, whose value is calculated at the beginning of a program run, then every drawing routine that uses it to define the width of a stem will necessarily produce a stroke of the same thickness.

Metafont's virtues as a language for handling the transitions between shape and appearance, though, give rise directly to the difficulty it faces as a general-purpose tool for typeface design: the nature of its user interface. Writing programs that specify the shapes of characters and determine their behaviour under rasterization is a very unnatural activity for most designers. As Charles Bigelow wrote, in the context of a discussion about desirable characteristics for a computer-based type design system, 'It is important to emphasize ... that designers think *with* images, not *about* images.'[11]

In a report published in 1985 I drew a distinction between *design systems* and *drafting systems* in type manufacture.[12] The defining feature of a design system, in the terms of that discussion, is that it places no restrictions on the type designer's work of developing original shapes for the characters of a script. The function of a drafting system, on the other hand, is to translate existing character shape specifications from one medium or representational mode to another. In the same report I distinguished between *graphic-mode* and *symbolic-mode* design systems. In a graphic-mode system, communications between the parties involved are carried on mainly by the exchange of graphic objects such as drawings or proofs of type. In a symbolic-mode system, on the other hand, communication is mediated entirely by alphabetical and numerical symbols. A type manufacturing system as described in Chapters 1 or 3 above will include a design system as its front end, and may also make use (as for example Monotype's matrix-manufacturing system did) of drafting systems as part of its production component. Generally

---

[10] *PostScript Language Reference Manual* (1990), ch. 4.

[11] From a discussion paper prepared for the digital typography group at Stanford in November 1983.

[12] *Designing new typefaces with Metafont*, report no. STAN-CS-85-1074, Department of Computer Science, Stanford, California (1985), p. 13.

speaking, there are no restrictions on the mode or modes in which a type manufacturing system or its components might operate.

In the Computer Modern project, Knuth used Metafont as a type manufacturing system that operated principally in symbolic mode. The design his programs generate is a reinterpretation of Monotype Modern Series 8A, not a reproduction of it: not least because the sanserif and typewriter variants of Computer Modern have only the most tenuous connection with the original Monotype design. Knuth, however, did not begin his work of reinterpretation in graphic mode, by making drawings in the conventional way. He went directly into symbolic mode, using projected images of character shapes as a basis for writing programs in the Metafont language that specified the different variants of his design according to particular groups of parameter settings. If there is a drafting function in Knuth's production system for Computer Modern it is implemented by Metafont's rasterizer, which constructs bitmap fonts for a particular writing resolution by interpreting the resolution-independent specifications in the programs.

In the Colorado project, by contrast, the design system embodied by Mandel himself produced precise graphic-mode specifications for character image configurations at a particular pixel size in the form of pre-digitized drawings. My use of Metafont was as a drafting system with some supplementary features. The translation of Mandel's specifications from graphic to symbolic mode, which was necessarily the first stage of the work, paralleled in many ways the capture by Bigelow's students of data from Zapf's drawings for the Euler typefaces. The novel feature of the Colorado programs was their reinterpretation of Mandel's single-size pixel diagrams into a form from which character configurations in a range of sizes could be derived, while retaining the characteristic pixel-level features and the precisely defined differences in appearance between variants that were the keys to the success of Mandel's design.

Conclusion

Nothing is more striking, over the years covered by this survey, than the progressive dematerialization of the means by which texts are prepared for reproduction. At one extreme, in 1915, are the thousand pages of hand-set type for Fortescue's *History*, waiting to be printed at R & R Clark's works in Edinburgh.[1] At the other are the resources used to produce this book, where the single concrete realization of the completed text that existed before printing was begun was the output from a laser imagesetter.[2] In between are the disappearance of three-dimensional punches, matrices and type that came with direct-photography photocomposition, and the disappearance of the photographic matrix with the electronic technologies that followed.

Over the same period the means used to produce the types with which text is composed have followed a similar course. The ranks of drawing desks or pantographs receding into the distance at Salfords date from the great days of the Monotype Corporation between the wars;[3] but even in 1918 Rudolf Koch's *Die Schriftgiesserei im Schattenbild*[4] shows 27 men, two women, two boys and two horses at work on the manufacture and despatch of foundry type. By contrast, the team that worked on the Colorado project, which in two years after 1995 produced all the type used for residential and business entries in telephone directories for most of the western United States, was made up at its largest of six people. The work was done in three different countries; the only concrete objects exchanged between the participants were character drawings and photocomposed proofs of type.

In some ways the end of the twentieth century has brought the business of type manufacture back almost to where it began. Claude Garamont cut the punches for the *grecs du Roy* himself and had the matrices justified by Paterne Robelot, whom he chose for the task because he was clever at it.[5] In the last couple of decades the development of computer-based typemaking tools and the world-wide web have meant that designers can now make and distribute type entirely on their own; though unless, like Garamont or the Colorado group, they are fulfilling a specific commission, marketing their work is still a problem.

---

[1] See Chapter 5.
[2] Digital presses are now becoming available which will print directly from computer files, with no need for platemaking.
[3] They are illustrated in the *Monotype Recorder* vol. 40 no. 3 (1956).
[4] *The typefoundry in silhouette*: reproduced by Andrew Hoyem in 1982 with a translation by Alexander Nesbitt.
[5] Harry Carter, *A view of early typography* (1969), p. 11.

For the manufacture and composition of printer's type, paradoxically enough, the first decade of the twenty-first century is a period of relative technological calm. The basic tools – PostScript, TrueType, networked personal computers, page makeup programs and desktop laser printers – all appeared in the whirlwind of the 1980s. Increased computing power has meant that more can now be done with them, and done more quickly; but the processes of type design, and the fundamental technologies that underlie them, are very much the same today as they were for Sumner Stone in the late 1980s.[6]

If typemaking tools changed beyond recognition in the early 1960s and again in the 1980s, there has been no change at all since 1445 or so in the task that types for composing text – or rather, the character images the types give rise to – are required to perform. The first objective in the design, manufacture, composition and reproduction of text types remains the same as it has always been: to put legible character images, legibly arranged, before the reader's eyes. It is the means of doing this that changed during the twentieth century, not the objective itself. The second objective – to give the type a voice of its own to speak with – has also remained the same, although changes in rendering techniques have had more effect on the difficulty of achieving it.

The problem of producing fonts that combine expressiveness and legibility at small pixel sizes has confronted type manufacturers since the arrival of desktop publishing in the mid-1980s. It stands in marked contrast to the apparent trend of development at the time, which was the rapid disappearance of mechanical constraints on the type designer's freedom of action. Addressing it has involved a great deal of software-engineering effort, exemplified in the design of hinting systems and of character-image specification languages such as TrueType; and the problem itself is not yet fully solved.

Although the strict constraints imposed by cam-and-lever mechanisms or stepping escapements are long gone, the type designer's work still has to be brought into harmony with the externally imposed requirements of one or another system for character-image rendering. Technical progress may make some of these less onerous as time goes by, but they are never entirely absent, and the whole gamut of image-rendering systems always needs to be borne in mind.[7] In the real world, type design is never a context-free activity.

---

[6] See Chapter 17. Donald Knuth's Metafont language, with its radically different approach to the specification of character image configurations, might have provided an alternative, and in many ways a better, approach to typemaking if the interface it presented to designers had not been so forbidding.

[7] This was a notable omission from the requirements for the Colorado project. The problems of rendering Mandel's designs on electronic displays did not form part of the original brief.

References

Adobe Type 1 font format. Reading, Massachusetts: Addison-Wesley, 1990.

Elizabeth Armstrong, *Robert Estienne, royal printer*. Cambridge: Cambridge University Press, 1954 (revised edition, 1986).

Nicolas Barker, *Stanley Morison*. London: Macmillan, 1972.

Paul Beaujon (Beatrice Warde), 'Eric Gill, sculptor of letters', *The Fleuron* 7 (1930).

Nazneen N Billawala, *Metamarks* (Computer Science Department report STAN-CS-89-1256). Stanford, California: Stanford University (1989).

Andrew Boag, 'Typographic measurement: a chronology', *Typography papers* 1 (1996), pp. 105–121.

Christopher Burke, 'The early years: 1900–1922', *Monotype Recorder* new series no. 10 (1997), pp. 4–13.

Harry Carter, 'Optical scale in typefounding', *Typography* vol. 4 (1937), pp. 2–6.

— *A view of early typography*. Oxford: Clarendon Press, 1969.

— *Fournier on typefounding*. Darmstadt: Technische Hochschule, 1995 (facsimile reprint of the Soncino Press edition, 1930).

Matthew Carter, 'Galliard: a modern revival', *Journal of typographic research* vol. 19 no. 1 (1985), pp. 77–97.

Matthew Carter: Bell Centennial. Type and technology monograph no. 1. New York: Center for Design and Typography, The Cooper Union, 1982.

Sebastian Carter, *Twentieth century type designers*. London: Lund Humphries, 1995 (second edition).

— 'Eric Gill: The man and his letters', *Monotype Recorder* new series no. 8 (1990), pp. 6–13.

Victor Corrado, 'High speed photo composing systems.' In *Report of proceedings, Computer Typesetting Conference, London University, 1964*. London: Institute of Printing, 1965.

'Designer's profile: Adrian Frutiger', *Print in Britain* vol. 9 no. 9 (1962), pp. 258–261.

T L De Vinne, *Plain printing types*. New York: Century, 1902 (second edition).

John Dreyfus, *The work of Jan van Krimpen*. London: Sylvan Press, 1952.

— 'Univers in action', *Penrose Annual* vol. 55 (1961), pp. 15–19.

— (ed.), *Type specimen facsimiles 1–15*. London: Bowes & Bowes and Putnam, 1963.

John Dreyfus, *Italic quartet*. Cambridge: privately printed, 1966.
— 'The evolution of Times New Roman', *Penrose Annual* vol. 66 (1973), pp. 165–174.
— 'Gill, Morison and Warde', *Monotype Recorder* new series no. 8 (1990), pp. 14–17.
— 'Giovanni Mardersteig's work as a type designer.' In *Into print*. London: British Library, 1994, pp. 139–189.
— 'Histoire d'une collaboration: Deberny Peignot, Monotype et la commercialisation du caractère Univers.' In A Marshall (ed): *La Lumitype-Photon*. Lyon: Musée de l'Imprimerie, 1995, pp. 155–165.
W A Dwiggins, *WAD to RR: a letter about designing type*. Cambridge, Massachusetts: Harvard College Library, 1940.
David Fishlock (ed.), *A guide to the laser*. London: Macdonald, 1967.
Henri Fournier, *Traité de la typographie*. Paris, 1825.
Pierre-Simon Fournier le jeune, *Manuel typographique*. Paris: Barbou, 1764.
Adrian Frutiger, 'Letterforms in photo-typography', *Journal of typographic research* vol. 4 no. 4 (1970), pp. 327–335.
— *Type sign symbol*. Zurich: ABC, 1980.
— 'Du plomb à la photocomposition: une mutation profonde.' In A Marshall (ed): *La Lumitype-Photon*. Lyon: Musée de l'Imprimerie, 1995, pp. 137–142.
— *Une vie consacrée à l'écriture typographique*. Méolans-Revel: Perrouseaux, 2004.
Eric Gill, *An essay on typography*. London: Sheed & Ward, 1936.
— *Autobiography*. London: Jonathan Cape, 1940.
'Eric Gill: master of lettering', *Monotype Recorder* vol. 41 no. 3 (1958).
F W Goudy, *Typologia*. Berkeley, California: University of California Press, 1940.
R L Graham, D E Knuth & O Patashnik, *Concrete mathematics*. Reading, Massachusetts: Addison-Wesley, 1989.
Robert Harling, *The letter forms and type designs of Eric Gill*. Westerham: Svensson, 1978 (second edition).
Rudolf Hell, 'Le Digiset, composeuse binaire électronique', *Caractère* vol. 16 no. 11 (1965), pp. 5–16.
Roger D Hersch, 'Font rasterization: the state of the art.' In Hersch, R D (ed.): *Visual and technical aspects of type*. Cambridge: Cambridge University Press, 1993, pp. 78–109.
Richard Huss, *The development of printers' mechanical composition methods*. Charlottesville: University Press of Virginia, 1973.
— *The printer's composition matrix*. New Castle, Delaware: Oak Knoll, 1985.

Allen Hutt, *Newspaper design*. Oxford: Oxford University Press, 1967.

Intertype Corporation, *Book of instruction*. Slough: Intertype Corporation, n.d.

A Javan, W R Bennett & D R Herriott, 'Population inversion and continuous optical maser oscillation in a gas discharge containing a He-Ne mixture', *Physical review letters* vol. 6 (1961), pp. 106–110.

Peter Karow, *Digital formats for typefaces*. Hamburg: URW, 1987.

— *Typeface statistics*. Hamburg: URW, 1993.

— *Font technology*. Berlin: Springer, 1994.

Donald E Knuth, *TeX and Metafont*. Bedford, Massachusetts: Digital, 1979.

— *The Computer Modern family of typefaces* (Computer Science Department report STAN-CS-80-780). Stanford, California: Stanford University (1980).

— *The TeXbook*. Reading, Massachusetts: Addison-Wesley, 1984.

— *Computer Modern typefaces*. Reading, Massachusetts: Addison-Wesley, 1986.

— *The Metafontbook*. Reading, Massachusetts: Addison-Wesley, 1986.

— *Digital typography*. Stanford, California: CSLI, 1999.

Paul Koch, 'The making of printing types', *The Dolphin* no. 1 (1933), pp. 24–57.

Jan van Krimpen, *On designing and devising type*. Haarlem: Enschedé, 1957.

— *A letter to Philip Hofer on certain problems connected with the mechanical cutting of punches*. Cambridge, Massachusetts: Harvard College Library, 1972.

E R Lannon, 'Computers and composition in the United States government.' In *Advances in computer typesetting: proceedings of the 1966 International Computer Typesetting Conference*. London: Institute of Printing, 1967.

LaserWriter [User manual for the Apple LaserWriter]. Cupertino, California: Apple Computer, 1985.

L A Legros & J C Grant, *Typographical printing-surfaces: the technology and mechanism of their production*. London: Longmans, Green, 1916.

Pierre Mackay, 'Typesetting problem scripts', *Byte* vol. 11 no. 2 (1986), pp. 201–218.

Macmillan archives. Cambridge: Chadwyck-Healey, 1982.

T H Maiman, 'Stimulated optical radiation in ruby', *Nature* vol. 187 no. 4736 (1960), pp. 493–494.

Ladislas Mandel, 'Il nuovo carattere Galfra per gli elenchi telefonici italiani', *Graphicus* vol. 59 no. 9 (1978), pp. 16–19.

Alan Marshall, *Ruptures et continuités dans un changement de système technique* (Internal publication no. 638.) Rennes: IRISA, 1992.

— (ed.), *La Lumitype-Photon*. Lyon: Musée de l'Imprimerie, 1995.

— *Du plomb à la lumière: la Lumitype-Photon et la naissance des industries graphiques modernes*. Paris: Éditions de la Maison des sciences de l'homme, 2003.

Edgar Lee Masters, *Spoon River anthology*. London: Werner, 1915.

' 'Monotype' matrices and moulds in the making', *Monotype Recorder* vol. 40 no. 3 (1956).

Monotype Corporation, *Book of information*. [Redhill]: Monotype Corporation, 1970.

— *Unit arrangements of "Monotype" composition matrices*. [Redhill]: Monotype Corporation, 1947.

Monotype Newsletter no. 75 (March 1965).

Stanley Morison (anonymously), review of Ch. Maurras, *Invocation à Minerve*, *The Fleuron* 5 (1926).

— 'Lutetia italic', *The Fleuron* 6 (1928).

Stanley Morison, *A tally of types*. Cambridge: privately printed, 1953 (edited by Brooke Crutchley and republished, 1973).

James Mosley (ed.), *Charles Earl Stanhope and the Oxford University Press*. London: Printing Historical Society, 1966.

— 'Eric Gill's Perpetua type', *Fine print* vol. 8 no. 3 (1982), pp. 90–95.

— (ed.), *The Manuel Typographique of Pierre-Simon Fournier le jeune*. Darmstadt: Technische Hochschule, 1995.

Joseph Moxon (ed. H Davis & H Carter), *Mechanick exercises on the whole art of printing* (London, 1683). Oxford: Oxford University Press, 1962.

Ray Nash (ed.) *Calligraphy and printing in the sixteenth century*. Antwerp: Plantin-Moretus Museum, 1964 (second edition).

Stan Nelson, 'Any fool can cut a punch...', *Matrix* 4 (1984), pp. 31–36.

Olivier Nineuil, 'Ladislas Mandel, explorateur de la typo française', *Étapes graphiques* no. 55 (1999), pp. 44–64.

G W Ovink, 'Two books about Stanley Morison', *Quaerendo* vol. 3 no. 3 (1973), pp. 239–242.

— 'Grandeurs and miseries of the punchcutter's craft', *Quaerendo* vol. 10 no. 2 (1980), pp. 164–172.

Christian Paput, *La gravure du poinçon typographique*. Paris: TVSO Éditions, 1998.

Annie Parent, 'Les "Grecs du Roi".' In *L'Art du livre à l'Imprimerie Nationale*. Paris: Imprimerie Nationale, 1973, pp. 55–67.

— *Les métiers du livre à Paris au XVIe siècle, 1535–60*. Geneva: Droz, 1974.

Charles Peignot (interviewed), 'Deberny Peignot: la belle époque de la typographie', *Caractère* vol. 20 no. 12 (December 1975), pp. 33–53.

Pamela Pfiffner, *Inside the publishing revolution*. Berkeley, California: Peachpit, 2003.

A H Phillips, *Computer peripherals and typesetting*. London: HM Stationery Office, 1968.

PostScript language reference manual. Reading, Massachusetts: Addison-Wesley, 1985 (first edition), 1990 (second edition).

J Randle, 'The development of the Monotype machine', *Matrix* 4 (1984), pp. 42–53.

Richard Rubinstein, *Digital typography*. Reading, Massachusetts: Addison-Wesley, 1988.

Lynn Ruggles, *Letterform design systems* (Computer Science Department report STAN-CS-83-971). Stanford, California: Stanford University (1983).

John Ryder, *The case for legibility*. London: Bodley Head, 1979.

David Saunders, 'The Type Drawing Office', *Monotype Recorder* new series no. 8 (1990), pp. 32–37.

— 'Two decades of change', *Monotype Recorder* new series no. 10 (1997), pp. 26–35.

A Schawlow and C H Townes, 'Infrared and optical masers', *Physical review* vol. 112 (1958), pp. 1940–1949.

Carl Schlesinger, *The biography of Ottmar Mergenthaler*. New Castle, Delaware: Oak Knoll, 1989.

Victor Scholderer, *Greek printing types*. London: British Museum, 1927.

Jonathan Seybold, 'An imagesetter for the rest of us: Apple's LaserWriter', *Seybold report on publishing systems* vol. 14 no. 9 (1985), pp. 3–24.

J W Seybold, *Report on cathode ray tube character generation devices*. Printing Industries of America Inc, 1969.

— *Fundamentals of modern photocomposition*. Media, Pennsylvania: Seybold Publications, 1979.

— *The world of digital typesetting*. Media, Pennsylvania: Seybold Publications, 1984.

David R Siegel, *The Euler project at Stanford*. Stanford, California: Department of Computer Science, Stanford University, 1985.

Fred Smeijers, *Counterpunch*. London: Hyphen, 1996.

William J Solimeno, 'Camex: leading the way to a total system', *Seybold report on publishing systems* vol. 14 no. 12 (1985), pp. 10–24.

Richard Southall, 'Electronics in typesetting', *Wireless World* vol. 74 no. 1389 (1968).

— *Designing new typefaces with Metafont* (Computer Science Department Technical Report STAN-CS-85-1074). Stanford, California: Stanford University (1985).

Richard Southall, 'Designing a new typeface with Metafont.' In Jacques Désarmenien (ed.): *TeX for scientific documentation* (Lecture notes in computer science, no. 236). Berlin: Springer, 1986, pp. 161–179.

— 'Towards the present-day font.' In A Marshall (ed): *La Lumitype-Photon*. Lyon: Musée de l'Imprimerie, 1995, pp. 143–154.

— 'Metafont in the Rockies: the Colorado typemaking project.' In Roger D Hersch, Jacques André & Heather Brown (eds.): *Electronic publishing, artistic imaging and digital typography* (Lecture notes in computer science, no. 1375). Berlin: Springer, 1998, pp. 167–180.

Gary K Starkweather, 'High-speed laser printing systems.' In Joseph W Goodman and Monte Ross (eds.): *Laser applications vol. 4*. New York: Academic Press, 1980, pp. 125–189.

Sumner Stone, 'The Stone family of typefaces: new voices for the electronic age', *Fine Print* vol. 14 no. 3 (1988), pp. 123–126.

C L Stong, 'How a persevering amateur can build a gas laser in the home', *Scientific American* vol. 211 no. 3 (1964), pp. 227–241.

Walter Tracy, *Letters of credit*. London: Gordon Fraser, 1986.

D B Updike, *Printing types: their history, forms and use*. Cambridge, Massachusetts: Harvard University Press, 1937 (second edition).

Lawrence Wallis, *Electronic typesetting*. Gateshead: Paradigm Press, 1984.

— *A concise chronology of typesetting developments 1886–1986*. London: Lund Humphries, 1988.

— 'Frank Hinman Pierpont (1860–1937): an unsung pioneer of mechanical typesetting', *Printing Historical Society Bulletin* vol. 36 (1994), pp. 8–14.

Beatrice Warde (as Paul Beaujon), 'Eric Gill, sculptor of letters', *The Fleuron* 7 (1930).

Beatrice Warde, 'Cutting type for the machines', *The Dolphin* no. 2 (1935), pp. 60–70.

John Warnock and Douglas K Wyatt, 'A device independent graphics imaging model for use with raster scan devices', *Computer graphics* vol. 16 no. 3 (1982), pp. 313–319.

Walter Wilkes, *Das Schriftgießen: von Stempelschnitt, Matrizenfertigung und Letterguß*. Darmstadt: Technische Hochschule, 1990.

Berthold Wolpe (ed.) *Vincent Figgins type specimens 1801 and 1815*. London: Printing Historical Society, 1967.

Hermann Zapf & his design philosophy. Chicago: Society of Typographic Arts, 1987.

Index

Accuracy
  in data capture from drawings, 157
  in hand punchcutting, 10–11
  in mechanical punchcutting, 26
Addison-Wesley, publishers, 185, 186
Adobe Systems Inc, 165–167, 169–170
  typeface licensing agreements, 173
Aldus Pagemaker, 171
American Mathematical Society (AMS), 101, 189, 200, 201
American Type Founders Company, 23–24
AMS Euler typeface family, 189–192, 197–198, 200–201, 202
  early fonts, 200
  Zapf's designs, 190–191, 198
    data capture for, 197–198
    Kim's Metafont programs for, 192
Appearance of character images
  effects on, of reduction in size, 33
  in hand punchcutting, 9, 31
  translation between character shape and, 28–33, 219–220
Apple Computer Inc, 166–167, 170–171
  and TrueType language, 169
Apple LaserWriter, see under Laser printers
Armstrong, Elizabeth, 12
Association Typographique Internationale (ATypI), 107, 108
  Charles Peignot and, 107
  Stanford working seminar, 198
Autologic Inc, 101, 146, 154

Bancroft, J S, 35
Barker, Nicolas, 53, 71, 72
Beaujon, Paul (Beatrice Warde), 53, 58
Bennett, W R, 161
Benton, Linn Boyd, 20–21
  his matrix-engraving pantograph, 23–24
Bézier splines, 166, 177, 179, 181, 202
Bigelow, Charles, 197, 221, 222
Billawala, N N
  Pandora typeface family, 202
Bills of font, 4, 47
Bitstream Inc, 157–158, 173
Boag, Andrew, 114
Burch, W I, 58, 66, 73
Burke, Christopher, 28, 43, 48

Calibre
  defined, 9
  distinguished from size, 9
  of Univers characters, 105, 114
  Schuchardt's investigations of, 9–10

Camex Corporation, 157–158
  BitCaster RIP, 165
  Breeze page make-up terminal, 165
  LetterIP input terminal, 158
  SuperSetter system, 165
Carter, H G, 3, 212
Carter, Matthew, 197
  typeface designs
    Bell Centennial, 144, 153
    Galliard, 159
Carter, Sebastian, 53, 56, 70
Caslon, H W & Co, typefounders, 42, 50
Character dimensions
  in Lumitype practice, 94–95, 97–98, 105
  in metal-type composition, 82
  Schuchardt's investigations of, 9–10
Character image data
  capture, from drawings, 157, 177
  digital, 144–146
  numerical, 147–148
Character image sizes
  and point sizes, in Univers, 118
  in Lumitype practice, 94–95
  in photocomposition, 136
Character shape
  specification, in PostScript, 169–170
  translation between image appearance and, 28–33, 219–220
Character widths
  in linecasters, 44
  in Lumitype machines, 94
  in Monotype system, 35–38
  matrix-case positions and, in Monotype system, 37
Clark, R & R, printers, 42–43
Clottes typeface, 210, 211
Colorado typeface family
  control of typographic parameters in, 209–212
  early design work, 206–208
  variants in, 217
  visual characteristics of, 206–208
Colorado typemaking project, 206–218
  direct-to-plate composition in, 211
  guidelines for entry typography, 217–218
  low-resolution imagesetters in, 209
  options for font production, 210–213
  use of TeX, in prototyping for, 217
Composing machines, hot-metal
  linecasters
    Intertype, 35, 45

Composing machines, hot-metal *continued*
 linecasters
  Linotype, 19, 44, 92
  Typograph, 27
 single-type
  Monotype system, 35–44
Composing machines, photographic
 digital-font
  Alphatype CRS, 193, 196
  Autologic APS series, 146, 200
  Digiset 40T series, 146
  Digiset 50T1, 143–145, 150
  Digiset 50T series, 146
  Dymo DLC-1000, 161
  Harris-Intertype Fototronic CRT, 146
  Linotron 404, 146
  Linotron 606, 146, 153
  RCA Videocomp 820 series, 146
 direct-photography
  Compugraphic 8200, 92
  Harris-Intertype Fototronic series, 90, 91
  Linofilm COL-28, 89
  Linofilm Europa, 92
  Linofilm KE18, 89
  Linofilm Quick, 90
  Linotype VIP, 88, 89, 92, 136, 149
  Lumitype-Photon 200/500 series, 81, 82, 84–86, 90, 121, 149
  Monophoto 400 series, 92, 149
  Monophoto 600, 90, 91
  Photon 561, 161
  Photon 713 series, 90, 126–128
  Photon Pacesetter series, 90, 91
  Photon Zip 901, 122–126
 'first-generation'
  Intertype Fotosetter, 80, 136
  Monophoto Filmsetter, 79, 80, 84, 86, 89, 108
 hand-operated
  VGC Photo Typositor, 139
 numerical-font
  Linotron 202 series, 148
  Linotype CRTronic, 149
  MGD Metro-Set, 148
  Seaco 1600, 147
 scanned-matrix
  Compugraphic Videosetter, 134
  Crosfield Magnaset, 132–135
  Linotron 1010, 129, 135
  Linotron 303, 131–132, 134–135
  Linotron 505, 92, 130–132, 134–135
Computer Modern typeface family
 first version, 189, 193–196
 new version, with Metafont84, 200–201
Computers
 Apple Macintosh, 166–167, 170–171
 Digital Equipment PDP series, 134, 145, 163

Xerox Alto, 163, 166
Cranach Press, 15
CTAN (Comprehensive TeX archive network), 203

De Vinne, T L, 19, 48
Deberny & Peignot, 93
 negotiations with Monotype, 107–112
 punchcutting patterns, 110, 111
Declarative hints, in PostScript fonts, 169
'Definitive outline', 159–160
Dentation, *see* 'half-bitting'
Désarmenien, Jacques, 202
Desktop publishing, 171
Device coordinate space, in PostScript, 167–169
Device independence
 in laser imagesetters, 165
 in PostScript, 167
Didot, Pierre l'aîné, 14, 18
Digital typography group, at Stanford, 199, 221
Discrete matrices, in photocomposition, 89
Drawings
 Dwiggins's, for Caledonia, 29–30
 Frutiger's, for Univers, 104–106
 Gill's
  for Gerard Meynell, 59
  Perpetua, for Stanley Morison, 53, 58
 in hand punchcutting, 14, 16
 in Lumitype practice, 98–99
 in mechanical punchcutting, 19, 22, 26, 28, 33, 219
 in production of the *grecs du Roy*, 13
 Mandel's
  for Clottes typeface, 210, 211
  for Colorado family, 206–208, 213–214
  for Galfra, 153
 pantographic reduction from, 21, 22
 'pre-digitized' drawings, 153, 214
 Stone's, for Stone family, 173–177
 Van Krimpen's, for Lutetia, 17
Dreyfus, John, 17, 53, 73, 74, 105, 106, 109, 118
 his negotiations with Deberny & Peignot, 107–112
Drost, Henk, 16
Duchâtel, Pierre, 12
Duplexing, of character widths
 in linecaster practice, 45–46
 in Photon 713 series, 127
 in Univers, 104
Dwiggins, W A, 33
 his design technique, 29–30
 typeface designs
  Caledonia, 29–30, 34
  Electra, 29, 46

Index

Dwiggins, W A *continued*
  typeface designs
    Metro, 29, 119
Electrotyping, in type manufacture, 20, 27
Emery, E, 80
Enschedé, Joh. en Zonen, 17, 71, 72–73
Estienne, Robert, 12

Fibre-optic faceplates, for CRTs, 148
Figgins, Vincent, 47–48
Fishlock, D, 161
Fleuron, The, see The Fleuron
Foata, Dominique, 202
Fonts
  in hand composition, 47–48
  in mechanical composition, 48–52, 155
  in photocomposition
    digital, 150–156
    direct-photography, 136–137
    numerical, 150–151
    scanned-matrix, 140, 150–151
Fortescue, J W, 42–43
Fournier, Henri, 11
Fournier, Pierre-Simon le jeune, 3, 47
  drawing character shapes
    in soft metal, 8–9
    on the punch, 9
  gauges
    for calibre and slope, 6
    for small capitals, 7
  testing character dimensions, 11
  typefaces
    Bâtarde coulée, 8, 9
    Caractères poétiques, 13
  use of smoke-proofs, 11
Frutiger, Adrian, 88, 94–96, 98, 99, 138, 176
  and design of Univers, 103–120

Garamont, Claude, 12–13
Garth, W W Jr, 109
Gauges, in hand punchcutting, 6–7, 10
  Fournier's, for small capitals, 7
  Moxon's method for setting, 6–7
  Paput's use of, 11
  Paul Koch's, 16
  Smeijers's, 10
Geschke, Charles (Chuck), 165, 166
Gill, Eric, 30–33, 120
  comments on Monotype punchcutting, 75
  drawings
    for Gerard Meynell, 59
    Perpetua, for Stanley Morison, 53
  typeface designs
    Joanna, 32
    Perpetua, *see* Perpetua typeface
Girard, Lucette, 99

Goudy, F W, 186, 187
  his matrix-engraving technique, 24
  University of California Old Style typeface, 33
Graphic Arts Research Foundation, 81, 109
Griffith, C H, 29
Gréa, René, 94

'Half-bitting', 154
Harling, Robert, 53, 66
Hell, Dr.-Ing. Rudolf GmbH, 143
Herriott, D R, 161
Higonnet, R A, 79, 80–82, 93, 121, 126
Hinting, in PostScript fonts, 169–170
Hobby, John, 199–201
  his Metafont technique for non-linear scaling, 213
Hofstadter, D R, 197
Huss, Richard, 21

Ikarus system, 157–159, 181, 199
Image transfer, in hand punchcutting
  by photoengraving, 16, 18
  by photography, 16
Index Medicus, 122
International Typeface Corporation (ITC), 173, 182

Javan, A, 161
Johnston, Edward, 14–16, 33
Jones, G W, 50
Justification, in hand matrix-making, 4, 9

Käch, Walter, 102
Karow, Peter, 157
Kerning
  in digital photocomposition, 152
  in duplexed designs for photocomposition, 127
  in linecaster matrices, 45–46
  in scanned-matrix photocomposition, 135
  in the Wicks typecaster, 45
  in Univers, 115, 116
Kessler, Harry Graf, 14–16
Kim, Scott, 192, 197
Knuth, D E, 114, 171, 185, 198–199, 201, 222
  Concrete mathematics, 201, 203
  diary entries for 1977, 185–187
  Josiah Willard Gibbs lecture, 188–189
  modifications to Euler characters, 201
  objectives for the TeX system, 187
  Seminumerical algorithms, 185, 186, 189, 193
    reaction to appearance of second edition, 195–196
  The art of computer programming, 185, 193
  The TeXbook, 187

Koch, Paul, 3, 16
Lanston Monotype Company, 72, 193
Lanston Monotype Corporation, *see* Monotype Corporation
Lanston, Tolbert, 35
Lardent, Victor, 41
Laser imagesetters, 161–165
   Camex SuperSetter, 165, 167
   device independence in, 165
   Monophoto Lasercomp, 161, 163, 165
   whole-page specification for, 164–165
Laser printers
   Apple LaserWriter, 166–167, 170–171
   Canon LBP-CX, 166
   Xerox
      9700 system, 163
      Dover, 163, 192, 194
Lasers, early work, 161
LaserWriter, *see under* Laser printers
Leavenworth, William, 20
Legros, L A & Grant, J C, 19, 21, 27–28, 48
Line justification, in hot-metal composition, 44
Linotype machine, *see* Composing machines, hot-metal
Logotypes, in linecaster practice, 45
Luce, Louis René, 13
Lumitype SA, 94
Lutetia typeface, 44, 53, 119–120
   comparison of hand-cut sizes, 17
   configurations of hand-cut **m**, 72
   Monotype version, 73–74
   Morison's *Fleuron* reviews, 72
   original cutting, 51, 71–72
   revised for Frick catalogue, 18
   Van Krimpen's drawings for, 17

Mackay, Pierre, 203
Macmillan & Co, publishers, 42–43
Maiman, T H, 161
Malin, Charles, 53, 56, 66, 71, 74–75
   correspondence with Morison, 54–55
Mandel, Ladislas, 98–99, 102, 162, 204, 205, 209
   his model of directory search task, 205–206
   'pre-digitized' drawings, 153, 214, 220
   typeface designs
      Clottes, 210, 211
      Colorado, *see* Colorado typeface family
      Edgware, 204
      Galfra, 153, 155, 204
      Univad, 204
   views on PostScript fonts, 210, 220
Marshall, Alan, 79
Matrices
   in typefounding, 4

Matrices *continued*
   linecaster, 19, 44–46
Matrices, photographic, *see* Photographic matrices
Matrix engraving, 23–25, 31–32
   Goudy's technique, 24
Matrix-case arrangements, in Monotype system, 37–40
Matrix-making, photographic, *see* Photographic matrix-making
Matson, Jack, 107, 109
Mergenthaler Linotype Company, 26, 35, 46, 48
Mergenthaler Printing Company, 21
Mergenthaler, Ottmar, 19, 27, 35, 44
Metafont, *see also* Metafont79, Metafont84
   and characters for computer terminals, 202
   and PostScript, differences between, 220–221
   as drafting system, in Colorado project, 222
   as symbolic-mode manufacturing system, 222
   beginnings of, 186
   control of image configuration in, 220
   first version of, *see* Metafont79
   interface to, 221
   'meta-design' and typographic quality, 199
   'meta'-ness defined, 189
   named variables in, 221
   pen metaphor in, 199, 203
   second version of, *see* Metafont84
   use of outlines, 198, 199, 202, 220
Metafont79
   and first version of Computer Modern typeface family, 189
   construction of Euler characters with, 197–198
   ddraw method for filling outlines, 197–198, 200
   virtual pens in, 194–195
Metafont84
   and AMS Euler typeface family, 200, 201
   and Colorado typeface family, 213, 215–217
   results compared with Metafont79, 200–201
   virtual pens in, 199
Meynell, Gerard, 58
Microsoft Corporation
   and TrueType language, 169
Mills, Dan, 197, 199
Models
   in hand punchcutting, 14–15, 18
Monotype Corporation, 26, 30, 48, 73

Index

Monotype Corporation *continued*
  hot-metal composing system, *see* Monotype system
  Super Caster, 108
Monotype system, 35–41
  matrix-case arrangements, 37–40
    in Univers variants, 114
  unit arrangements, 40–41
Morison, Stanley, 27, 32, 53, 71–73, 119, 181
  correspondence with Charles Malin, 53–55
  objectives for Perpetua and Lutetia, 74–75
  relationships with Monotype works, 76
Mosley, James, 41, 53, 57, 58, 59, 66, 69
Moulds
  in Monotype system, 36–38
  typefounder's, 4
Moxon, Joseph, 3, 47
  corrections, in punchcutting, 10–11
  drawing on the punch, 7
  his method for setting gauges, 6–7
  on casting type, 5
Moyroud, Louis, 79, 80–82, 93, 121, 126

Nash, R, 3
Nelson, Stan, 3
Non-linear scaling, of character images, 212
  John Hobby's technique for, 213

Ovink, G W
  on Jan van Krimpen, 76
  on Rädisch's technique, 18

Page description languages (PDLs), *see* Page specification languages
Page make-up terminals, 164
  Camex Breeze, 165
Page specification languages, 164
  PostScript, 165–172
  Xerox Interpress, 165
Pantographs
  in wood-type manufacture, 20
  matrix-engraving
    Benton's, 23
    Kämpf machine, 24
    pattern-cutting, 21, 28
    punchcutting, 20–23, 75
Paput, Christian, 3, 16
  his use of gauges, 11
PARC, *see* Xerox Palo Alto Research Center
Parent, A, 12, 13
Patents
  Benton's, of 1885, 21
  Higonnet and Moyroud's
    des cartes and *des fentes*, 85, 90
    for character positioning by flash timing, 121

Patents *continued*
  Pierpont's, for projection microscope, 27
  Starkweather's, for polygonal mirror in laser scanning, 163
Pattern-making, in mechanical punchcutting, 21–23, 28
Patterns (templates)
  in hand punchcutting, 14, 15, 18
  in mechanical punchcutting, 26, 219
Paxton, W, 174
Peignot, Charles, 93, 102, 107–111
  and ATypI, 107
Penrose Annual, 118
Perpetua typeface, 53–71
  design finalized, 67
  experimental italic, 31
  fate of original drawings, 58
  final version, 70
  first Monotype cutting, 60, 67, 68, 75
  Gill's contributions
    corrections to Malin's cutting, 58
    drawings for Gerard Meynell, 59
    original drawings, 53
    remarks on 18-pt **y**, 66–67
  Malin's cutting, 56, 67, 69, 71
  Monotype trials, 61–64, 65, 66, 68, 69, 71
  new Monotype sizes, 64
  round terminals, in Monotype cutting, 60–61
  titling capitals, 70–71
  type from Meynell drawings, 59, 68
Pfiffner, P, 166
Phillips, A H, 79, 129, 135, 143
Photocomposing machines, *see* Composing machines, photographic *and* Laser imagesetters
Photocomposition
  character selection mechanisms, 79, 90
  escapement systems, 80, 83, 86
  film transport mechanisms, 80, 83
  optical systems, 79
Photoengraving
  in cutting of Lutetia punches, 18
  in hand punchcutting, 16
Photographic matrices
  disc
    Lumitype-Photon, 85, 86–87, 136
    segmented, 90, 91
  discrete
    Linofilm Europa, 92
    Monophoto 400 series, 92
    Monophoto 600, 90
    Monophoto Filmsetter, 80
  filmstrip
    Crosfield Magnaset, 133, 134
    Linotype VIP, 88–89
    Photon 713 series, 126–127

Photographic matrices *continued*
  'grid'
    Linotron 1010, 129
    Linotron 303, 132
    Linotron 505, 130
Photographic matrix-making
  camera masters, 87, 88
  intermediate images, 88, 132, 133
  Lumitype-Photon camera, 86–87
  stages of reduction, 88
Photography, in hand punchcutting, 16
Pierpont, F H, 27, 60, 61, 66, 71, 74, 76
Plantin, Christopher, 3
PostScript, 165–172
  and device independence, 167
  and Metafont, differences between, 220
  character shape specification in, 166, 169–170
  device coordinate space, 167–168
  hinting, 169–170, 220, 221
  imaging model, 166
  path specifications in, 220–221
  scan conversion, 166
  screenfonts, 175
  Type 1 font format, 169–170, 220
  Type 3 fonts, 210, 220
  unit widths in, 168
  user coordinate space, 167–169
Prince, Edward Philip, 15–16
Printer's point, values for, 114
  in PostScript, 168
Processing effects, in photocomposition, 83
Punchcutting
  hand, 3
  mechanical, 21–25
    Updike's views on size ranges in, 48, 160
    using cardboard patterns, 23, 111–112

Rädisch, P H, 17, 72–73
  cutting of Lutetia punches, 18, 51, 72
  his use of photography, 18, 72
Randle, J, 119
Raster image processors, 165
  Adobe's, for Apple LaserWriter, 166
  Camex BitCaster, 165
Raster scans, in photocomposition
  digital, 144
    varying resolution of, 146
  numerical, 148
  whole-page, 161–163
Rasterization, 150, 151
  effects on image configuration, 211, 220
Reid, Brian, 165
Representational modes
  in fontmaking, 150–151

Representational modes *continued*
  in type design systems, 221–222
  translation between, 150–151
Ribaudeau Dumas, typefounders, 55, 56
Richmond, Wendy, 158
RIPs, *see* Raster image processors
Rogers, Bruce, 32
Rubinstein, Richard, 154
Ruggles, Lynn, 157
Ruzicka, Rudolf, 29

Sanders, J H, 161
Saunders, David, 28, 53, 71
Sauvage, Lucien, 93
Scan conversion, 150
  in PostScript, 166
Schawlow, A, 161
Scholderer, Victor, 13
Schuchardt, Jochen, 9–10, 168
Script appearance space, in typeface classification, 138, 140
Set value
  in Lumitype practice, 83–84
  in Monotype practice, 35–36
Seybold, Jonathan, 171
Seybold, J W, 79, 143
Sidewall breakdown, in linecaster matrices, 45
Siegel, David, 198–200
Smeijers, Fred, 3, 9, 10, 120
Smoke-proofs
  compared to PostScript proofs, 182
  in hand punchcutting, 4, 10, 11, 31, 33
Solimeno, W J, 165
Spencer, Herbert, 118
Standard Generalized Markup Language (SGML), 171
Stanford University, California, 163, 171, 185
Stanhope, Charles, 45
Starkweather, Gary, 163
Steltzer, F M, 41
Stempel, D AG, 21–23, 25, 88
Stone typeface family, 173–182
  corrections on proofs of type, 180
  'Stone Relaxed', 176
  'the very first drawings', 175
Stone, Sumner, 173–182, 197
Stong, C L, 161

Telephone directories
  combined listings in, 218
  Mandel's model of search task, 205–206
  residential listings in, 218
    structure of entries, 204–205
    variability of entry content, 208–209
Teletypesetter (TTS) system, 46, 164
Terminals, page make-up, *see* Page make-up terminals

Index

TeX
  beginnings of, 186
  in production of *Seminumerical algorithms*, 193
  in prototyping for Colorado project, 217
  metal-type composition as model for, 187
The Fleuron, 53, 58, 66, 70, 72
Thibaudeau, François, 53
Townes, C H, 161
Tracy, Walter, 18, 24, 41, 46, 72, 181, 212, 219
Translation
  between character image appearance and shape, 28–33, 219–220
  between representational modes, 150-151, 157
TrueType character image specification language, 169
Twombly, Carol, 197, 199
Type 1 font format, *see under* PostScript
Type bodies, in traditional type manufacture, 47–48
Type design systems
  communication in, 14
  distinguished from drafting systems, 221
  models in, 13, 14, 16
  representational modes in, 221–222
Type manufacture
  digital, 152–155
  mechanical, 19–34
  numerical, 156–159
  photographic, 86–89
  traditional, 3–11
Type manufacturing systems
  communication in, 12
  defined, 6
  in production of the *grecs du Roy*, 12
  responsibilities in, 15, 219
Typeface classification
  by appearance characteristics, 138
  Lumitype numbering scheme for, 96
  Vox's scheme for, 96
Typefaces
  and photolettering machines, 139–140
  and scanned-matrix photocomposing machines, 140
  defined by sets of appearance characteristics, 138
  in mechanical type manufacture, 49
  in photocomposition
    'first-generation', 136
    direct-photography, 137
Typefaces, by manufacturer
  Adobe
    Helvetica Neue, 168
    Stone, *see* Stone typeface family

Typefaces, by manufacturer *continued*
  Autologic
    Athena, 154
  Deberny & Peignot
    Europe, 94, 102
  D Stempel AG
    Optima, 32
  Lanston Monotype Company
    Modern Series 8A, 193, 201, 222
  Letraset
    Aachen, 159
  Linotype
    Bell Centennial, 144, 153
    Caledonia, 29–30, 34
    Caslon Old Face, 45
    Electra, 29, 46
    Galliard, 159
    Helvetica, 119
    Metro, 29, 119
  Lumitype
    Baskerville, 102, 137
    Bodoni, 102
    Clarendon, 100
    Garamont, 102
    Modern, 100
    Univers, *see* Univers typeface family
  Monotype
    Baskerville Series 169, 137
    Caslon Series 128, 43, 51
    Clarendon Series 12, 50
    Garamond Series 156, 44
    Gill Sans family, 107, 119
    Gloucester Old Style Series 99, 41
    Gravura Series 533, 41
    Grotesque Bold Condensed Series 15, 41
    Grotesque Series 11, 50
    Grotesques Series 215 and 216, 107
    Imprint Series 101, 41, 42, 43, 50, 76
    Joanna Series 478, 32
    Lutetia Series 255, *see* Lutetia typeface
    Modern Series 1, 35–36, 46, 48, 50
    Old Face Series 20, 42
    Old Face Series 45, 42
    Old Style Bold Series 544, 41
    Old Style Series 2, 36, 48, 49
    Perpetua Series 239, *see* Perpetua typeface
    Plantin Series 110, 28, 41, 42, 50, 76
    Poliphilus Series 170, 53
    Scotch Roman Series 137, 43
    Times New Roman Series 327, 41, 42, 181
    Univers, *see* Univers typeface family
    Veronese Series 59, 41
Typefaces, by name
  Aachen, 159
  AMS Euler, *see* AMS Euler typeface family

Typefaces, by name *continued*
  Athena, 154
  Baskerville
    Lumitype version, 102, 137
    Monotype version, 137
  Bâtarde coulée, 8, 9
  Bell Centennial, 144, 153
  Bodoni
    Lumitype version, 102
  Caledonia, 29–30, 34
  Caractères poétiques, 13
  Caslon Old Face
    foundry type, 50
    Linotype version, 45
    Monotype Series 128, 43, 51
  Cheltenham, 41
  Clarendon
    Lumitype version, 100
    Monotype Series 12, 50
  Colorado, *see* Colorado typeface family
  Computer Modern, *see* Computer Modern typeface family
  Cranach Press italic, 15–16
  Edgware, 204
  Electra, 29, 46
  Europe, 94, 102
  Folio, 119
  Futura, 94, 102, 119
  Galfra, 153, 155, 204
  Galliard, 159
  Garamond Series 156, 44
  Garamont, 102
  Gill Sans family, 107, 119
  Gloucester Old Style Series 99, 41
  Gravura Series 533, 41
  Grecs du roy, 12–13
  Grotesques
    Bold Condensed Series 15, 41
    Series 215 and 216, 107
    Series 11, 50
  Helvetica, 119
  Helvetica Neue, 168
  Imprint Series 101, 41, 42, 43, 50, 76
  Joanna Series 478, 32
  Lutetia, *see* Lutetia typeface
  Metro, 29, 119
  Modern
    Lanston Monotype Series 8A, 193, 201, 222
    Lumitype version, 100
    Monotype Series 1, 35–36, 46, 48, 50
  Old Face Series 20, 42
  Old Face Series 45, 42
  Old Style Series 2, 36, 48, 49
  Old Style Bold Series 544, 41
  Optima, 32
  Perpetua, *see* Perpetua typeface
  Plantin Series 110, 28, 40–42, 50, 76
  Poliphilus Series 170, 53
  Scotch Roman Series 137, 43

Typefaces, by name *continued*
  Stone, *see* Stone typeface family
  Times New Roman Series 327, 41, 42, 181
  Univad, 204
  Univers, *see* Univers typeface family
  University of California Old Style, 33
  Veronese Series 59, 41
Typefounding, by hand, 4–5

Unit arrangements, in Monotype system, 40–41
Unit widths
  in Lumitype system, 94
  in Monotype system, 35–39
  in PostScript, 168
Unitary matrices, in photocomposition, 89
Univers typeface family, 103–120, 138, 176
  calibres in, 105
  comparisons between variants, 113–117
  matrix-case arrangements, in Monotype versions, 114
Updike, D B, 14, 48, 72, 160
US West Dex Inc (USWD), 204, 205, 210, 211, 217, 220
User coordinate space, in PostScript, 167–169

Van Krimpen, Jan, 53, 71–74, 119–120
  drawings for Lutetia, 17
  relationships with Monotype drawing office, 32, 76
Vergecio, Angelo, 12–13
Vernier acuity, 169
Vibert, punchcutter, 14, 18
Voskens, Dirck, 8
Vox, Maximilien (Samuel Monod), 96

Wallis, L W, 80, 90, 92, 137, 144, 163
Warde, Beatrice, 27, 30, 53, 75
Warnock, John, 165, 166
Wicks typecasting machine, 45
Width allocation systems
  for Linotype scanned-matrix machines, 151
  Lumitype, 94, 110
  Monotype, 35–36, 110, 113
  Photon, 94
Wilkes, Walter, 23
Willimann, Alfred, 102
Wyatt, D K, 166

Xerox Palo Alto Research Center (PARC), 163, 165

Zapf, Hermann, 189, 197, 222
  typefaces
    AMS Euler family, 189–192, 197–198, 200–201, 202
    Optima, 32

Colophon

This book was produced with Donald Knuth's TeX page-formatting language, briefly discussed in Chapter 18. It uses D C Brotsky's YTeX macro package, with extensions by the present author. The index was compiled with Pehong Chen's MakeIndex program, from the LaTeX macro package.

The fonts with which the book was composed are from Sumner Stone's ITC Stone family, generously donated by their designer.

The text was written and formatted on Apple Macintosh computers, and submitted with the illustrations for imagesetting as a set of files in Adobe Systems' portable document format.